HISTORY IN PRACTICE

HISTORY IN PRACTICE

Second Edition

Ludmilla Jordanova

Hodder Arnold

A MEMBER OF THE HODDER HEADLINE GROUP

First published in Great Britain in 2000
Second Edition published in 2006 by
Hodder Education, a member of the Hodder Headline Group,
338 Euston Road, London NW1 3BH

www.hoddereducation.com

Distributed in the United States of America by
Oxford University Press Inc.
198 Madison Avenue, New York, NY10016

The advice and information in this book are believed to be true and
accurate at the date of going to press, but neither the author nor the publisher
can accept any legal responsibility or liability for any errors or omissions.

British Library Cataloguing in Publication Data
A catalogue record for this book is available from the British Library

Library of Congress Cataloging-in-Publication Data
A catalog record for this book is available from the Library of Congress

ISBN-10: 0-340-81434-9
ISBN-13: 978-0-340-81434-5

2 3 4 5 6 7 8 9 10

Typeset in 10/12 New Baskerville by Servis Filmsetting Ltd, Manchester
Printed and bound in Great Britain by the MPG Books Group

If you have any comments to make about this, or any of our
titles, please send them to the feedback section on
www.hoddereducation.com

For all my students –
past, present and future

CONTENTS

LIST OF ILLUSTRATIONS

ACKNOWLEDGEMENTS

For the second edition of *History in Practice* I have reorganised some sections, added a chapter and inserted some new material, principally on the following themes: the relationships between both archaeology and geography and historical practice; history via the internet; and globalisation. I have also sought to broaden the geographical and chronological range of the examples given.

It is a pleasure to renew my thanks to all those who contributed to the first edition of this book, which was published early in 2000. In preparing the second edition I am especially grateful to my fellow historians at Downing College, Cambridge – Paul Millett, David Pratt and Richard Smith – who have been a source of inspiration, information and insight. A recent stint on the Council of the Royal Historical Society was not only hugely enjoyable but also exceptionally valuable for thinking about the discipline of history in its current forms. The President during that period, Jinty Nelson, has been a friend and mentor of remarkable generosity and wisdom. William O'Reilly and Richard Rathbone both agreed to speak to me about how the discipline of history is changing – I appreciate their kindness. In doing this sort of work, I have inevitably been a magpie, taking ideas here, there, wherever. My warm appreciation therefore goes to all those who allowed me to chat with them about 'doing history'. Paul Kerry's enthusiastic feedback on the first edition has been both delightful and extremely helpful. I owe a special debt to Jacqueline Rose, of Clare College, Cambridge, who has given me so much invaluable help and support in preparing this edition. My gratitude also goes to Chris Clark, Ruth Deyermond, Richard Fisher, Alex Hemming, Ian James, Helen Macdonald, James Montgomery, Dang Phong, Rachel Reeves, David Reynolds, Susan Reynolds, Margit Thøfner and Christopher Wheeler for help on specific points. Mel Leggatt has encouraged my nascent interest in the role of information technology in the practice of history, made many useful suggestions and offered a great deal of practical help, for which she receives my warm thanks. The staff of the Centre for Research in the Arts, Social Sciences and Humanities have shown amazing degrees of patience and tolerance while I manifested those signs of derangement characteristic of an academic finishing a book.

For reading drafts I thank Kenneth Fincham and Catherine Hurley, and for help with preparing the index Alix Jordanova and Paul Green. I have benefited from endless encouragement and support from Kenneth Fincham, Catherine Hurley, my beloved daughters Alix and Zara, Andy and Jila Peacock, Joad Raymond and Lauren Kassell, and many other friends whose loving kindness has sustained me. The dedication to my students stands – the rewards of teaching are inexpressible; in particular I thank the graduate students who participated in the interdisciplinary seminars at the Centre for Research in the Arts, Social Sciences and Humanities, University of Cambridge, and the history students at Downing College, Cambridge.

Cambridge and Edinburgh have provided wonderful environments in which to think about the practice of history, the presence of the past, the uses of memory, the organisation of academic life and the display of historical items. It might be thought absurd to thank places, but it is quite appropriate to be thankful for them and for their marvellous copyright libraries.

I remember with affection two historians, Roy Porter and Simon Collier, who were important to me and who have died since the first edition of this work was published. It is only now that I am coming to appreciate more deeply how much I owe to Roy; I miss his inspiring dedication to historical labour and his exemplary ability not to take things too seriously. Simon wrote to me in the most wonderful, encouraging way about *History in Practice*. I shall always be grateful to him for that, for insisting on the centrality of extra-European history and for demonstrating that a dance, the tango, was a proper subject for historical scholarship. I remember too my mother, from whom I learned to love teaching, who would have liked to be a historian, and who died in December 2003. The illustration on page 177 may be read as a tribute to her engaged curiosity about just about everything – a valuable trait for any historian.

Cambridge and Edinburgh
July 2005

Introduction

I should like to begin with my own vantage points. This is not the result of an autobiographical urge, but rather of the recognition that readers are entitled to know where I am coming from. If I am to advocate self-aware history, I should strive to practise it, and if, like all historians, I believe in the significance of context, I should attempt to provide some for this volume.

After secondary school, my first meeting with history was through studying the history and philosophy of science in the late 1960s. While this field was certainly concerned with the past, at that time it was driven by an agenda set largely by the natural sciences. Encountering history in the company of philosophy was significant – the combination allows the critical analysis of ideas to be central to historical practice. While undertaking doctoral research on French biology of the late eighteenth and early nineteenth centuries, I started to become aware of the possibility of a closer integration between history and the history of science, without being at all sure what this would entail. I have been greatly influenced by others who, more sure-footedly, pursued these possibilities. As a result of their endeavours, the history of science and the history of medicine are now much more integrated with general history, although they remain distinct subfields, which are frequently pursued by those with some training in the sciences or medicine.

One of the big developments in the history of science has been 'science and literature', which brought literary critics, with their distinctive assumptions, methods and goals, into close contact with historians of science. This encounter with text-based approaches has been enormously important to me. So too was the 'discovery' of anthropology, which historians of science made in the late 1960s and the 1970s. It enabled them not only to value other belief systems that were, by modern standards, 'unscientific', but also to appreciate the power of simultaneously maintaining a critical distance from, while sympathetically entering into, other cultures. For me this remains the kernel of historical practice. In the late 1970s I started thinking about the objects and images that are produced in the course of scientific and medical activities, and this led me to art history. Like the history of science, the history of art is a separate field with its own journals, professional associations and intellectual frameworks. Art, like science, carries an aura that sometimes acts to discourage its full contextualisation, yet both domains can only be understood if placed in a rich historical context. This constitutes an important project, since everyone in the past used their visual experience, the traces of which, accordingly, afford general historical insights. All these areas may be distinct, but they have much to learn from each other, and the terrain they inhabit is not neatly packaged to meet modern disciplinary distinctions. These interdisciplinary experiences inform my ideas about the discipline of history, which, I shall argue, possesses nonetheless its own distinctive character.

The periods on which I have worked also shape my view of history. Much of my work has been concerned with the second half of the eighteenth and the first half of the nineteenth centuries, although I have worked a little on adjacent eras. At the University of Essex I was involved with some early modern survey teaching, and my interest in that ill-defined period was extended by the strong group of early modernists at the University of York. I am intensely conscious, however, of never having studied ancient or medieval history. In spite of this, I hope that some of the concerns of historians working on earlier periods are reflected in this book. By the same token I have tried to think about contemporary history. In ways I explore in chapter 5, we have all sorts of mechanisms, conscious and unconscious, for shaping and imagining the past. These privilege some themes, times and approaches and marginalise others. The models each historian finds appealing have a great deal to do with 'their' period, as well as with their own political, social and economic views.

The institutions within which historians learn, teach and do research should also be considered. I did not belong to a university history department until I joined the University of Essex in January 1980, as a lecturer in a department that was devoted to comparative history in the early modern and modern periods. In each year undergraduates took a survey course, starting with the sixteenth to eighteenth centuries in the first year, and culminating in recent times for final years. The commitment to comparative history had two highly positive effects. The first was a constant attention to the concepts and categories, the frameworks, analytical procedures and theoretical ideas that making systematic comparisons demands. The second was daily contact with historians of the United States and Latin America, Russia, China and Africa, as well as with Europeanists. In addition, a high proportion of the students were 'mature'; many had left school early and had considerable experience of the workplace and strong views about topics such as equality, class and gender, which play a central role in discussions of the past. My next post in the history department at the University of York brought a fresh set of experiences: colleagues working in medieval history and close links with art historians and literary historians. The history curriculum was also organised in a highly distinctive manner, requiring all undergraduates to take a course on the 'discipline of history', for example. When I joined the University of East Anglia in 1996, I was no longer in a history department, but working alongside archaeologists, anthropologists and art historians, a situation that prompted reflection on geographical and temporal reach as well as on material culture studies. As I write this I am involved in helping to promote interdisciplinary research in the arts, humanities and social sciences, in a university with a large and strong history faculty as well as numerous historians in other parts of the institution. The interplay between the study of history broadly defined and other fields is thus at the forefront of my mind. When this book is published, I will once again be a member of a history department and thinking about the ways in which the evidence provided by visual and material culture can be fully integrated into historical thinking.

The pursuit of history is, whether practitioners choose to acknowledge it or not, a political occupation. For the entire time I have been doing historical work, politics has loomed large in every aspect of it, from the relationships between the wider political world and research undertaken, to the micro-politics of academic institutions and sub-fields. It seems to me not just natural but proper that professional energies should be concerned with the most cherished values out of which politics is built. Thus I am proud to call myself a feminist historian, because thinking about gender relations, their history and their future from a woman's perspective has been a central part of my life. All this occurs in specific contexts that may be called political in that they involve the allocation of resources and esteem. I make this point about the pervasiveness of politics for historians partly because any book about the practice of history has to tackle the question of 'bias'. All human beings have biases of one kind or another and to pretend otherwise is simply dishonest. There is no such thing as unbiased history, but there is such a thing as balanced, self-aware history. Bias becomes a problem when it prevents historians from being judicious and from having a measure of creative, critical distance from their work. For historical writings to be informed by our passions and values is not just inevitable, it is good in that it lends them energy. But passions and values should also be constantly subjected to scrutiny; they need to be tempered by evidence – for a conviction to be heartfelt need not imply it is unreflexive. Our attention should therefore be directed to the definition, selection and interpretation of evidence. It is pointless to hold up an ideal – unbiased history – which is simply unobtainable.

Historians are present in the histories they make in many different ways, in their prejudices, their passions, their commitments, beliefs, persuasions and life experiences. Even when these are idiosyncratic, they can offer insights into the discipline as a whole. Inseparable from these values is a sense of what is most precious in the discipline, of how it can and should develop. This book has been written in a spirit of passionate enthusiasm for the study of the past. While it is not a requirement for the job, most historians love what they do. It is a paradox of historical study that it demands intimate involvement with one's objects of study; such involvement, precisely because it is a form of love, can lead both to sympathetic identification and to the myopia that comes from being too close. The discipline has another complex face: a self-aware intellectual distance that makes analysis possible, but which can be impersonal, stolid and, frankly, pompous. It is extremely difficult to say at all briefly what the defining characteristics of history are, although knowing eclecticism and analytical flexibility are major features. Integrating apparently diverse sources and approaches to produce more holistic accounts is an important goal of the discipline. For me, this is bound up with what is often meant by 'cultural' history. Cultural history is also hard to define, but it always gives priority to mental processes, to what are usefully called mediations, in any historical study.

When scholars articulate their aspirations, they naturally reveal their personal visions – and by 'personal' I do not mean 'idiosyncratic' (since these visions may be shared by many practitioners), but 'close to the heart', integral to a given biography. Let me give a specific example. It was only in the course of writing this book that I realised how deeply permeated my view of historical practice has been by the history and philosophy of science in which I was trained, and by an approach to scientific and medical knowledge that is often called social constructionist. As a result I have stressed the social construction of historical knowledge and its production within communities, now of a fairly structured kind, that are in turn rooted in institutions, nations, political groupings, and so on. What counts as successful history depends on the context in which it is being judged, and the most helpful way of thinking about such matters is in terms of trust, not truth.

Because of persistent misunderstandings on the matter, it is crucial to be clear about what does *not* follow from this position. I am not suggesting that there are no clear standards by which historical work can be judged, or that history as a discipline cannot engage with the material, embodied worlds of past times. I counsel against a smooth, thoughtless, naive transition between the sources and the claims historians make, just as I do against taking the sources themselves at face value. Behind the work done in this vein in the history and philosophy of science was a desire to unsettle received views of science. So long as it is done well, that is, within a sophisticated intellectual framework, such unsettling is all to the good – and so it is with history. In both their teaching and their research, historians should, responsibly, unsettle their audiences, provoking them to think harder and deeper about the human condition.

Since historical knowledge is produced socially within communities, and because that knowledge is given some status, those who produce it have ethical obligations as well as intellectual ones. We are not free to say whatever we like about the past, because historical claims have entailments for which their makers are responsible. These responsibilities are a complex matter, and a full discussion of them is beyond the remit of this book, but in discussing public history I shall sketch in some of the main issues.[1] If I have one wish for the future of the discipline it is that it may continue to embrace the possibilities for which 'public history' stands as shorthand. This involves, for example, a willingness to write for the general public and to collaborate with museums and the media. No group is better placed than historians to demonstrate to the public how fatuous and dangerous are the crude moral polarities that are so often invoked in history's name, and how simplistic it is to think that unambiguous lessons from history exist, which provide simple formulae according to which present policies can and should be formulated. Taking account of history is quite different from claiming to draw 'lessons' from it, although the language of lessons continues to be bandied about. As I was completing the first edition, notions of a 'just war' in the Balkans were being tossed around. Now, six years later, in the wake of the Iraq War, this idea continues to have an awful currency. Where does the notion of a 'just war' come from and how has it been used previously? The answers will not give governments recipes, but they should give citizens a greater level of understanding of how things come to be and of the manipulative uses of history, as well as its significance as the first step towards change.

It follows from everything I say here that 'history' cannot speak with one voice, indeed that public history should not do so. Historians are subject to the same forces as everyone else, although their professional and scholarly training encourages them to temper their emotions, to channel their commitments and to be as balanced as possible when making judgements. Nonetheless, they see the world in diverse ways; there is indeed no consensus on matters of substance, and historians will never achieve full consensus. I do not see their wider role as one where they are saying, as it were, the 'right' things, or the same things. Rather historians should foster informed debate about the past, and encourage people to think critically about evidence and what it does and does not reveal. In other words, political pluralism is essential, and in this sense I am against 'political correctness' in one of its meanings. So, diversity of *opinion* among historians is inevitable. What historians share is their commitment to the critical evaluation of evidence, to meticulous reasoning and to disclosing their sources, acknowledging their scholarly debts.

Healthy pluralism is built upon openness. I do not conceal my own interests and preferences, so readers will perceive that my sympathies lie more with the left than with the right. However, my position does not make me automatically uninterested in or disapproving of conservative history, so long as it, like its radical counterpart, is done well. I may not always 'like' it, but I can certainly respect it. Indeed, it is vital to be stimulated into deeper reflection by views that challenge one's own. One of the things that most upsets me is styles of women's history that make simplistic, universalistic claims about the oppression of women. This is poor history and it is also poor politics; these shortcomings are not forgivable just because we might be 'on the same side'. Disagreement should not be solely about ideological conflicts – it should also be about the *quality* of scholarship and about the uses to which that scholarship is put. Ideological conflict is inevitable, although it is important to be open and constructive about it. Never ever should such disagreements be personalised or allowed to get nasty, leading to the blocking of jobs or publications, for instance. Most historians will witness some such behaviour over the course of their careers: for example, at seminars and conferences. It is wholly to be condemned, and conveys to young historians the impression that besting people, putting them in their place, is acceptable. Passions can be lived and expressed in vigorous debate without such destructiveness.

Another point, which requires explanation, follows from my position. It is sometimes thought that to study a historical phenomenon is to approve of it. While this is not an entirely unreasonable assumption – I do, after all, stress historians' identifications with what they study – it is too crude. Intellectual curiosity is aroused in all manner of ways – by concern as well as by approval. So the study of Fascism, totalitarianism and dictatorships, for example, does not imply that historians share the value systems they are examining, although the widespread curiosity about extreme forms of power, and the violence that tends to accompany them, does require some explanation. People often mistake *description* and analysis for *prescription* and advocacy. Giving an account of a state of affairs is not to advocate it. When historians write they cannot do so without 'bias' or 'objectively', but it does not follow from the fact that they are interested parties that they are being advocates or prescribers. If historians do indeed use their historical research inappropriately, they must be censured for it. By inappropriately I mean *without* due regard to evidence and other scholarly work and without a transparent apparatus, or for dishonest ends. I accept that providing a full apparatus is a problem in popular works, but if publishers and their referees are responsible this should not cause overwhelming difficulties.

Historians' differences are indeed inevitable, and the mere fact of their existence should not undermine the discipline's capacity to be active in public debate, so long as the points I have just made are taken fully into account. The discipline must be pluralist in terms of the topics and approaches that are pursued. Fashion, a theme of chapter 8, is an issue here. I would not say that fashion is a bad thing – that would be a waste of breath – but I would say that it is in the interests of the discipline to keep a wide range of activities going, including ones that may seem obsolete or boring to some practitioners. For example, there has been a trend towards placing ever greater emphasis on the history of the last 150 years or so, with the result that students have often studied restricted periods of time. This limits them intellectually, and curricula that offer all students a wider chronological range are highly desirable. By contrast, at a popular level, archaeology and ancient civilisations, such as Egypt,[2] exercise wide appeal, while areas with continuing, perhaps growing allure, such as medieval history, which now has its own magazine, are not taught at all by some history departments.[3] Obviously it is good for newer forms and styles of history to be available to students, but it should not be at the expense of established ones. In my opinion, economic history, and areas that demand familiarity with quantitative methods, continue to be particularly vulnerable in this respect. It is always hard to work out how it is that fields change in the image and value they are given, but it is evident that they do. Rather than capitulating and agreeing that students should get whatever they want, we need to mount clear intellectual arguments about why a given area or approach is important.

Economic history (like some others fields) is a fundamental part of the discipline, of which all students *ought* to have some understanding. This is because the subject matter of economics, which studies the generation and distribution of resources, is intrinsic to the manner in which every society functions. There are only a limited number of such 'structural' phenomena and they lie at the heart of history, which, as a discipline, aspires to make general statements about past societies. Faced with a choice between courses on the history of sport or the history of animals and those on economic, political, social or intellectual history, I would hope students would be able to see that the latter are likely to be of more *general* use than the former. This is not at all to diminish the interest of the former; it is simply to recognise that their role in the discipline is different. A course on the history of dress does not afford the same kinds of insight as one on the history of government. One is not 'better' than the other, but they do occupy different positions within the discipline. However, one *is* more fundamental and general than the other. We would not insist that, *instead* of studying sonata form, musicologists should look at paintings of performers or the history of subscription concerts, inherently interesting though they are. The latter simply would not give them the basic tools they need to go on to other topics in the field, although they could be useful extensions once some kind of groundwork was in place. Cultural history and the history of intellectual traditions are integral parts of this groundwork because they provide insights into the way the world is experienced in other times and places. Thus they help in relation to phenomena, such as religion, that many students find increasingly baffling.

Inevitably there is no consensus on what such historical groundwork should cover, in which countries and over which centuries, but it is essential to debate what that groundwork would ideally look like. For me, it should cover economic, social and political history, together with major intellectual traditions in several countries (including the student's own), at least two continents and over more than three centuries. It should do all this in a fairly systematic fashion, through compulsory core courses, which act as a kind of spine to which flesh is added in optional courses. I would like to see 'skills' integrated into all history teaching. I would also like to see an understanding of the discipline itself integrated in a similar manner. It has always puzzled me why historians are not more 'historical' in relation to their own professional practices. It is not hard to train students to ask basic questions of any item they read, including secondary sources. 'When was it written and in what circumstances?' should be asked of all secondary sources, without exception; by systematically doing so we build up a sense of changing historical practices and of where we have come from in intellectual terms.[4] This would be a logical extension of both critical reading and placing of phenomena in context, which are basic historical skills.

Curiosity about where 'we' have come from is an important aspect of the historical enterprise. When I used the word 'we' at the end of the previous paragraph, I meant those who identify themselves as historians, including those studying history at university level. But broader groups are also addressed by historians. It is generally recognised that curiosity about the past is a widespread phenomenon, met in an amazing variety of ways, of which the discipline of history is just one. I have found the idea of conversation useful here. Thus, it could be said that although historians are constantly in conversation with each other, with their predecessors and with their sources, they also talk to other interested parties, on behalf of whom they write and teach. These matters are rarely made explicit, although I would argue that they become more visible in relation to some utterly exceptional historical phenomena, such as the Holocaust. In fact, 'the Holocaust' is a term that has come into general use relatively recently – it is a shorthand used in innumerable historical conversations. 'Interested parties' include the societies in which historians function. This is not to say that every person at a given time and place is consciously interested in history – if only. But it seems that in public discourse there is a dependence on claims about the past; hence my stress on the ethical dimensions of historical practice.

The argument about the centrality of history in public discourse suggests that historians have the function of bearing witness. Generally they do not do so directly; rather they operate where direct witnessing is not available. The notion of bearing witness has strong religious connotations, including the idea that direct observation of divine powers has a special status in the transmission of beliefs. I would like to invoke another aspect of the idea – doing something on behalf of others. It seems to me that historians have been given considerable privileges and rights, even if people do not always listen to them. The contemporary role of historians is especially significant given the growing recognition of the emotional and social value of memory and commemoration. Our historical practice should reflect these functions and responsibilities, which have come about precisely because what actually happened is constantly being used and called into question. If history were solely fiction, *and* universally recognised as such, we would hardly care so much about its practice. An awareness of history as a made narrative is perfectly compatible with recognising both its genuine significance and its capacity to speak meaningfully about past times. The future of history lies in practitioners and their publics possessing an awareness of its limitations *and* a confidence in its intellectual strengths and achievements.

While I accept that historians need and want to be highly specialised, I hope we never lose sight of major 'structural' elements, of broad sweeping themes, of motifs that persist for centuries. I also hope we can be inclusive with respect to sources and approaches, and creatively cultivate wide audiences. The goal of inclusiveness requires careful consideration, however. Let me give a concrete example. I argue that the discipline should be keeping alive and actively promoting areas such as economic history because they contribute not just to the substance of history, but to thinking about structural issues within societies. Yet this book cannot engage with traditions of history writing that have developed over many centuries in, say, China or India. In this sense it is not inclusive. To be inclusive in the sense of embracing many cultures presents challenges to any individual historian. Writing about such complex matters without having studied and thought about them deeply would be impertinent. Ways of writing history are inseparable from language, literary and cultural traditions, political formations, and so on. For the majority of historians, global inclusiveness is simply not feasible, and tokenism is, to my mind, offensive.[5] Yet it would clearly be totally wrong to pretend other traditions did not exist. A useful analogy comes from the history of science. Non-specialists are frequently astonished to learn how ancient and sophisticated were the forms of natural knowledge developed outside what is too frequently reified as 'the west'. Joseph Needham's life's work was to bring the riches of Chinese scientific and medical traditions to a wider audience.[6] Similarly, we need, and will certainly profit from, work on other ways of doing history provided by people who are genuinely steeped in them, as Needham was in the civilisation of China. Thus the goal of inclusiveness should go hand in hand with a humble appraisal of each historian's limitations.[7] I am vividly aware of mine; hence I write out of what I know and have experienced, and make no pretensions to have done otherwise. If inclusiveness is interpreted mechanistically, as an obligation to mention something because it is there, the results will be intellectually shallow. Openness, together with a sense of historical practice as provisional and limited, might be a good way of thinking about these issues.

While no historian can ever be totally open, they can cultivate this trait in themselves and in others. Openness is about emotional and intellectual receptivity, whether this concerns the types of sources used, their content, the ideas of others or methods and approaches. In setting up historical problems for research, a degree of open-endedness is essential, otherwise there is a risk of simply confirming what was already thought. It is in this spirit that parts of the world hitherto unfamiliar to particular communities and new perspectives are best approached. The underlying motive should be generating fresh historical insights. It would be possible to think about this issue in terms of comparative approaches to history, which involve taking a range of cases for comparison, because doing so will shed light on a specific historical problem. In this way, historians can expand the areas they work on in a realistic fashion, and the selection of regions is driven by tough intellectual considerations. Furthermore it should be axiomatic that excellent language skills and first-hand familiarity with countries being studied are part of this more open approach to historical practice.

An individual's reasons for working on the areas they do are bound to be mixed. They generally include an assessment of what others are likely to be interested in over the coming years. Since historians depend on their audiences, they have, it seems to me, always had an eye on the future. Far from being immersed in a fusty past, unaware of what is going on around them, historians stand firmly in the present, as mediators between past and future. The notion of usable pasts is now common currency. Hence it is fitting that historians come to see their field as helping to create understanding and identities that are future-orientated.[8] If I seem to be constantly giving priority to public history this is because it is a logical extension of what goes on inside the discipline. Throughout *History in Practice* I evoke six features of the discipline that seem to me to be of paramount importance. First, its modes of operation should be transparent; second, eclecticism is acceptable and desirable; third, historians need to be judicious; fourth, they must embrace a range of approaches and subjects; fifth, rigid polarisations, such as that between those who are for and those who are against theory, should be eschewed; and, finally, consciousness-raising is crucial, so that practitioners better understand their own traditions and procedures. All these features suggest to me that there cannot and should not be rigid boundaries around the particular set of academic practices named 'history'. The public implications of historical practice are profound and would benefit from constant critical evaluation, whether academic historians like it or not. Most of us practise history not just because we love doing so but because we believe it matters to *everyone* precisely what accounts are given of the past. An integral part of being a historian is having a fair and honest sense of one's own practices, which should be reflected in every single piece of speaking, teaching and writing one undertakes. *History in Practice* attempts to bring some of the key issues of historical practice to a wide audience. In this respect it is a modest contribution to public history: it aims to combine balanced and reasonable claims with a certain openness about personal commitments.

There are, however, limits to openness, which I have evoked in a utopian spirit. Naturally there is much about any writer that can never be known, sometimes for lack of evidence, and always because of the complexity of the unconscious. Readers still need to know, more or less, where an author is coming from. Here I am sketching in where my own interests and enthusiasms lie, and hinting at my methods of working. Closely bound up with all this is my imagined audience. I have deliberately tried *not* to imagine myself writing for my peers, but, on the one hand, for general readers and, on the other, for students. Those who teach courses on historiography and related areas will, I hope, read the book, but it is not primarily aimed at them. Furthermore, it is best read as a series of interconnected arguments and taken as a whole. I am not conveying information, but working through ideas. One reason for treating the volume as an entity is connected with the manner in which I originally wrote it: I started at the beginning and developed the ideas in the sequence in which they will be read. Brief examples serve to amplify key points; other examples would have done equally well.

A few further words of explanation are in order at this point. *History in Practice* is designed to provoke the reader to think about the processes through which the kind of knowledge called 'history' is made and used. It leaves much unresolved because there are no simple resolutions to most of the questions I pose. The discipline is intriguing precisely for this reason. It is also a vast domain and I make no pretence to cover everything – that would be absurd. I can only apologise for the book's limitations and hope that these are understood for what they are: human frailty combined with an unwillingness to pretend to experience and knowledge I do not possess. I have also sought to provide positive rather than negative instances to illustrate key points. In the relative privacy of the seminar or tutorial we can dismantle the work of others and see how it might be done otherwise, but in a work of this kind explicit criticism of named historians would be out of place.

In explaining the type of arguments that follow, it is best to be perfectly open about what this book does *not* do. For instance, it is not about the philosophy of history, which examines the nature of arguments, the use of concepts, theories and evidence, and evaluates these abstractly. Inevitably we will touch on these issues, especially in chapter 4, but they are not the centrepiece of the book. Nor am I responding to the challenge of postmodernism or of any other theoretical framework. Although I hope to convey how the practice of history has changed in recent years, I am not defending the discipline or engaging with particular theoretical issues. *History in Practice* is not a handbook that tells readers how to be better historians, do research more effectively or get published. It would be wonderful if it raised the awareness of those starting out as historians, but it does not contain recipes for improvement. Finally, it is not a history of history; no attempt is made in the pages that follow to provide a narrative overview of the ways in which either history writing or the historical profession have changed over the centuries.

History in Practice has three principal goals: to give readers a sense of the issues in the discipline; to place the field in a wider context; and to sketch in what historians actually do and how and why they do it. Thus it is more an 'anthropology' of history, in that it tries to make sense of the practices and ideas of a distinct group of people, without being overly prescriptive about what historians ought to do. Yet it is not an ethnography – a detailed account of directly observed behaviour – for it works at a more general level than that term implies. This book does not ignore the question of standards. I believe that it is both possible and essential to discriminate between 'good' and 'bad' history. So, the interest in an 'anthropology' of history should be taken as meaning not simple observation, but a sympathetic account of what doing history is all about, which includes critical evaluation as an integral part of the enterprise.

While it is inevitable that writing history involves making value judgements, I do not believe that all value judgements are equally acceptable, or that all accounts of the past are equally valid. In a book of this kind it is necessary to make generalisations that cannot be supported by voluminous notes. In order to write it, I have undertaken as wide a range of reading, observing, listening, teaching and talking as possible. It would be neither feasible nor appropriate in a book of this kind to footnote all that. The book's apparatus, the support for my arguments, takes two main forms. References for the small number of direct quotations are always given in endnotes, which also make the general claims of the text a little more concrete. The further reading includes items that I have found relevant in writing the book and that will offer readers further insights into the themes with which it deals. Accordingly it is divided into sections reflecting the organisation of the text.

I would like to suggest a metaphor through which *History in Practice* may be approached. Perhaps it can be understood as a sketch map – an apt metaphor if history is a field – which is helpful in finding one's way around, locating basic markers and also appreciating the terrain.

1

History in general

HISTORY AND DISCIPLINES

The word 'history' has a number of meanings, and a wide range of connotations, some of which are charged with intense emotion. We use it to invoke the authority of precedents, to refer to what is no longer relevant, to endow objects with value and status, and to mobilise longings for better worlds. Since one of the main meanings of history is simply 'the past', then almost any association with past times can be transferred to 'history'. Yet there is another rather different way of defining history: as the *study* of the past. In this sense history is an academic discipline. Chapter 1 looks at the nature of academic disciplines with history in mind.

I have indicated that *History in Practice* has three main aims: to convey a sense of the issues in the discipline; to place the field in a wider context; and to indicate how historians actually practise. These aims already imply some of the answers to the questions 'what is an academic discipline?' and 'what is the nature of history in particular?' My first aim implies that fields share intellectual preoccupations, and in this sense they are communities built around ideas of one kind or another, where members are constantly conversing, in their writings as much as in their direct contacts. One result of this is that publications are never free-standing (although they are often seen this way), but rather are parts of elaborate conversations with other historians, living and dead. They are also conversations with governments, political parties, interest groups, and so on. As this book constantly makes clear, publications work at many different levels, so that, in addition to participating in conversations, they stake out territory for their authors, speak to contemporary concerns and contribute to the creation of imaginative frameworks through which the past is felt, as well as thought about.

The second aim, to place the field in a wider context, implies that disciplines, like those who practise them, cannot be seen as isolated; in reality there are no ivory towers in which academics and their productions exist, detached from the world. In recent decades the practice of history has become ever more closely bound up with politics, with the popularisation of history, with ideas of heritage and with the changing priorities of nation states. The demands of intellectual rigour, to which all disciplines are subject, are not incompatible with extensive engagement with a wider world. The study of history is intimately connected with social, political and economic institutions, such as museums, the educational system and government. It is equally closely related to cultural life, that is, with television, fiction, drama, poetry, radio, film, art, and so on. For centuries elites have recognised that the past is usable, as a resource, an instrument through which it is possible to persuade, cajole and moralise. Groups that have felt themselves to be subordinate, oppressed or marginal have taken up the same tools, hence the development of oral history, labour history, black history and women's history, of history from below and 'subaltern studies'.[1]

My third aim, to indicate what historians actually do, implies that the discipline of history is best understood as a set of practices, rather than as a constellation of beliefs or theories, or a stable body of subject matter, for example. History, the discipline, is indeed about what historians do. This formulation is not circular, as might appear at first sight. Rather it signals that there is no essence of the discipline, which is made up of what members of the community agree will count as such. Through the institutions that regulate academic disciplines in a variety of ways, conventions are formed about who counts as a historian and what counts as academic history. Of particular importance in this respect are schools, universities, professional groupings, government bodies and specialised publishers. This is not to say that disputes do not constantly arise. They occur precisely because, on the one hand, our investments in how the past is interpreted are so great, and, on the other, because our interests in it are so diverse. They also arise because there are never clear boundaries around academic subjects: these are imposed on the 'raw' materials, in a manner that reveals more about scholars and scholarship than about the past itself. Nonetheless, most people who earn their living as historians agree on what the general rules for generating sound knowledge of the past are – for the selection, use and citation of sources, for example – and disputes frequently revolve around whether these have actually been followed. Beyond that, historians differ on academic matters as much as they do on political ones. They are united, not by the *content* of what they believe, but by their commitment to the importance of studying the past, by their participation in shared activities, and by their conviction that certain ways of proceeding produce reliable historical insights. Thus the discipline of history is a complex array of practices, and these practices are underpinned by an infrastructure. Just as modern societies need to be understood in terms of the structures – such as transport, banking and health services – which enable them to function, so academic disciplines need to be placed in the context of their support systems and institutional bases, and it is to these that I now turn.

INFRASTRUCTURES

There are a number of elements that need to be distinguished in the infrastructure of history: training; professional organisations; government agencies; employment; marketing; and the dissemination of ideas and information. There is, inevitably, some overlap here – for example, schools and universities are places of training and employment, and in most countries they interact extensively with government agencies. Nonetheless, it is useful to distinguish these areas in order to be able to think about them as clearly as possible, since they give rise to distinct issues. Before discussing these elements in more detail, two general points need to be made. The first serves to draw attention to the *variety* of ways in which individuals, groups and nations use, shape and respond to the infrastructure of intellectual life. Historians make choices, to belong to one professional association rather than another, for example. In Britain we have two main national organisations: the Historical Association, founded in 1906, which embraces both professional and amateur historians, and the Royal Historical Society, founded

1.1 Extracts from the American Historical Association website

Most professional organisations now use the internet to publicise their activities. The format, visual style and content chosen convey a great deal about their self-image. In the case of the American Historical Association, the emphasis is on its government mandate, its broad constituencies, the responsibilities of historians, the professional services offered to members and the public significance of history.

in 1868, which elects to the fellowship those with scholarly publications on historical topics. Decisions about joining such bodies express an individual's assumptions about priorities in the study of history and how they are best expressed. Many, including myself, would see populist and scholarly organisations as complementary. Neither organisation, however, is as politically up front as the American Historical Association (AHA), founded in 1884, a huge and powerful body, which publishes the prestigious and widely read *American Historical Review* (1895).[2] Issues around gender, race and class, both as subjects within history and as professional matters, have been foregrounded by the AHA, as they have been by many historical organisations in the United States. The British organisations, while they seek to represent the interests of historians broadly defined, are considerably less political and often more traditional – the Royal Historical Society had its first ever woman president in 2000–4, for instance. In one sense the History in the Universities Defence Group (HUDG), which was founded in the Thatcher years, is more 'political' than the other national organisations in Britain, in that it engages directly with government policy, claiming to speak on behalf of university historians as a whole. Yet it is not partisan in the sense of espousing party-political lines, not least because this would be divisive, and hence weaken its position. So, not only do individuals make choices, but historians in different countries exercise their choices in markedly different contexts.

One element referred to above was the dissemination of ideas and information, and this includes the press. Daily newspapers in France devote considerable space to historical issues. When the prominent historian Fernand Braudel died in 1985, a number of papers discussed him and his contributions at considerable length – far greater coverage than is imaginable in Britain or the USA. Nonetheless, books about history, especially biographies and anything to do with heritage matters, are widely reviewed in British newspapers and magazines. Thus when we think about the practice of history in France, we should bear in mind the larger environment, especially the ongoing, passionate debates about revolutionary traditions, which partly account for the distinctive French preoccupation with the past and those who recount it.

The second point follows directly: while there is considerable room for individual choice and collective manoeuvring, attitudes to history are nonetheless strongly shaped by institutional structures and the ideologies that go along with them. We can illustrate the point by thinking about attitudes towards Germany and Japan, especially in those countries that won the Second World War. National stereotypes have proved extraordinarily persistent, and they manifest themselves in a number of forms, from imitating accents to huge generalisations about a nation's character and culpability, and a reluctance to learn certain other languages. While some might say that this is no more than popular prejudice, I would reply that such feelings are reinforced by institutions such as schools, newspapers and the media, especially by the film industry, which, in the years following the war, constructed, using visual images, language and music, a quite particular set of responses to the events of 1939–45.[3] Such values, selectively reinforced by the infra-structure of the discipline, have real consequences for the manner in which history is practised. *Styles* of education, which go far beyond the *content* of history syllabuses, play an extraordinarily important role in setting the most basic terms through which children think about and imagine the past.

EDUCATIONAL SYSTEMS

The study of history is an important part of most educational systems. It is identified as a major subject in conventional curricula, and this is because, in most countries, knowing about the past is valued as, on the one hand, an important component of a well-educated mind and, on the other, a source of useful insights for the modern citizen. Later on I shall examine the idea of 'lessons from history', which underlies many educational arguments about why the subject should be widely taught, and which is often invoked as a major defence of the field. I am referring to widespread assumptions about the value of school history here because the vast majority of the population first encounters the subject at school. Ideas about the past, the degree of interest it holds and the esteem given to those who study it, are subsequently further shaped by the mass media, especially by newspapers, historical fiction, film and television, and by leisure industries, a growing sector that selectively markets historic experiences.

The educational system also trains historians. In this respect it is less a pur-veyor of governmental and general ideological values than the structure that determines what the next generation of teachers and researchers will be like. For some, school history is simply part of the furniture; for others, it is prep-aration for a career. The history taught in schools changes with historical fashions and responds to political imperatives. For example, it is only rela-tively recently that school history has given less weight to political history and communicated a wider range of historical styles, including reminiscence and oral history. The shift towards studying direct testimony places heavy stress on the notion of empathy with historical actors. The concept of living history, of dressing children up in order that they can behave more like people in the past 'really' did, has a marked effect both on general attitudes to history and on the way historians think about their professional activities. Re-enactment is promoted in museums, and hence is related to public history, which will be discussed in chapter 6. There is a simplistic literalism here, which needs to be seen in the context of broader educational trends. These imply that the past was not really foreign and mobilise superficial notions of historical ac-curacy. They also make assumptions about class and about historical agency, for example, by advocating listening to a wider variety of accounts – those of so-called 'ordinary' people, rather than those of elites, who were far better placed to record their views in enduring forms. The implication is that history is not just made by those in charge but by those with less overt power. Going along with this are a number of more subtle shifts in ideas about the ownership and uses of the past. The idea that groups, especially non-elite ones, own their past and need to engage with it as a means of constructing

1.2 A line of Confederate troops advances in a re-enactment of the Battle of Gettysburg, July 1995, Gettysburg, Pennsylvania.
The re-enactment of battles has become a popular activity for participants and audiences alike. Yet such performances offer limited historical insights given that they are highly selective and have been purged of most risks. They reveal how parts of the past remain alive for a long time and how seductive the idea is that we can experience it vicariously.

more satisfying identities in the present, is now pervasive, and quite evidently it is political at its core, as is clear in the concern with post-colonial identities. It is sustained and popularised by organisational structures, which convey values through the teaching of history. These are contentious matters and we shall encounter them in many different forms in the pages that follow. Are female historians uniquely well placed to study women's history, or can men do it too? Is the study of Jewish history in the post-Holocaust world to be undertaken by Jews alone, or can it be undertaken legitimately by any interested historian, regardless of background?[4]

Educational systems do not speak with one voice. In Britain, which has a legally enforced national curriculum, the teaching of history is used to explore concepts of nationhood, which operate in tension with people's history. An interest in nationhood tends to return politics and political leaders to centre stage, and to approach the past teleologically via the nation state, which then becomes the goal towards which earlier processes are seen to be leading. Hence modern nation states are presented as the norm, the proper state of affairs, and this assumption is not only sustained by history teaching in schools and universities, but is also propagated by activities outside education, such as the organisation of sporting events and international diplomacy. School history sets in place basic notions about the past, thereby defining the terms in which both the general public and historical professionals think about the subject.

The contrast between Britain and the United States is instructive here. The persistence of the British monarchy and its highly controversial nature, especially over the last couple of decades, sustains an extraordinarily high level of popular interest in kings and queens of all periods, one result of which is a strong association between nation and monarch. Notions of citizenship have only arrived on educational agendas recently, while the complexities of ethnic and regional identities across the British Isles are not dealt with systematically, leaving the way open for media stereotypes to persist. Admittedly, issues like 'the Irish question' are unavoidable, but the point remains that persistent tensions between England and Wales, for example, are accorded no priority in the national curriculum.[5] In the USA, by contrast, where political identity is predicated on a conscious act of nation creation, which made the subjects of imperial Britain into citizens of an independent new republic, the history of the nation is presented quite differently, and far more explicitly in terms of citizenship. However strong the cult of presidents may be, it differs markedly from the British obsession with their monarchs. How ethnic identities are to be understood historically is an increasingly explosive question, which is constantly being rehearsed at every level of American society. These processes are beginning in Britain and the rest of Europe. The fierce recent controversies in France, with its long tradition of citizenship, over whether female school pupils could wear 'Islamic dress' brought religion, culture, history and education to the fore in the most dramatic ways.[6] The United Kingdom is not the only country that reinforces a cult of the monarchy and national identity in education. The Danes, Swedes and Norwegians are keenly interested in their royal families, and the Danish government is currently seeking to reinforce a sense of national cultural identity in schools.

However hot a political topic the teaching of history in schools is, university courses have a considerably more far-reaching effect on the values, attitudes and intellectual frameworks of professional historians. Furthermore, what is taught in universities varies dramatically within and between countries – far more, I would venture, than in the sciences, and possibly even more than in other humanities subjects. These variations indicate where some of the main issues lie in the discipline of history at the moment. The following variables would seem to be the most important: the periods and countries covered; the balance between primary and secondary sources; the degree to which teaching is organised thematically; the extent to which it raises openly political and theoretical issues. Naturally these relate to the *content* of history, but they also relate to its organisational framework, and they do so in three main ways. First, institutions of higher education possess administrative mechanisms for approving courses that staff wish to offer. Within both the formal and informal cultures of these institutions some subjects are deemed suitable, and others unsuitable, for teaching to undergraduates. We can immediately appreciate how important these mechanisms are when we notice that many history departments held out for a long time against offering courses in women's history, and many in Britain and Germany still offer nothing on race and ethnicity or on oral history. It is significant that 'new' subjects are seen as threatening, and that organisations find ways not just of resisting them but of presenting them as less intellectually demanding, as overly modish, in fact, as not 'proper' history. I put new in inverted commas because sometimes, as in the case of women's history, the subjects are not actually new at all. Professional historians have been writing on this subject for as long as there have been professional historians. What was 'new' about women's history was its overt association with a populist women's movement, that is, with feminist agitation about equal pay, sex-based discrimination, childcare provision and control over reproduction, which posed a threat to the academy that is still being worked through. Feminism remains a contested term, and gender relations continue to be a site of social, economic and political conflict. Nonetheless, as more women and men who are sensitised to these issues get academic jobs, and precisely because gender matters are now debated so widely, the composition of committees changes, and proposals that would previously have been seen as way out are accepted. I am not saying that curriculum innovation is automatically 'good' and resistance to it 'bad'. However, curricula do need to change and mobilise fresh energies, and the manner in which this is resisted illuminates cherished assumptions within a discipline and an institution. At the same time, change always brings costs and valuable perspectives can be lost in the process.

The second way in which organisations shape the content of history, the provision of resources, is particularly relevant to university-level teaching. New areas of history demand extra resources, such as tapes, CDs, DVDs, computing facilities, access to specialised software and to costly online resources, videos, slides, new books and periodicals. Yet despite increasing participation rates, it seems that the boom time for education is over worldwide. This is not to say that governments are less committed to education – certainly their rhetoric to this effect remains strong – but recent shifts in the world economy have squeezed spending in this area, and many countries are working with infrastructures, such as libraries, that are weak by any standards. Even 'first-world' countries are concerned to keep budgets for education under tight control, while also seeking to improve the general skills levels of their populations. 'Skills' here means literacy, numeracy and analysis, as well as an ability to use information technology efficiently. There are many ways in which computers have come to play a part in the practice of history, and their provision has become a major component within history's infrastructure. The internet, by providing access to library catalogues and holdings worldwide, interactive websites and huge amounts of information, has become a particularly significant part of that infrastructure. At the same time there is an expansion of the sheer *amount* of history being produced, with more journals and books in circulation than ever before. The result is intense pressure on resources, and, although so far this has probably not prevented the introduction of new fields or courses, it does shape the experience students have of working at more advanced levels. Especially significant in this respect is the degree to which students have access to both primary and secondary sources – the most effective university-level education involves experience of using a wide range of both types of material.

The third way in which organisational issues inform the content of history concerns 'demand'. General shifts have certainly taken place in recent years, as a result of which the ideologically charged language of the market has become dominant; a trend that is particularly marked in higher education. Education policies have changed along with the rhetoric. History is in the marketplace; the point applies to universities as much as to publishing, for example. Ultimately courses do respond to student demand, which itself is shaped by prior educational experience, by career opportunities, by personal commitments and by the political environment. The more universities offer open choices to students – who are, in effect, putting together customised degree schemes – the greater the impact of 'the market' will be. Naturally, perceptions about career choices are particularly relevant here, and there seems to have been a general trend in higher education towards vocational subjects, presumably due to increased pressure on employment opportunities. Yet choices are not only driven by instrumental demands; for example, there has been a general decline of interest in economic history, despite it being high on 'relevance' to many careers, whereas there is increasing demand for courses on culture in general and the mass media in particular, where related careers are dramatically oversubscribed. Humanities students may now be increasingly sceptical about quantitative methods and lack the skills to master them, but there is also a sense that economic history is less exciting and cutting edge than other historical areas. We can note these trends and try to explain them, but historians should also be mounting strong intellectual arguments to demonstrate the importance of subjects, such as economic history, which are perceived as less alluring. In a state of anxiety about their income, institutions sometimes allow less fashionable fields to decline, precisely because they do not seem to be what students want. However, if such areas are promoted vigorously within departments and universities, this can often shift patterns of demand.

Academic disciplines work, then, within elaborate organisational frameworks, by which they are shaped. And these frameworks, although they have the inertia of institutions behind them, are also subject to change. Many different types of change affect academic disciplines: a good example of the point is the naming of departments and degree-level courses. History is currently taught under many umbrellas, some of which do not even have the word 'history' in their titles. The rise of area studies, where history, along with other humanities and/or social science disciplines, is applied to a specific geographical region, is a case in point.[7] This trend is indicative both of alterations in which parts of the world are thought worthy of specialised investigation, and of changes in the relationships between history and other disciplines. The surge of interest in the Soviet Union during the cold war is a noteworthy phenomenon, and Russian studies brought together histor- ians, linguists, sociologists, economists and political scientists. Despite renewed conflicts with far-reaching implications in areas formerly part of the Soviet Union, Russian studies as a field has shrunk. In area studies the kinship between history and other disciplines tends to come to the fore. For the purposes of area studies, such as American studies, Latin American studies, and so on, history is one of a range of approaches, which are com- plementary. Generally, language teaching, which is otherwise declining in the context of history, is part of the package. Outside Germany, German history is a relatively small field, especially in the English-speaking world, partly because the language is not widely taken up. This is an ironic situa- tion given the huge interest in twentieth-century Germany. Nonetheless, there are strong attempts to promote some more 'exotic' languages, espe- cially when, like Japan, the areas in which they are spoken are politically and economically powerful – African languages, for instance, have not exercised similar appeal. Research on Chinese history, for which the language is essen- tial, is thriving. As a result, excellent English-language works are available that can be used in undergraduate teaching.[8] The appeal of languages and geographical areas needs to be seen in a wider cultural context, which, through art, music and literature, shapes aesthetic preferences. These general responses affect the practice of history.

Gradually, since the Second World War, those parts of the world that are both politically sensitive and economically significant – Russia, Africa, Latin America, Asia – have come under the area studies approach. Which areas are favoured at any given moment depends in part on patterns of colonial development – the current interest in both India and the Caribbean among British scholars reveals much about the ways in which those zones entered the national consciousness, often through family memories and traditions, coming as much from a sense of guilt as from pride. Hence, which geo- graphical areas seem important for scholarly work depends on where you are standing. To historians in Britain the notion of 'British studies' seems rather odd: the *Journal of British Studies* (1962) is an American publication, which publishes important articles on British history. Each country tends to privilege its own history, although the degree of reflexiveness involved is quite variable. Yet to designate an area suitable for interdisciplinary studies implies a tinge of exoticism; hence area studies are not based on our own region but on zones that are already 'other' in some way. Area studies are by no means uniformly distributed across universities, and tend to be found in institutions already committed to interdisciplinary work and sensitive to the political imperatives behind historical scholarship. They can also be a form of international relations, with the country or region being studied offering funding incentives and, through cultural diplomacy and institutes, promot- ing conferences and exhibitions that bring the attention of scholars else- where to that particular part of the world. By these means geographical regions can be promoted as interesting, and worth visiting and trading with, that is, as players on a world stage.

Many universities still have separate history departments and teach degree courses in history that would be more or less recognisable to students from earlier generations. Yet the organisational environment has changed markedly. In countries, such as the United States, which have for a long time had a modular approach to degrees, together with mechanisms for preventing early specialisation, the idea of studying one field as an undergraduate for three or four years is foreign. A more focused model persists in many European countries, including Britain. Although most British courses are now modular, few rules exist to prevent specialisation, so that in practice students rarely take the range of options, within history and across disciplines, that students in North America do. Nonetheless, organisations are increasingly encouraging interdisciplinary ventures – at least, there is much rhetoric to this effect.

Another significant development is the tendency in recently founded institutions to put different humanities disciplines together in general departments called 'Humanities', 'Combined Studies' or even 'Theoretical Studies'. Distinguished historians may well be teaching under such rubrics, although what they do is not necessarily signalled as 'history'. This fosters a thematic approach rather than a descriptive one. A course entitled 'European history 400–1200' or 'History of the British Empire and Commonwealth' would exemplify the latter approach. Often thematic courses are enticing because they cut the historical cake in fresh ways, thereby encouraging students to consider new approaches and unfamiliar angles. A course on 'Themes in early modern cultural history' signals to students that they are being offered something distinct from a political, social or economic narrative. 'The Northern Ireland troubles' prompts participants to think about painful and intractable matters that remain part of contemporary affairs, and is as relevant to those interested in politics and religious studies as it is to historians.[9] Many institutions offer courses on 'Revolution', which encourage students to consider both the similarities and differences between, for example, France in 1789 and Russia in 1917: in other words, to think comparatively. This allows students to become more analytical about the relationships between economic difficulties and political protest, about what makes regimes weak, about charismatic leaders, about politically active classes, about theories of revolution, and so on. Yet if themes are taken out of context, if feminist movements are not placed in the context of other attempts at political reform, for instance, or if the scientific revolution of the seventeenth century is not compared with other intellectual and social changes of the period, partial vision results. Of course, the same arguments apply to descriptive courses, where countries, regions or periods are too often taken as self-evident and treated in isolation from one another, and a privileged place is given to political developments as if these somehow *are* the history. The ideal situation is to have a mixture of courses and approaches, which is precisely what very large departments of history achieve. But for most institutions this is simply not possible, and their ethos, organisation and approach to disciplines will determine the overall approach taken to the teaching of history.

So far I have sketched in some of the parameters which determine how the educational arm of the discipline is organised, and I have stressed that within these the variations are huge. However, across most countries, there are common elements in the ways in which professional life is organised, and these apply to history just as to other subjects: the centrality of the school curriculum; the need for most school teachers to have a university degree and a teaching qualification; the existence of a system for research training, which qualifies people to teach at more advanced levels; government involvement in funding and in standards; professional bodies that bring historians together for conferences, lobbying and publication.

ORGANISATIONS FOR HISTORIANS

Many different types of organisation exist to help historians in some way or another, from local ones that promote the use of archives in their area to international ones that sponsor huge meetings of professionals from all over the world. Since the levels of specialisation have increased so markedly in most fields in recent years, the proliferation of organisations is hardly surprising. It reflects the wide range of people, professional and amateur, with an interest in the subject, and the expansion of jobs related to history – not just in educational institutions, but in government, the media and museums. Rarely do such organisations have a single function; they exist to promote ideas and people, and they become especially significant when resources are limited. Professional bodies have particularly varied functions, some of which are more openly acknowledged than others. They often protect the interests of a field, for instance, by expressing an opinion on proposed changes in government policy. They serve to bring that field to the notice of peers, scholars in cognate disciplines and, sometimes, the general public. Frequently they sponsor journals, so that in some sense the journal represents and thereby becomes one public face of the professional grouping or learned society. By such means they help to define what counts as 'history', so that articles published in the *American Historical Review* or the *Transactions of the Royal Historical Society* (1876) come under the remit of 'history'. This function is especially important when fields are changing and new sub-fields grow up – being able to get an article on a 'new' topic into an established journal means more than the publication of an individual piece: it signifies something about definitions of history. New organisations and journals are instruments of legitimation, endowing their founders with 'career capital'. Thus professional bodies help to define their disciplines; they also create communities and a concomitant sense of being part of an intellectual network, by means of conferences, newsletters and other publications.

It follows then that many people come to see themselves as historians, not just by earning a living and/or publishing, but by belonging to groups that affirm their occupational identity. Along with this go more directly professional functions, such as networking to make contacts that help secure jobs, assist in publication and develop careers. Some societies advertise jobs and see it as their role to ensure that institutions do not cut 'their' subject, that the best young scholars are appropriately placed and that women and minorities get a fair crack of the whip. Professional bodies, in other words, help historians develop an ownership of their subject, to debate issues, to promote a general sense of the value of history and to forge their identities in the process. We can see these working in presidential addresses and inaugural lectures, when distinguished members of the field have a chance to address their fellows and lay out key issues. Many members will strongly identify with those figures and use their words to affirm or adjust their own sense of themselves as historians, just as many may disagree and will clarify their identity by contrast. All these processes are characteristic of the ways in which professional middle classes establish and maintain their positions.

It can be quite expensive to join a professional body and some can only be joined by invitation or by submitting one's name for election. Since they have a variety of roles, there is considerable variation between them according to which ones are predominant. New fields and scholars who fear they may be marginal are especially reliant on groups of like-minded people running conferences, perhaps publishing proceedings, and generally publicising their activities in order to achieve respectability and legitimation. Some such groups see themselves as radical and oppositional, for example, the Oral History Society in Britain and the group which founded *Radical History Review* (1975) in the United States; they strive for a public voice and some sort of recognition. The recognition of peers is just as important as recognition by governments, universities, funding agencies, and so on. Historians affirm the value of the discipline by bonding with the like-minded, and then show the wider world the nature of its achievements. Knowledge is shared, and displayed, in professional bodies, and thereby the quality of what is done is, hopefully, improved. But the more subtle functions, such as networking, bonding, affirming, and so on, are just as significant. It is vital that these bodies have public faces; they stand at the interface between highly specialised forms of knowledge production and the wider world.

PUBLISHING

History, like other disciplines, relies on the open dissemination of findings, which takes many forms, including electronic ones. The relationships between historical practice and the internet is discussed in chapter 8. Publishers, part of huge multinational industries, play a central role in academic life; hence the discipline of history is closely bound up with and dependent upon them. The general assumption is that for something to count as knowledge, whatever the field, it has to go through a series of evaluations and checks, such that authors are felt to be somehow accountable to their readers. At the most basic level this is why scholarly works have footnotes and bibliographies, so that their claims can be verified by those who wish to do so. Footnotes also indicate the range of sources the author has consulted, and it is open to critics, such as book reviewers and referees for journals and books, to argue that authors have missed important categories of sources, or misread those they have consulted. This is why undergraduates are taught how to evaluate evidence and to provide full citations for quotations. At least, that is the theory; in practice, the situation is rather more fluid. Who you are certainly has an impact on publication, especially if earlier publications have been successful. But what, we must ask, does 'successful' mean in this context? It can mean that many people have read and used the item in question, or that it has been highly influential on the work of others. Scepticism is important here given that many 'bestsellers' are hardly read and have achieved that status by exceptionally aggressive marketing; and supposedly objective indicators, such as citation indexes, can be misleading. In any case, we should distinguish between commercial and critical success, and then acknowledge that a number of communities pass judgements on any particular publication – peers are only one such. So when we are told that a book is 'successful', 'brilliant' or 'bad', careful probing is called for.

Authors who are already well known find it easier to secure good publishing deals. When it comes to books, little work is refereed totally 'blind', that is, with the referee having no idea at all of the author's identity. Some publishers, like a number of journals, do still seek to do this, but my impression is that much is published that has not gone through these procedures in their most rigorous form. In any case, effective operation of the blind refereeing system depends on a number of factors, such as the genuine impartiality of readers, which is inevitably hard in one's own field, while those who work in more distant areas may not be able to pick up problems. The system also depends on authors being willing to accept the need for any changes suggested. More prosaically it depends on authors genuinely disguising their identity when writing, which is in fact quite hard to do, although it is somewhat easier for younger scholars who have not already published a great deal and are less established in networks. Giveaway signs like 'this is based on my thesis' or 'see my earlier article on . . .' can be difficult to eliminate totally. My hunch is that the most prestigious journals still operate this system as strictly as possible, given the inevitable difficulties I have mentioned, such as the existence of relatively small and closed scholarly communities. Even so, it does not follow that articles rejected by prestige journals are 'worse' than those they do publish. For instance, rejects may fail to conform to the house approach to history or be on subjects the editor and/or editorial board do not happen to find particularly interesting. Hence simple claims to quality in scholarship need to be viewed sceptically. Nonetheless, the goal of transparency – openness in relation to sources, approaches, decision-making and interpretation – remains important.

We can put these points in a different way by mentioning the continued importance of patronage, including in publishing. Most institutions connected with history see themselves as meritocratic, but it does not follow that patronage is unimportant. In a competitive world selection is necessary, and in any case it is impossible for selection criteria to be perfectly rational. It is well known that in obtaining academic jobs the referees are of crucial importance – are they powerful in the field, known to be discriminating and perceptive? do they write for too many people and risk devaluing their currency? do they really know the candidate – is he or she generally respected? The same considerations apply in publishing, where historians will often recommend those whom they wish to promote, such as their own doctoral students, to a particular publisher, just as they will encourage them to speak at conferences, make sure that they get invitations to address the research seminars of other departments and meet influential scholars. Series of books edited by one or a small group of historians is one particularly clear way in which patronage can be exercised at the same time as a field is shaped. Many university presses have such series, which indicate academic priorities.[10] Among academics these points are commonplace; they are less familiar to undergraduates, who often take a publication at face value, without thinking about the patronage relationships involved, which have a real bearing on what is published, who is publishing where, and how the work is promoted. That is why informed readers turn first to the preface and acknowledgements of any work, where the author generally indicates who their most significant mentors and teachers were, and how they place themselves in a field.

Publishing is a vast, complex industry, which operates at an international level.[11] While the details of the composition and functioning of this industry are not strictly relevant here, it is vital to bear in mind the diversity of presses that publish history books, and to have some understanding of their different commercial and intellectual goals and their distinctive lists. They occupy specific niches in the market. While no publisher can ignore commercial factors, many, especially of the long-established university presses, continue to undertake costly and/or highly specialised publishing ventures that other companies simply would not be prepared to entertain. A good example of this is the new *Oxford Dictionary of National Biography* for Britain, an expensive, ambitious project that was undertaken by Oxford University Press. It drew on new scholarship, and also on new value systems – many more women are now being included, for instance.[12] The same press produced the *Oxford Encyclopedia of Economic History*, a collaborative enterprise that attempts to map the field.[13]

There are other approaches to producing reference books: for example, Routledge publishes a number, which are bought extensively by libraries and sometimes put into paperback.[14] On the whole, Routledge tends to keep books in print for a relatively short time and to publish in areas of wide immediate interest. Publishers develop market niches and their choices have a considerable impact on the content of what is published, especially on how books are used within the educational system.

When people think about educational publishing, the notion of a textbook springs readily to mind. While these are used a lot in schools, and at all levels in the sciences, law, economics and medicine, their role in the study of history, especially at university level, is considerably more problematic.[15] Four key assumptions typically underlie textbooks: that there is stability in a subject over time; that in different locations more or less the same subject matter is being taught; that it is appropriate to feed students 'pre-digested' material; and that there is sufficient consensus on key issues to make such volumes viable. Commercial considerations permitting, textbooks can be revised and updated regularly, although it is hard to imagine that this could be done more often than every five to six years. And even so, the basic premises of the work would remain the same. There is a certain innate conservatism in the very notion of a textbook, not just in terms of content, but in pedagogic philosophy. Textbooks can be rather distant from primary sources and, although some include short extracts, this is unsatisfying to more advanced students. There are document collections, which can be very useful, especially when they contain material otherwise unavailable to those without the relevant language. Nonetheless, textbooks present a viewpoint, which, by the very nature of the genre, readers are discouraged from contesting, whereas a monograph, that is, a specialised scholarly work presenting the findings of original research to those who are pretty expert already, can evaluate diverse approaches to a subject and acknowledge the depth of intellectual divisions, even if, in the end, it puts a particular case with a distinctive type of authority. Many monographs are pitched at a level that undergraduates find difficult. Because textbooks generalise, synthesise and seem to speak with authority, they can be somewhat bland. Since they seek to be fair and uncontentious, the sparkle, the sense of what the stakes are in divergent views of the past, sometimes gets lost. It is important to recognise the special form of publication that they represent, often making their publishers a great deal of money, and to develop the critical skills to evaluate the distinctive type of distillation that they constitute. Textbooks need to be understood in terms of professional structures and disciplinary infrastructures.

We can usefully compare textbooks with survey histories. Textbooks are written expressly for a defined educational level and purpose. Surveys, which typically cover significant swathes of time and a range of topics, may become textbooks, but can be more polemical.[16] As with textbooks, the reader has to take a great deal on trust in reading any survey history: that the examples have been carefully and well chosen; that the author has not simply followed what others have claimed or been uncritically reliant on secondary sources; that they have taken account of recent research and approaches, and so on. Some historical surveys come to wield huge influence. An excellent example of these points is the clutch of books by Eric Hobsbawm: *The Age of Revolution* (1962), *The Age of Capital* (1975), *The Age of Empire* (1987) and *The Age of Extremes* (1994). These have become established and venerated, although the perspective from which they were written, that of a committed Marxist, is one with which only a limited number of readers sympathise. So, what makes a particular book become a standard? There are no simple answers to this question, but it must be posed if we are to think at all critically about historical publications and, by extension, about how views of the past gain acceptance and change.

We shall return to these issues throughout the book, but they need to be mentioned here for two reasons. First, there are many different genres of historical writing, and each has its own place in the publishing industry and is an important element in the infrastructure of history. We need some understanding of the differences between genres of writing and, more particularly, how they win over readers. Second, publications are never received in isolation, and often, when they gain acceptance, it is because they fit in, mesh with other assumptions about the past. To return to the example of Eric Hobsbawm, you do not have to be sympathetic to Marxism to be convinced of the power of economic forces. Although his books are not narrowly economic, they are built around distinct phases of capitalism. Economic history may not be perceived as the sexiest field within history, but many historians, like members of the general public, are at heart economic determinists. It may well be that the revival of interest in his books over the last few years says more about attitudes to wealth and consumption than about the so-called decline and death of Marxism.

At the other end of the accessibility scale are learned journals, which usually come out several times a year and publish specialised articles on new research. In practice, historical journals are incredibly diverse, with some publishing pieces that are *recherché* by any standards, while others, such as *History Workshop Journal* (1976) and *Radical History Review*, contain many types of article, including 'think pieces', film reviews, obituaries and responses to exhibitions, precisely in order to respond to all aspects of 'history' and to keep their audiences as wide as possible. They also publish research articles, but the whole style of these journals is designed to open up diverse historical issues and to avoid narrow, elitist exclusivity. Many journals place no *a priori* limits on the subject matter of articles – anything 'historical', interpreted broadly, is eligible: *Annales* (1946) and *Past and Present* (1952), for example. But others have narrower agendas, to promote research into a given country, region, field or period: *Journal of Italian History* (1978), *Journal of Pacific History* (1965), *Journal of Modern European History* (2003), *Journal of Historical Geography* (1975), *Social History of Medicine* (1988), *Accounting, Business and Finance History* (1990), *Le Moyen Âge* (1888), *Seventeenth Century* (1986), *Victorian Studies* (1957) and *Journal of Contemporary History* (1966). The huge proliferation of fields, sub-fields and associated periodicals poses a number of problems connected with the fragmentation of knowledge and audiences. For any given piece of research, what is the appropriate audience? This question is made quite pressing by research assessment exercises, by trends towards interdisciplinary history[17] and by the relative difficulty of getting work accepted by the general historical journals, many of which enjoy high reputations but, since they cover the whole of history, receive huge numbers of submissions and have to be extraordinarily selective. Since journals are presented as the latest thing, students are often surprised at how long it takes for the whole process to occur, from initial submission to final appearance, which includes refereeing, making revisions suggested by referees, having the revisions accepted, checking proofs, and so on – and that assumes the first journal contacted accepts the piece! One to two years is not uncommon. Some journals, such as the *Economic History Review* (1927), publish the dates

INSTRUCTIONS TO AUTHORS

1. Submission of typescripts
Three copies of each typescript should be sent to the Editors, together with the originals and two photocopies of any statistical tables and maps.

The Editors will notify authors as soon as possible about the acceptability of a paper, but will not enter into correspondence about papers considered unsuitable for publication. Neither the Editors nor the publisher accept responsibility for the view of authors expressed in their contribution. Authors may not submit to *German History* a typescript that is under consideration elsewhere.

Articles should be between 7,000 and 10,000 words in length. Authors of accepted papers should submit an abstract (up to 250 words) for publication with the article.

2. Typescript layout/disks
All material should be on A4 or quarto paper, in double-spaced typing, and on one side of the page only. Ample margins should be left. Each page of the typescript should be numbered. In Notes and Reviews, all material should be incorporated into the text: there should be no footnotes. In articles, footnotes should be numbered consecutively and placed together in double-spaced typing on a separate page or pages at the end. In Notes and Reviews, the author's name should appear at the end on the right-hand side, with his/her institution on the left. In articles, the author's name and institution should appear at the beginning, immediately under the title. Quotation marks should be single; double quotation marks should be used only to indicate one quotation within another.

Disks should only be provided after the manuscript has gone through all the review and editing stages, when the data should be copied on to a clean newly formatted disk. Each disk should be identified by the first author's name and article title and give details of the hardware and software used.

3. Illustrations
All maps, diagrams, figures and graphs should be submitted in the form of completed artwork suitable for reproduction. They should be identified and separate from the typescript (with a list of captions on a separate sheet), and their place in the text should be marked.

No illustration (*including caption*) will be given more space than the text area of the journal page, i.e. 191 mm × 112 mm. Figures should ideally be drawn for a reduction of one-third, i.e. 3:2.

All costs for reproducing figures in colour must be met by the author.

4. Tables
Tables should be typed on separate sheets. Indicate in the margin of the text where the tables should be placed.

5. References
These should be kept to the minimum. Books are italicized (underlined in typescript), e.g. F. L. Carsten, *Princes and Parliments in Germany* (Oxford, 1959). In second and subsequent references to a work, an abbreviated title should be adopted, e.g. Carsten, *Princes*, p. 72. A reference to an article in a periodical should include (after the author's name and the title of the article and the title of the journal) the volume number (arabic), date in brackets, and relevant page numbers, e.g., 'The False Joseph II', *Historical Journal*, 18 (1975), pp. 467–95.

6. Copyright/offprints
In submitting a paper to *German History*, an author recognizes that, on its acceptance for publication, its exclusive copyright shall be assigned to the Germany History Society and operated on the Society's behalf by the publisher. In consideration of this provision, the publisher will supply the author with 50 offprints of his/her paper. The publisher will not put any limitation on the freedom of the author to use material contained in the paper in other published works of which he/she is author or editor. It is the author's responsibility to obtain permission to quote material from copyright sources.

7. Alterations to articles
Any amendments or corrections should be sent to the Editors (or Review Editor) as soon as possible after any author receives notification of acceptance for publication of his/her article. Because of the high cost of correction, the Editors reserve the right to reject alterations in proof. To avoid delays in the production of the journal, contributors will be asked to return their proofs promptly. Proofs are not sent to authors of reviews.

www.germanhistoryjournal.com

1.3 Instructions to contributors, *German History*
Each academic journal has a more or less distinctive style, to which layout, typeface and type of footnotes make a contribution, as do subject matter and historiographical preferences. Each journal uses different publishing conventions, generally laid out as a set of rules in each issue or available on request. It can prove extremely time-consuming for scholars to make sure that each time they submit an article to a journal they have abided by the house rules. Note that in the case of *German History* these cover issues such as the assignment of copyright, an important aspect of intellectual property (IP). In the age of the internet, IP is an increasingly significant issue.

of initial submission and final acceptance for each article, although this is more common in the sciences. Constraints, such as word limits, that are imposed by the article format, as well as by each individual periodical, mean that this is a genre with strong conventions, although these are invisible to the uninitiated. At the same time, periodicals are often the place where intellectual disputes can be slogged out, precisely because they come out several times a year and often encourage this type of exchange.[18]

Many other types of publication bear on the practice of history, including those designed for broader audiences, such as magazines and newspapers. In many countries it is quite common for academic historians to write accessibly about current affairs in order to bring out the historical issues implicit within them. Book reviews appear in many forms and they can generate exceptional heat, since they are one of the places where strong opinions can be expressed legitimately; these are unavoidably somewhat personal, given that they are directed at named authors. From the publishers' point of view, the more controversy the better; from the authors' point of view, attacks on their work or reputation are exceptionally painful. It is vital to remember the diversity of publications and their audiences, the range of ways in which history is presented to a larger public, and the complexity of the publishing infrastructure.

RESEARCH

So far in this chapter I have referred to 'research' as if it was self-evident what this term meant. In fact it is rather loose and under-determined in its meaning. One implication of the term 'research' is the discovery of fresh materials and novel insights. Originality is supposed to be an important element. Yet it is often unclear to what extent research is original, given the huge amount of history being written in so many different places. So how is it possible to assess the degree of originality involved? Material on the internet is particularly hard to evaluate. And is 'research' primarily about the investigative process, through which sources are gathered and read? What about the process of writing, through which interpretative frameworks are developed? Any new materials or information by themselves are not necessarily particularly significant; rather it is the ways in which they are used and connected up with previous accounts that really matter. Although previously unstudied public records are released regularly, only infrequently do newly available archives change historical assessments radically. Sometimes this is simply because of the information they contain, but more often historians have to work extremely hard at making sense of such evidence, and a good deal of research effort is expended on finding theories, concepts and approaches that will do the business.

Although it is potentially misleading to think of historical research in terms of 'data', the phrase 'raw data' is nonetheless revealing. It suggests the importance of preparation, cooking and digestion, and that is precisely what writing, together with the thinking and puzzling that precedes it, does. In fact, as we shall see, sources are rarely 'raw'. These issues are clearly central to the skills historians deploy, which will be discussed in chapter 7, but they also bear on the infrastructure of a discipline which, to be called a discipline at all, has to support research. There are three main ways in which research is made possible: by institutions, mainly but not exclusively of higher education, giving their staff time, money and library facilities specifically in order to undertake research; by dedicated organisations, either governmental or charitable, giving grants to individuals, groups or institutions to defray the costs of research; and by individuals using their own time and resources. Thankfully 'private scholars' still exist and many of them do very distinguished work indeed. The first two forms of support for research come with strings attached. Sometimes these are overt: for example, most grant-giving bodies expect transparency both in terms of financial management and regular reports. Universities may impose fewer overt conditions, but pressures connected with research assessment exercises and other markers of status, or indeed with non-research duties, significantly affect what and how much research is done. Access to primary materials is a major issue, although the possibility of downloading more and more resources from the internet is beginning to make a difference. Yet historians also depend on other kinds of sources, such as archives, many of which have never been microfilmed or transcribed – some have not even been fully catalogued – while others may be difficult to get access to. The costs of travelling to work on sources of which there are no copies, and of photography, should not be underestimated.

It is evident that historians who work close to great library collections are at a tremendous advantage. This is why large, rich universities in 'new' countries, such as Australia, Canada, New Zealand and the United States, have pursued active acquisitions policies, generating in the process some of the finest rare book and manuscript collections in the world. Yet even the greatest libraries have their limitations, and historians who work on parts of the world that are distant from their own, poor or politically unstable, probably have the hardest time; furthermore, these tend to be the areas of which the 'developed' world is most ignorant. They include much of Latin America, much of Asia (especially central Asia) and a significant proportion of Africa. Of course, such historians face other problems – the unfamiliarity of readers with the basic historical and geographical contours of their area; language difficulties; and the need for special interpretative tools and frameworks – that go far beyond the questions of infrastructure with which we are concerned primarily here. In his recent history of Bolivia, which begins with the pre-Columbian era, Herbert Klein acknowledges these issues.[19] The lack of resources for some types of history and the failure to recognise their importance – maybe even a sense of their threat or irrelevance – are related. It is usually more comfortable to work on and read about situations with which we are already familiar from direct experience. This would include, for instance, the distant history of one's own country or region, where political lineages, institutions, buildings, landscape and music act as links between then and now.

1.4 Ironbridge Gorge
Ironbridge Gorge is a spectacular site, which combines natural beauty with an engineering feat. The varied displays and activities available to visitors, while they work hard to offer historical insights, are nonetheless carefully manicured versions of 'the Industrial Revolution'.

BRIDGE

Most of this chapter (and, indeed, much of the book) has been concerned with the discipline as it is practised within specialised institutions, and hence with professional history of one kind or another. Despite the growing enthusiasm for world histories, mentioned in chapter 8, the discipline is increasingly fragmented and specialised; it covers such broad terrain that those inside it tend to forget how inaccessible most of it has become. The view from inside is indeed only a partial view. The leisure industry, for example, supports the endeavours of historians, through theme parks, museums and galleries, popular publications, films, television and radio, and all those shops that market the past. It may surprise some readers that I used the word 'support' above. I do not mean to imply that these admittedly diverse branches of the heritage and leisure industries expressly set out to contribute to the discipline of history, although many in museums and galleries certainly do see their roles in this way.[20] I am suggesting that these industries are inevitably connected with the ways in which the past is conceived, experienced and studied. Indeed they contribute to it materially. One particularly pertinent example comes to mind – Ironbridge Gorge in Shropshire, England, described as 'the birthplace of the industrial revolution' and now a UNESCO World Heritage Site. It is simultaneously a successful commercial enterprise, a significant area for industrial archaeology, and a vast display connected with a defining process for British identity. Such a venture depends upon the industrial revolution being 'remembered' with interest, as a phenomenon that could occasion visual pleasure and general curiosity, precisely as a heritage issue. This is a relatively recent phenomenon, as is the growth of interest in industrial archaeology. No doubt restored pumping engines have long exercised a particular appeal, perhaps akin to that of steam trains, but Ironbridge is a completely different phenomenon. This trend is closely connected with a growth of interest in the history of everyday life that is being packaged carefully. I do not want to claim that one came before the other; leisure industries and academic disciplines are subject to similar social and economic forces. But whether the past is presented in documentary terms or openly fictionalised, the heritage industry is part of an infrastructure too, helping to make available and promote ideas, words, objects, images and buildings that contribute to a widely diffused sense of the past. Academic disciplines exist in these larger contexts, and this is most obviously the case with history. Yet 'history' is also a huge idea, with many facets; chapter 2 maps these in more detail, especially with respect to their content and approaches.

2

Mapping the discipline of history

THE DIMENSIONS OF A DISCIPLINE

Academic disciplines have a number of dimensions, and so far I have dealt with one of them – the organisational base or infrastructure, which is similar for most fields. I have alluded to the other dimensions of a discipline and called them its content. But the content of history is not as straightforward as it seems. In a way, the past is the content of history, but this concept is so vast and inchoate that it hardly helps us to be clearer about the nature of the discipline. We can observe that, in general, disciplines tend to be composed of methods, approaches, theories and bodies of knowledge. Superficially, defining history as a body of knowledge appears attractive; it fits well with the fact that a great deal about the past is known, and with the existence of accumulated wisdom about how to make sense of it. There are two problems with this formulation, however. First, it assumes a finite field with relatively clear boundaries. 'History' includes so much, and has such fluid edges, that the idea of a delimited *body* of knowledge is not really appropriate. Second, it fails to take account of the radical differences between accounts of the past that historians give. To the extent that historians share anything, it is less an intellectual corpus than a combination of a commitment to the value of historical study and a shared sense of how relevant sources should be handled. To be sure, we produce historical knowledge, but there is no body of historical knowledge that underpins the whole field. Knowledge implies intellectual stability. Although this is indeed present for historical fields that have been studied over long periods of time, the discipline is made up of hugely diverse areas and it is currently addressing a wide range of topics, such as sexuality, food and sport, which had not been studied systematically before. So, given the size of the discipline, the range of sources and issues considered, and the diversity of historical practice, defining its content as a body of knowledge is unsatisfactory.[1]

2.1 Statue of Anne Frank, by Mari Andriessen, in the Westermarkt, Amsterdam
Anne Frank is a 'living' presence for many people today. The figure by Mari Andriessen at the Westermarkt in Amsterdam emphasises Anne Frank's youth. James Young discusses Anne Frank's memorials in the collection of essays he edited: *The Art of Memory: Holocaust Memory in History*.

Perhaps, then, there are characteristic methods and approaches. History is a notoriously eclectic discipline, methodologically speaking; as a result, it uses a wide range of approaches and is constantly drawing on other disciplines. While I want to suggest that there is something distinctive about the discipline, we do not, I think, get any further in our discussion of its *content* by pressing on its methods. So what about theories? This is a difficult issue. The phrase 'theories of history' refers to claims both about what has determined temporal change and about the basis for the entire discipline, and it has a dated ring to it.[2] Most professional historians are deeply sceptical that there can be any one overarching way of explaining change.³ The range of cases such a monolithic interpretation would be expected to cope with is simply too vast for a single theory to possess sufficient explanatory power. In this respect the discipline of history is totally unlike the natural sciences; they possess bodies of theory *and* knowledge without a mastery of which one cannot be said to practise them at all. In thinking about the content of history we must turn elsewhere. I propose that we consider two other dimensions of the discipline – its sources and the manner in which it is divided up. This chapter pays particular attention to the intellectual organisation of history and to the assumptions about historical practice implicit within it. One of the most characteristic features of the discipline is the elaborate, overlapping classifications of the types of history it contains, which, as specialisation proceeds apace, become ever more complex. It is precisely because history covers so much territory that navigational aids are required. In any case, a subject that includes numerous subjects and approaches, as well as practitioners, has to be divided up; understanding what underlies those divisions, an appreciation of how and why they change, and a grasp of the nature of the constituent parts is indispensable.

BASIC MATERIALS

The starting point for this chapter must be the basic materials out of which history is composed. Although historians use disparate sources, their engagement with their chosen ones is so fundamental a part of historical practice that it must be considered early on in our discussions. Before going any further two preliminary points are in order. The first concerns serendipity and sources. Many sources have survived accidentally. They are always vulnerable to mishaps such as fire and flood, they have often been destroyed wilfully, and simple neglect accounts for a great deal of loss. Furthermore, many sources have been created with no particular view of their permanence in mind. Although most institutions have deliberately sought, with an eye on the future, to generate accounts of their activities, many other areas of human life are less self-conscious. Even where there have been attempts to leave records for posterity, they remain vulnerable. Of course, there have been countervailing forces, and documents that promise rights, rewards and recognition have been preserved by many social groups, who often put them to quite different uses from those their originators intended. Nonetheless, there is a significant element of serendipity involved in the survival of historical sources, which extends even to official papers. What does survive to be used by historians by that very token wields influence, yet it can be unclear how it fits into larger patterns. This should be known as the 'Anne Frank' effect, after the Jewish girl who hid from the Nazis in Holland during the Second World War. Her diary became a bestseller in many languages, to the extent that she became an icon and a legend. It only became known much later how carefully the diary had been edited and how profoundly this determined readers' responses.⁴ Since her diary was published, many other first-hand accounts have been found, providing a whole new context in which a source that was once seen as exceptional must be interpreted. The passion of the debates about Anne Frank and her legacy provide a vivid sense both of the weight sources carry and of their accidental nature.

The second point extends the theme of the accidental quality of sources. The motives for leaving a permanent trace are hugely diverse, and it is one of the historian's tasks to reconstruct them in so far as this is possible. Relatively few sources were constructed with future historians in mind; many were produced in settings where academic disciplines did not exist, and they largely stem from the messiness of lives as they are lived – and that includes institutions and arms of government. These points are obvious, but there is no harm in reminding ourselves of the anachronism of taking sources and making them work for the discipline of history as it has been developing over the last hundred years or so. To put the same point differently – in the sources themselves, there is little or nothing of what we know as 'history'. In this respect history differs from law and music, where the sources and the discipline share some kind of mental framework, and from the natural sciences where the distinctions between sources (nature) and the operations performed upon them are relatively clear. The matches between history and its sources are custom-made by scholars; sources nonetheless constitute a major element of the content of historical accounts. The sheer diversity of sources is one of the discipline's most notable features.

Historians rely heavily on written evidence, although objects and images can be equally relevant. Written evidence is found in many different forms – too many to characterise in general terms since any trace of the past is potentially a useful source for historians. When we talk about sources, it is conventional to divide written ones into 'primary' and 'secondary'. Primary sources are taken to be original documents, raw materials, direct evidence of the era being studied, while secondary sources are those created by historians and other commentators upon the past. Hence, writings *about* the past, which are what most students and non-professionals rely on, are generally considered secondary sources in that they result from the study of and reflection upon another type of material that was produced *in* the past – primary sources. Hence Magna Carta, the charter of liberties granted to the English people by King John in 1215, is, according to this distinction, a primary source, while a book about Magna Carta is a secondary one.[5] Medievalists use chronicles a good deal; these were often compiled retrospectively, mainly by monks, who were preparing them for a patron and, hence, for a purpose.[6] Such monks are a bit like historians, using documents to construct an account determined by circumstances. Yet we value their accounts as primary sources, since they were so much closer to the worlds they chronicled than we are, providing along the way testimony to their own attitudes and values. So, in one sense, medieval chronicles are primary sources, in another, secondary sources. The same argument applies to the New Testament, especially as biblical scholars stress the gap between the events recounted and the acts of writing them down. There are many instances

2.2 Twelve-hundred year old Qur'an displayed for the Muharram Festival, Srinagar, Kashmir.

As the very words of Allah, the Qur'an is divine. Muharram is the first month of the Muslim year. The 10th is thought to be the day on which Noah left the ark; verse 23 here mentions Nuh (Noah). We might view this as a visually appealing, legendary document. Its significance is kept alive by its active religious life. The Hazratbal Mosque, built 1619, in Srinagar, the city of the sun, is the repository of a single hair of the Prophet Mohammed, exhibited on certain days of the year. The contrasts with Magna Carta, which has long held mythic status in English history, are instructive.

where materials shift between being a primary and a secondary source. For example, a project on the development of the historical profession would use writings about the past, conventionally designated secondary sources, as primary sources. E.H. Carr's *What is History?* is for a student of twentieth-century attitudes to the study of history, of E.H. Carr's oeuvre or of recent British historians, a primary source.[7] Similarly, when Roy Porter wrote a book on Gibbon, the great eighteenth-century historian of the Roman Empire, his primary sources were Gibbon's own writings and those of his contemporaries about him.[8] The *content* of the original sources Carr or Gibbon used would be relatively uninteresting; rather it would be the way they worked that was in focus. Like all historians, these authors relied on the findings and ideas of commentators; this rather common situation indicates that too rigid a distinction between primary and secondary sources is pointless. A certain collective moralism surrounds historians' use of sources, with primary ones being regarded as somehow 'better' and reliance on secondary sources being deemed weak. This is because the former are considered to lie closer to the past. There is nothing inherently wrong with using mixtures of primary and secondary works, so long as the status of different types of sources for a given project is made clear. We shall explore this issue further in chapter 4.

So, the very terminology 'primary' and 'secondary' can be misleading, and the ways in which this is so need to be made perfectly explicit. The words I have used in relation to primary sources should have indicated the difficulty. Terms such as 'original', 'raw' and 'direct' imply a special kind of authority that comes from first-hand testimony, from closeness to the events themselves. This may well be true – a description of a tomb or a plot of land by someone who has seen them is likely to be more reliable than a second-hand account. But this is a relatively trivial form of accuracy, and next to it we have to consider the possibility that those bearing direct testimony are also interested parties, who shape the evidence even as they are recording it. Furthermore, memory, as we know from experiences in law courts, is a notoriously fragile faculty. These 'adjustments' may happen either consciously or unconsciously or from a combination of both factors – being very close to something can also mean that you see it less clearly. Thus the division between primary and secondary sources can be treacherous. Much of the historian's skill consists of being able to imagine how sources are constructed and using those very processes, as well as their manifest content, to reach sensible conclusions.

The materials from which history is made are, therefore, diverse and we need to be able to appreciate the richness and the limitations of each type. One characteristic of outstanding historical scholarship lies in the creative and self-aware use of the complexities of evidence. This involves conveying to readers something of the processes by which sources have been produced, so that they are not presented as static documents with self-evident authority, but rather emerge as layered assemblages that testify in a variety of ways. Although these skills are taught in universities, they begin to be properly acquired only at the postgraduate level, leaving undergraduates to receive historical evidence extensively pre-packaged.[9] As a result, the ways in which evidence has been found, selected and used, how authors have chosen a particular genre to write their work up in, which audiences they have targeted and the tacit assumptions upon which their work rests, tend to be obscured. A critical reader needs to be able to think through these issues, and one obvious first step is to ask what kind of history any given piece of writing constitutes. Before discussing kinds of history further, I want to acknowledge the less tangible ways in which sources inform historical accounts. We can best speak of these in terms of the emotional responses historians experience when working with their sources, and especially those upon which they rely most heavily. These responses are complex and certainly cannot be summed up in a few words, and yet they infuse everything historians do. The idea of identification may be useful in evoking the profound connections that scholars experience with their sources, so much so that they may feel themselves to be 'inside' them. Such persistent historical perfumes, which elicit quite individual responses, are not to be understood as good or bad. They should not be romanticised, but they must rather be acknowledged, discussed and, where possible, evaluated as inherent in the practice of history.[10]

KINDS OF HISTORY

The first point to note when thinking about kinds of history is how varied are the criteria by means of which the discipline is divided up. One of the main ones, according to *period*, goes right to the heart of the field because it works with notions of causality and time, which are central to historical explanation; these issues will be discussed in a separate chapter. Other criteria include: *methods* – for example, oral history and demographic history; *theories*, such as psychohistory; *places* – urban history, the history of specific regions, countries or continents, for instance; *type of human being* – women's history, history of childhood, Jewish history, labour history; and *institutions* – church history, history of public policy or welfare states, for example. These are not mutually exclusive categories; each historian probably thinks of themselves and their work in terms of more than one. But, largely through journals, such types of history do define fields, and historians are constantly classifying each other in these ways, which are dense with political meaning and central to identity construction. Thus, a historian who worked on the schooling of girls in the nineteenth century could be a social historian, a historian of education, a women's historian, a feminist historian or a historian of the country or period in question. They might use different labels for different purposes, but the one that expressed most precisely what they felt was the core of their intellectual identity would be highly significant. Each of the possibilities just given carries distinct political as well as intellectual connotations.

The most familiar division of the discipline, however, is not according to any of these criteria. Indeed it is quite a challenge to work out precisely what the force behind this most conventionalised of distinctions is. I refer to the notion that there are three basic kinds of history – political, social and economic. Do we regard these as levels of analysis, as complementary aspects of a society or as distinct phenomena? What do you do about the fact that the boundaries between them are evidently blurred, and yet they seem to be 'right', 'natural' or 'obvious' categories?

It is not difficult to see some of what lies behind the separation of political history. Most obviously, countries have generally been led by individuals, together with small elites – in many parts of the world for a very long time. Thus 'politics' is easily identified and is often seen as what really counts. Since successful monarchs, military leaders, and so on, not only displayed charisma but explicitly invited their subjects to identify with them and to see the person and the political identity as different facets of the same coin, these forms of power can readily be described. Leaders reinforced their position by the panoply of symbolic forms, such as coins, that supported a political order in whose name war was made and laws enacted. The notion of political history as a distinct kind of history appeals to common sense. Although it is often claimed these days that there could be a political history of just about anything – that is, a history that focuses on power relations – the connotations of 'political history' as the history of rulers, governments and dominant groups is still strong. It remains, in effect, history from above. A related assumption is that this type of history is totalising – it unifies a given historical situation by giving priority to state-centred phenomena. As a result, we are encouraged to comprehend a whole era, a whole area, via its politics – indeed phrases such as 'the age of absolutism' reinforce the point. There are historians who want to keep the specific flavour of political history by retaining its connotations of *high* politics and by resisting the idea that political history can be applied to any facet of a society. Diplomacy, constitutions and local government would all come under the rubric 'political history' as conventionally defined, yet these are less fashionable topics now than they were only a couple of decades ago. 'International history' is a term now used to cover what used to be diplomatic history, in an attempt to give the field a new look and identity.[11]

Military history illustrates a number of points about kinds of history in general and about political history in particular. The phrase itself suggests the detailed discussion of wars and strategies, battalions and battles. This is what continues to elicit great interest among the general public – the re-enactment of battles and the transformation of their sites into 'heritage' locations are further manifestations of that interest. These phenomena are 'political' in that wars, especially in the modern era, are generally waged by or on behalf of states, the leaders of which are closely involved in their execution. Typically they involve large numbers of fighters, who are enlisted in the name of politically powerful institutions – such as king and country, nation, the republic, the church. The polity in question has to offer further support – economic and moral at least – in modern times coordinated by governmental organisations. At first sight, nothing could be more political. The history of these phenomena can be written in many different ways, however. These will not necessarily be of the kind suggested by the term 'military history', as demonstrated by Paul Fussell's *The Great War and Modern Memory*, a study of soldiers' responses to the First World War.[12] This hugely successful and influential book found another way of talking about the war, from the bottom up and with an attention to texts. The proliferation of fiction about that particular war is a well-known phenomenon. Pat Barker's *Regeneration* trilogy, based on an exceptionally rigorous use of archives, prompts further reflection on the boundaries of history, war and politics.[13] I shall return to the significance of military history in chapter 8.

A strong commitment to political history conventionally defined has to be justified by the idea that politics is a special class of human behaviour, which may be distinguished from social and economic phenomena, and is capable of affording historians a privileged insight into the past. Yet the merest reflection suggests that politics, even of the most elite kind, always was bound up with more general prosperity, with sources of revenue, such as taxation, and with forms of expansion, such as imperialism. While many economic phenomena, such as the operation of local markets and of household economies, have relatively little to do with high politics, it is hard to imagine politics not depending in some way on the nature and sources of the wealth of elites and rulers. Inevitably, the more that societies possess structured institutions, the easier it is to separate out different kinds of histories. Thus we could argue that political history is to be defined principally in terms of the apparatus of government, statecraft and their modes of operation. In societies that lack such defined structures, the notion of political history would accordingly become considerably more fluid and, in fact, might not serve any useful role at all. Presumably it would simply refer to the study of the most powerful people within the society in question.

We should note another problem with the tripartite political/social/economic model. The adjective 'social' is related to the noun 'society'. The word 'society' is commonly used to invoke a sense of a totality, while avoiding the use of more loaded and historically specific terms, such as nation, which carry culturally and chronologically specific connotations. Naturally, I am not claiming that the term 'society' is totally neutral, only that its long-established use in the social sciences as an inclusive term for a structured collectivity, without specifying the precise form it takes – nation, tribe, city state, ethnic grouping – makes it handy for historians. Yet the very concept of 'society' is considered by some to be ideologically loaded. Society does indeed express something more than country, region and area, which do not imply any sense of humanly-based cohesion, since diverse peoples can find themselves in geographical proximity to each other. 'Society' implies the existence of repeated patterns and motifs, indeed of coherent connections between constituent elements – coherent, that is, to those who study them. We need a *relatively* neutral word to evoke one type of unit that historians and social scientists study, and it is reasonable to suppose that aspects of that unit are linked to each other, that patterns emerge when groups of human beings live, work and reproduce together – the existence of such patterns is in fact what makes historical generalisations possible.[14]

How, then, can social history, if it is the history of societies, apparently refer to only *one* of their aspects? One possibility is that 'social' has taken on specialised meanings, thereby losing some of its inclusiveness.[15] So, what, in practice, does social history include?[16] The question can be tackled in three ways: we can see social history as an approach rather than denoting particular subject matter; we can seek a distinctive set of topics that it addresses; and we can understand it in relation to other kinds of history – for example, as a sort of remnant. If social history is an approach, then it can be connected with the conviction that the lives of ordinary people, not just elites, should be studied; that weight should be given to lived experience; that complex relationships between people, no matter what kind, should be explored; that whatever phenomena societies throw up should be investigated historically. That is, taking its cue from social theory, it examines structures and patterns across societies. According to this reading, social history *is* inclusive in its methods and approaches, and the relationship between social and society seems relatively coherent.

If social history is a particular set of topics, then there is indeed a problem. Most topics have political and economic dimensions, so what kinds of human behaviour are inherently 'social'? Those with *less* politics and economics in them? On this reading, social history might become the history of leisure and family life, which is precisely how some of its critics see it. Here 'social' means interactions between people and groups of people, especially in daily life and of the masses. To my mind, if we define social history in this way, the connections between 'social' and 'society' become confused. The concept 'society' begins to lose its inclusiveness, and it is hardly logical to claim that some human activities are more 'social' than others. The third definition of social history is as what was left over from other more defined, and possibly more prestigious, forms of history – precisely a remnant. By this account, it is *not* the history of politically powerful elites *nor* of forms of government; *nor* is it about the operations of the economy and its supporting institutions. Here the links between 'social' and 'society' are at their most fragile, since there is no attempt to conceptualise them at all. Rather 'social' comes to mean ordinary in its pejorative sense: what is mundane, unremarkable, insignificant, especially for national or world trends.

I do not think there can be a simple definition of social history, and indeed, as the field has developed, there have been persistent confusions and heated controversies over precisely these issues. This is not to say that social history is incoherent, rather that its key concepts, which I take to be 'society' and 'social relations', have been constantly contested both because they originally emerged out of specific theoretical models and because these models were highly politicised. Marxism, to take a model central to social history, contained assumptions about how societies worked – for example, about the fundamentally exploitative nature of class relations. Some commentators obviously worried that social history was really social*ist* history, while for many of its exponents that was precisely its allure![17] The most rigorous social historians have continued to debate the theoretical and conceptual issues raised by 'society' and its cognates.

HOLISTIC HISTORY

One possible way of overcoming the problems I have been discussing would be to embrace *histoire totale,* that is, a more explicitly holistic approach to the past, which is often associated with the French 'Annales' school.[18] The *Annalistes* were open to thematic history, to studying a wide range of human phenomena, and to collaboration with other disciplines – hence their intellectual embrace was notably generous. One problem such an approach throws up is what the focus of historical analysis should be – a community, a town or a region? Can *histoire totale* be done thematically – could you write the total history of an idea, an object or an occupation? The most celebrated example of this approach is Braudel's magisterial study of the Mediterranean.[19] He took a geographical region as his focus. It is a region with a rather special history, one that could be considered pivotal, not just for the development of Europe but for the relationships between Europeans and other parts of the world – the Orient, Africa and, in due course, the New World. Furthermore, Braudel worked with distinct historical levels and with a generous time-span, a *longue durée*, and this helped him to solve what is always the most challenging problem for large-scale projects – how to establish a clear and coherent framework through which a book can be organised. Braudel's whole approach to history is inclusive – the environment, economics and social structures as well as 'events, politics and people' – and this led him to distinguish between different types and paces of change.[20] Those who take a relatively short period as their object of study will be unable to attend to those shifts that take place extremely slowly; hence decisions about the length of time to be covered automatically give priority to some kinds of phenomena and explanations over others. The shorter the time covered, the more limited are the historian's options. Defenders of micro-history point out the advantages of small-scale work, for instance in recreating everyday lived experience. A notion such as *histoire totale* helps historians to think about questions of scale and focus, and about the entailments of choices concerning the kinds of history we practise. When 'second-wave' social history got off the ground in the 1970s, it did not go down the path of *histoire totale*, but of highly focused thematic or community studies on relatively restricted chunks of time.[21]

In its most rigorous form, *histoire totale*, like *longue durée* history, is little practised now. Yet the ideals they embodied are not dead. There are small numbers of historians who are deliberately trying to write for wider readerships, for those outside the academic world, and who are seeking to make their books a good read. This is a significant trend in a number of respects. For example, it exemplifies a 'revival of narrative' to use Lawrence Stone's phrase, an interest in telling stories with which readers can identify.[22] Simon Schama's books are an example of this trend. His *Citizens*, published to coincide with the bicentenary of the French Revolution in 1989, examines the revolution from the point of view of its participants. It is neither a political history nor a social history, but a mixture of whatever is available in order to show what it was like to be there. It is not *histoire totale* in the sense that Braudel's works are. But it is embracing, wide-ranging, trying to move out of rigid categories, such as political history, which, in the case of the French Revolution, would involve charting the changes in regime, the nature of revolutionary leadership, the legislation introduced, the military campaigns, and so on. Precisely because it does not address such matters, the book could be criticised for lacking a sense of the structural elements that made up the revolution. Here, as in Schama's other books, there is an emphasis on culture and on themes that can be traced in many different forms.[23]

To the extent that holistic history is still being practised now, it takes two principal forms: biography and cultural history. I will return to cultural history shortly. Although biography could be understood as a literary genre, it is far more than this. Taking a person as the unit of analysis is to adopt a quite particular historical approach, one that emphasises individual agency and sees the subject as a point at which diverse historical forces converge, while taking the span of a human life as a natural period of time. Biography can cut across arbitrary divisions between historical fields and approaches. There are two prerequisites for a viable biography – its subject must command more than specialist interest and there must be sufficient material available. Admittedly the second prerequisite restricts the field somewhat, although it should be remembered that sources do exist for a surprisingly wide range of biographical studies. Nonetheless, it is worth noting how many influential figures destroyed or heavily censored their papers, and how many relatives have either done the same or refused historians access to privately held materials.

The nature of biographical writings has changed markedly over their long history. Whereas leaders – especially political and military ones – used to be favoured, and most subjects were given hagiographic treatment, in recent years biography has become the vehicle for sophisticated historiographical approaches, including psychoanalytical ones.[24] The critical evaluation of a life is now more acceptable and biographies remain extremely popular with general readers. In a single individual's life we see many factors at play – the expected political, social and economic ones, of course, but also education, kinship and friendship networks, leisure activities, reading, work, and so on. In this way, reconstructing a life can be a form of *histoire totale* on a limited scale. It tells a story according to a pattern which most people find deeply satisfying – a life story has an intuitive appeal that should not be sneered at. Whereas biographies used to be thought of as conventional and frumpy, it is now becoming clear how rich in historical insights they can be.[25] Furthermore, a key feature of all historical writing is made manifest in them – the desire, even the need, to identify with our objects of study. The process of identification is facilitated when those objects are people with whom one has to engage both intellectually and imaginatively. A fantastic example of all these points is Anna Funder's *Stasiland*, which weaves together oral history, autobiography and contemporary history, to produce a chillingly vivid account of life in East Germany after the Second World War under the surveillance of the secret police, the Stasi. A number of life histories form the core of the book, but they are not narrated in chronological order, rather they are 'portraits' of people, stitched together through the intense encounters the author has with her subjects, as the shredded Stasi files are being painstakingly reassembled so that their subjects can know what was said about them. She is also 'painting a picture of a city on the old fault-line of east and west', while reflecting on the elaborate, selective ways in which memory works.[26]

So far in this chapter I have been addressing three points. The first is that history is so huge, in terms of its subject matter, its sources and its scope, that it has to be divided up in order to make it manageable. The second is that there are many different ways of accomplishing this; all contain significant assumptions, which shape the historical writings that result. Third, precisely because the divisions between different kinds of history are problematic and arbitrary, there have been attempts to write about the past in a more satisfying manner. I have characterised these as holistic and given the example of biography. I have also suggested that cultural history, which is now enjoying an unprecedented vogue, is another manifestation of the wish for forms of history which recreate the range of experiences and imperatives to which all human beings are subject. Cultural history has shown itself to be open to a variety of theoretical perspectives that place the nature of human consciousness at the very heart of scholarship. In this case the coherence or sense of wholeness that is sought by a number of historical traditions is found in human mental processes, since all historical phenomena are mediated by them.[27] It is important to compare very different ways of slicing up the historical cake.

FRESH FIELDS

Many new fields of history have emerged since the Second World War, and at first sight this looks like the result of processes of fragmentation and specialisation. There is certainly some of this involved – the expansion of higher education, for instance, has increased not only participation rates but also the numbers of university teachers. Not all teachers of undergraduates have had to do research, but now the trend is precisely in this direction, as teaching becomes valued less than research and as institutions compete for status and resources. In the humanities research is a matter for individuals, hence it is experienced as what is most properly one's own, even as a species of private property. It goes without saying that the academy is also committed to sharing knowledge freely and openly, and hence tensions constantly arise between this rather utopian goal and the need for researchers to make claims about originality in their research, which can be damaged if they pass findings around too freely before anything is published. The development of new fields can be seen as one way of creating distinctive niches, via specialisation, for the ever increasing numbers of historians. But there is another way of approaching the matter. New fields do not have to be seen just in terms of splitting a subject up to serve the interests of its practitioners; sometimes their formation is motivated by political concerns that require objects of identification.

The development of women's history is an excellent example of the complex investments in new fields. Historians have long been interested in women and, specifically, in whether women have a distinctive social role and, hence, history. This much is clear in eighteenth-century writings, which preceded the interest in the rights of women that is characteristic of the 1790s, and the growth of movements to reform women's legal and social status of the nineteenth century.[28] Yet the main impetus for women's history as a distinct field did coincide with 'second-wave' feminism, when more women were trying to make academic careers in institutions that were heavily male dominated. To this extent the development of women's history could be seen as a move that served the interests of aspiring female historians. Yet many of the early pioneers of this phase of women's history were men, and there were no guarantees that the new field would provide employment for women – in fact, there are still very few jobs designated as women's history positions in the UK, despite the fact that many people consider themselves to be working in the field. There are a lot more posts in the USA, where academic life built on politicised identities has been considerably more successful. In many parts of Europe, women's history is a tiny and somewhat marginal field compared to more conventional historical areas, although it has gained significant ground in Scandinavia.[29]

Two other closely related issues were involved in the efforts to establish women's history as a recognised field – issues that come up in many new areas built around identity politics. The name 'women's history' implies recognition of the value of the category 'women' for the purposes of historical research. It constitutes a form of legitimation, not just for an academic activity, but for the group that is its focus. Giving value is a political process, and women's history endows with significance both women and those who study their past. The second issue brings us back to identification. Having a separate field facilitates the identification of historians with those they study, and, by extension, the identification of their readers with women in the past. It also helps historians build up their own identities in dynamic interaction with both their academic peers and political movements with shared concerns. Similar processes have been at work in the development of black history, which, like women's history, makes an important contribution in furnishing role models and acting as a vehicle through which painful experiences can be understood historically. Inevitably new fields also raise ethical issues: should historians apportion blame retrospectively? Should they seek out and celebrate people who can be used as role models? Should they seek to change present-day values by retelling the past? These are difficult questions, which are impossible to answer in general terms, since much depends on the context in which they arise. It is inevitable that new fields of study will be doing complex cultural work, and by that token they are likely to be controversial. Precisely because they contain demands – pay attention to this social group, recognise oppression, take my point of view seriously – they are felt to be threatening, strident and lacking in solidity by those working within well-established areas of history. A good example of these points, which brings out the complexities to which I am alluding, is the history of childhood.[30] This area of history has arisen in the context of unprecedented interest in psychoanalysis and child abuse; there is a particularly high moral ground to be occupied here. Given that there are relatively few direct testimonies from children themselves, the opportunities for slippery forms of identification are particularly great. The feelings of both those who promote and those who resist new fields are to be taken seriously, although it is rarely possible for all the stakes involved to be openly acknowledged. Such conflicts are probably unavoidable, although they can and should be conducted with as much humanity and understanding as possible.

Historical research stems from many impulses, and historians are often deeply emotionally engaged with both their subject matter and their approaches. This makes for high levels of commitment, which are not amen-

2.3 *The Sick Child* **by Gabriel Metsu (***c.* **1665)**
Simon Schama used considerable amounts of visual evidence in *The Embarrassment of Riches*. Francis Haskell offered a persuasive critique of his approach, using this Dutch painting from the seventeenth century as an example. Historians are often tempted to treat 'realist' images as windows onto past worlds.

able to rational analysis, and for an intolerance towards those who do not share one's values and may even be opposed to them. Greater tolerance and respect for deep commitments is required, which might be easier if historians were more accustomed to speaking openly of their emotional investment in their work. Yet openness can be extraordinarily hard to achieve given the depth of political divisions among practitioners of the discipline. In these situations it is vital to be able to turn, dispassionately, to evidence and to firm ideas about its appropriate use, which involves both ethical and intellectual considerations. The alternative is trying to fight the matter out in terms that are ultimately unresolvable because they rest on matters of *belief* and not of *evidence*. Yet since beliefs are so important, there are bound to be conflicts. The extent of French collaboration during the pro-Nazi Vichy regime, which was established in 1940, is an interesting example. Feelings on the subject continue to run high – the very notion 'collaboration' implies moral taint, all the more so in what is widely regarded as a 'just war'. It is remarkable that the museum dedicated to the history of the French resistance in Lyon manages to handle the issue extraordinarily well, partly by presenting a great deal of evidence while acknowledging its emotional power.[31] Although I have linked these matters with the development of new fields, this is simply where they are most obvious; they arise in traditional areas too, especially where participation in political regimes now widely condemned is at issue. More generally, when fields change and the maps of a discipline are redrawn, then occasions arise for reflecting upon settled assumptions.

GEOGRAPHICAL BOUNDARIES

So far, when taking examples of sub-fields, I have used those which bring to the fore categories of human beings that claim special attention and elicit special forms of identification: women, blacks, Jews, children, and so on. I could have chosen other examples: workers, gays or slaves, for instance. But history can also be divided up according to other criteria. I want to consider some of these now, four in particular: regions, approaches, themes and theories. After the political/social/economic schema, the most common division is by place, which often involves an area that is now a nation state. We should note, however, that less professionalised forms of history pay particular attention to local areas, to regions that are considerably smaller than nation states, often of long standing in terms of their names and boundaries, and administratively important when it comes to organising records and archives.[32] In part this reflects the vitality of amateur local history and the strength of local pride. Equally it reveals long-standing scholarly traditions in which the past of a delimited area is examined by archaeologists, antiquarians, genealogists and architectural historians, as well as by 'historians'.

Countries are taken as obvious units of analysis, despite the fact that national boundaries are rarely neat at all. We can make the obvious point about disputed and changing borders, and add that within national boundaries questions of language use, ethnicity, religion and regional variations may be so contentious that any sense of unity becomes exceedingly fragile. For French, Chinese, German, Mexican or Italian history to be meaningful notions, historians require conceptual frameworks that hold disparate phenomena together. To lump historical processes together because they occurred in areas we *now* name France, China, and so on, is intellectually weak. Accordingly, it is possible to return to the unifying effect of political structures, and argue that if there is a single governmental apparatus, head of state and systems for law, health care, education, and so on, then it is meaningful to speak of Greek history, Spanish history or Egyptian history. Historians are becoming increasingly attentive to the complexities of just these issues. Yet at undergraduate level they are rarely raised, and many students take courses in French history without being aware either of the complexities of 'France' or of the ways in which prior assumptions about 'France' shape the work that is carried out. It is frequently taken for granted that French history is characterised by the existence of a strong state, hence areas where this was resisted, ineffective or simply not operative are played down. (It is equally surprising how often France means just Paris.) In contrast, British historians until recently have tended to imagine that during the period of French absolutism, Britain was characterised by a weak state apparatus. Revisionism on these issues strikes at the very heart of a sense of national identity.[33] In the British case this has involved the idea that we are laissez-faire at heart, although there is considerable evidence to the contrary from many historical periods. Yet this invented self-image still sets the terms in which (some) history is practised, and it is significant, I suspect, that few of the great theorists of the state have been British.

The problem is that we think of places as self-evident – geography is simply there – and tend to neglect the intricate historical processes through which they have been constructed. The point applies not just to countries, but to all the geographical units that historians use.[34] The solution is to pay more attention to the ways in which these were defined and imagined in the period we are studying. Yet learned journals based on countries tend to cover all periods, producing a certain homogenising effect, especially in cases such as Germany and Italy where unification is rather recent. The nation state is often taken as a norm, and hence the goal towards which earlier processes were moving. This kind of teleology is unhelpful and encourages anachronism.

The big plus of area-based history is that it encourages researchers to think about diverse historical phenomena in relation to one another.[35] We have already discussed holistic history, and it seems that, despite the existence of work such as Braudel's, area-based history works best when it takes entities smaller than countries. It is particularly effective for zones or topics where a nation state is not the most meaningful unit. The approach has been especially generative when cities are used as case studies. However, it would be over-specialised to define sub-fields in specifically local terms. Where local archives are particularly rich, historians may use them repeatedly, but with a variety of historical problems in mind. It would be these problems, rather than the location of the archives, that defined the kinds of history they were undertaking.[36]

METHODS AND APPROACHES

The second form of division is by method or, more loosely, approach. Two contrasting examples will help to clarify the issues involved – quantitative

history and oral history. While the use of quantitative techniques in historical analysis is not new – debates about the effects of the Industrial
Revolution using statistical measures have been going on for ages – its significant growth has been since the Second World War, with the hugely
increased impact of the social sciences on the discipline of history. There are
a number of arguments for the use of statistical methods in historical
research.[37] They are exceptionally well suited to the study of groups, since it
is possible to examine meaningfully aggregates that would otherwise be
dealt with impressionistically. Collective phenomena, if I can put it that way,
come into their own. A closely related argument is that a degree of precision
is offered by quantitative techniques that would not otherwise be available.
Demographic work on age at marriage or on illegitimacy rates exemplifies
the point since it enables historians to think about the nature of sexual activity among the young in more than vague and anecdotal ways. When age at
marriage is high, illegitimacy rates low and reliable contraception unavailable, historians have to reflect upon mechanisms of social control and
varied forms of sexual expression. They can also examine periods of social
transition with these issues in mind. Hence, another argument for quantitative techniques is that they reveal trends over long periods of time. There
are a number of reasons why long-term trends are important. They provide
a perspective that affords precise insights into periods of stability and
change, and they reveal just those slow, almost imperceptible shifts that historians otherwise find difficult to conceptualise. Thus they also open the way
for comparing different types of historical change, which work at different
paces, and historians hopefully become more careful when it comes to
assigning causes to significant shifts. Furthermore, better understanding of
long-term trends highlights the frequent discrepancies between perceptions
of change and change itself. For example, there were widespread anxieties
about population decline in many countries during the eighteenth century.
Demographic evidence reveals that no such decline took place, and in
England, for example, there was unprecedented growth. This insight is
useful, not so that we can chastise eighteenth-century commentators for
being wrong, but so that we can pay attention to the ways in which attitudes
take hold and are to be explained. Just invoking what is 'out there' clearly
will not do.[38]

Building historical work around quantitative methods is not unproblematic; it depends upon the quality of information available.[39] Consistency
is a particular problem here; for long-term trends to be meaningful, the data
across time and place have to be strictly comparable, and changes in their
nature (mode of gathering, criteria for inclusion, and so on) can undermine
general conclusions based upon them. How such information is interpreted
and what it is thought to demonstrate are equally contentious issues. Roger
Schofield explored precisely such an issue when he asked what can be
inferred from maternal mortality data about how women felt about child-
birth. It is a particular challenge to find evidence concerning the relationships between human beings' *subjective* sense of risk and *statistical* risk as

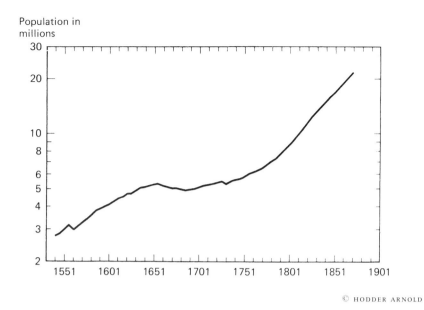

Population in millions

2.4 Estimate of English population totals, taken from Wrigley and Schofield, *A Population History of England 1541–1871* **(1981)**
This relatively simple graph offers an immediate sense of population trends from cursory visual inspection. The table referred to as the source for the graph consists simply of lists of numbers, the interpretation of which demands quite different intellectual skills. Wrigley and Schofield's *Population History of England 1541–1871* presents a wealth of quantitative material in diverse formats and thereby illustrates the huge range of ways in which data can be gathered, used and interpreted.

painstakingly reconstructed by demographers.[40] Claims about changes in women's attitudes would have to be documented using different types of evidence. Any sense of risk is a complex cultural phenomenon, which cannot simply be read off from the known occurrence of a particular event. It is both useful and important to know that maternal mortality was considerably less frequent than is usually supposed, but the wider conclusions we draw from this are less obvious. One productive route is to use such information as a stimulus for general historical reflection, so that quantitative materials are interpreted in the light of and after comparison with diverse qualitative ones. The limitations of quantitative sources are sometimes insufficiently appreciated, perhaps because they appear 'scientific'; it is vital to analyse critically the manipulations to which they have been subject before they reach the printed page. It is unfortunate to isolate quantitative from qualitative work; they are best seen as complementary. However, specialisation, especially in the skills needed to do first-rate quantitative work, tends to work in the opposite direction.

While there are close links between quantitative methods and economic history, many historians who work on economic phenomena do not in fact use statistical methods and vice versa. Economic history is potentially an extremely broad field: 'the history of actual human practice with respect to the material basis of life'.[41] We could say that economic history concerns itself with production on the one hand and consumption on the other. In spite of the concern with such huge, all-pervasive issues, economic history remains too little integrated with other approaches. Whereas 'quantitative history' signals that specific methods are involved, 'economic history' implies privileging one dimension of human life; it is therefore regrettable that it is often presented as impersonal. I would see economic history as more an approach than a method, although there are phenomena most historians would happily agree to call 'economic' – taxes, trade, the prices of commodities, for example – and by that token the field possesses distinctive content. Yet economic history can draw on the powerful and highly theorised discipline of economics; indeed some economic historians practise in departments of economics.[42] The use of economic theories (which tend to emphasise the rational choices of individuals) within the discipline of history raises a number of difficult issues, since they depend on models of human nature, the implications of which are rarely explored sufficiently deeply. Invoking economic theory does not solve the question of what sustains conventional definitions of economic history. As we observed in the case of political history, the defence of economic history must rest on 'economic' being analytically distinguishable and useful for historical explanation. It may well be that, as with quantitative techniques, the skills are sufficiently specialised that designated groups of historians, who are looking less at individuals in the past as economic actors and more at trends, aggregates, and so on, are required. Nonetheless, some clear idea of the work done by the concept 'economic' is vital. We might say that methods and approaches such as these examine certain *levels* of historical phenomena most effectively, but this notion in turn requires careful scrutiny.

The notion of levels of historical phenomena could also be applied to oral history – a clear example of a method-based division in the discipline. Oral history is based on the idea that powerful insights can be derived from people talking about their experiences. It therefore gives a certain status to memory, no matter how complex or uncertain this mental faculty may be. It also assumes that everyone's memory is valuable and of potential historical interest. Although it is possible to do elite oral history, the voice of the past (to use Paul Thompson's phrase), is that of the humble, of working men and women, who did not have power as this has usually been defined, but who did have rich experiences of social change, family, work, politics, and so on, that offer a distinct historical perspective.[43] So 'experience' is a key word for oral history, but it is experience evoked retrospectively by speaking about the past. Arguments in favour of this method would include the point that it offers access to phenomena that are otherwise close to invisible. The complexities of household management would be a case in point, and many health and reproductive matters were experienced in private and were inaccessible to historians until women, especially, were interviewed. The *quality* of human relationships in the past can be effectively brought to life by oral history techniques, which do not depend on literal accuracy, but on getting inside people's heads. Where accuracy is an issue, oral evidence should always be cross-checked with other sources. Although potentially a highly sophisticated technique, oral history can nonetheless be widely practised, and is, in a number of senses, a democratising approach to history.

One potential danger associated with oral history, however, is that of over-identification with those being interviewed, a point that links in with issues in other historical fields – the cult of authenticity and romanticisation. Neither of these is confined to the practice of history, although they are especially important issues for historians whose professional training and surrounding culture encourage them to seek truths and authentic evidence, which become all the more precious if they have been garnered with much effort. A person speaking to a historian of their own experience generates an especially direct kind of evidence, which is all the more valued if it comes from those who were not previously considered significant historical actors. And if such testimony contains, as it so often does, accounts of suffering and deprivation, of heroism and stoicism, then our romantic sensibilities are readily engaged. This does not necessarily involve seeing the past as *better* than it was – a shallow interpretation of 'romantic' – but it may create an emotional aura that affects the resulting scholarship. Such emotional invest-ments have their generative side, but they can also reinforce simple moral polarities, which are necessarily, given what we know of the human condi-tion, strategic fictions.

THEMATIC HISTORY

The tenor of my remarks about method-based history implies that it is a somewhat artificial way of organising historical research. There is a point of view according to which the most satisfying accounts of the past involve a wide range of materials and of methods, and that, in any given piece of research, the two should be brought into harmony with one another. One possibility is to take a theme as the organising principle – for example, an idea that has been important and influential and that has many facets. The clearest early examples of such work came out of the history of ideas, although it must be admitted that they privileged written texts of a some-what elite kind.[44] Arthur Lovejoy's classic book *The Great Chain of Being*, first published in 1936, took a pervasive model of creation and traced its history from classical times through to its demise with the development of evolu-tionary theory at the very end of the eighteenth century. Here, as in his other writings, Lovejoy used a wide range of written, although not archival, sources.[45] The emphasis in the history of ideas has tended towards 'high' culture, although there are many themes that bring together more diverse aspects of societies. Perhaps it is significant that *The Past Is a Foreign Country* was written by an American geographer. David Lowenthal's wide-ranging book looks at evidence from buildings, railway stations and museums, as well as from more expected sources, in order to examine the ways in which the past is imagined and represented, in fiction and in poetry as much as in historical writings. It would be hard to know exactly what kind of history this is, although there is now a growing literature on what could be called 'heritage issues', an area in which historians have only recently become active.[46] A somewhat different kind of thematic history has been undertaken by Keith Thomas, for example, in his *Man and the Natural World* (1983). The theme – how human beings have treated nature over several centuries – is evidently huge, and it is the occasion for bringing together disparate topics, sources and issues. Thomas constructs a sort of bricolage, assembling huge numbers of examples, quotations and anecdotes in the service of his theme. Such thematic history is bound to be less easy to control and to organise in a linear fashion than more conventional types of history. It is best seen as a supplement to other forms rather than a substitute for them. Since it can cut the cake in original ways, it can be used heuristically, in generating ideas and reappraisals, as *Man and the Natural World* certainly did. Current interest in the history of animals, for instance, while it owes something to 'animal liberation' movements, is productive because it offers an unusual vantage point, made possible by attending to themes and preoccupations of the past that do not fit into tidy packages.[47] A wonderful example is Mark Jenner's study of seventeenth-century attitudes to dogs, who were often slaughtered in times of plague, which is designed to open up responses to the disease from a new perspective.[48]

THEORY-BASED HISTORY

Fresh perspectives have many points of origination, sometimes in theories. Most people see history as a relatively untheorised discipline, although whether this is good or bad depends on your point of view. It also depends on the country in which you received your training. Historiography in the English-speaking world, in contrast to the more overtly theoretical French, Italian and German traditions, tends to emphasise the empirical dimensions of history. Although (some) historians work closely with theoretical perspectives, this does not tend to take the form of producing theories of history – at least, it did not do so in the twentieth century.[49] The major theorists of society have not been historians. Whatever tradition they are trained in, historians are more accustomed to searching for particularities, to spotting what is unique or special about a situation, than to noting its kinship with other cases. The latter is precisely what comparative history as a method sets out to do, but there is hardly *a* theory of comparative history.[50] Until about 20 years ago, most people would have come up with Marxism if asked to name a theory important to the practice of history. Now there appear to be few attempts to develop Marxian historiography further. We could interpret this shift in a number of ways. It could indicate disenchantment with the world view that Marxism represented. It could suggest that its key elements have already been incorporated where they are useful. Perhaps just fragments of Marxism remain alive.[51] It is possible that, because of cultural shifts, historians have lost interest in the leading themes of Marxism, such as class struggle and the nature of production, because they ceased to be apt for the world we now inhabit. Intellectual fashions do change, as a result of which theories fall out of favour, less because of explicit criticisms than because they are no longer vital and relevant.

Over the same period there has been a dramatic growth of interest in psychoanalysis. Although still regarded with suspicion in some quarters, it has become an accepted part of the historian's theoretical armoury, especially in the United States, where many large history departments include a psychohistorian on the staff, and where special training courses are available to scholars who want to use psychoanalysis in their research but have no wish to develop clinical skills.[52] Yet most people, and scholars are no exception, think psychoanalytically without being particularly aware of doing so. Many of the explanations we give of behaviour in everyday life owe much to what are now commonplace assumptions about how the unconscious works. Since a significant proportion of historical explanation rests on such assumptions, psychoanalysis has found its way into historical practice. However, many historians still have little direct knowledge of psychoanalytic thinking or of the significant differences between its principal traditions: Freudian, Jungian, Kleinian and Lacanian. There have been attacks on psychoanalysis in history, as there have on psychoanalysis in general. Readers may find it helpful to remember that the use of psychoanalysis does not have to be doctrinaire, but can be quite flexible, where the starting point is the historical problem. I would advocate that historians adopt the more flexible posture, and employ assumptions about psychology and behaviour knowingly wherever possible.[53] The implication of my position is that the creation of separate sub-fields can generate rigid and artificial divisions – it is much better for historians to be open to a range of theoretical perspectives, so long as they develop a critical purchase upon them.

Historians need to be able not just to recognise and name specific theoretical perspectives, but to have some idea of the properties of theories in general. Theories work at a meta-level, that is, they are more general and abstract than empirical detail. They offer frameworks designed to explain a wide range of phenomena. It follows, then, that theories tend to have a certain predictive quality – in the case of psychoanalysis, it can be claimed that specific types of psychological damage will have particular effects. In practice, clinicians and historians work back from the effects to the putative causes. Psychohistory tends to emphasise childhood experience and its effects on later life without paying sufficient attention to the specific historical context, and for some historians this is reductive.[54] We might say, however, that psychoanalysis broadly defined takes the complexities of the mind seriously and in this way helps historians to develop more satisfying ways of understanding human actions and experience. It is also one possible way of exploring the significance of metaphors and symbols, which often attain their power precisely because of their ability to tap into the unconscious.[55]

There are two commonly voiced objections to the use of psychoanalysis in history. The first is that it is an individualistic method, which may possibly work in relation to individuals about whom a great deal is known, but that it fails when it comes to group phenomena. In fact, many analysts, building on earlier psychological work, have thought about collective psychology, and psychohistorians have addressed precisely this issue in studying how totalitarian leaders can command support, for example. The second objection is that it is wrong, if not downright impossible, to psychoanalyse the dead, and that the method is especially inappropriate when it is applied to societies that were themselves innocent of psychoanalytic ideas. The latter point always seems to me to be particularly obtuse – theories are designed to be general, to be applied to a wide range of cases, and if they are productive theories they do not just apply to the period in which they were formulated. The *unconscious* did not come into being in the late nineteenth century; it has existed for as long as there have been human beings.[56]

BRIDGE

'History' is not a defined body of knowledge but an abstract idea with many meanings. Thus when we think about it as an academic discipline, it can easily seem overwhelming – it just includes so much that it is difficult to imagine where its coherence lies. I have argued in this chapter that there are a number of ways in which we can examine what is going on in the subject matter of the discipline in order to have a sketch map of it. Some of these involve thinking about the raw materials and how they are used. Others involve reflecting upon the method or theory applied to those materials. Yet others involve trying to work out how the discipline has been divided up and what these divisions mean for our understanding of the past. Partly they make research practicable, but they are also vehicles for powerful emotions and investments, for claims about how the past is best approached. In these respects history has much in common with other disciplines, upon which it has at times been extremely reliant. We may imagine cognate fields as resources for historians, or indeed as threats, since the study of the past is by no means the exclusive domain of history. In the following chapter I examine the complex and sometimes fraught relationships between history and its near neighbours.

3

History and other disciplines

DISCIPLINES IN HISTORY

History has not always been a discipline – a term that implies elaborate institutional, professional and communications structures. Before it became a separate field of study, history was a form of writing, in fact it was many forms. At its most simple, 'history' means description, as in 'natural history', which provides accounts of the natural world. It is worth remembering that Pliny's great *Natural History* was not just about animals, plants and minerals, but also about history, biography, art history, and so on.[1] For the Greeks histories were narratives of significant human doings, especially of wars. For the literate of medieval times, history was composed of chronicles, which described kinship relations, the distribution of property, the successes and travails of Christianity, conflicts between lords and the fate of kings. Lives of saints and martyrs (hagiographies) were also important. In the centuries that followed much historical scholarship was undertaken, but not by professionals called 'historians', since these did not exist. Rather it was produced by men (largely) who had other interests, concerns, professions and jobs; they were travellers, men of the church, doctors and lawyers. History was perceived as integral to theology, the gathering and study of antiquities, the practice of medicine and the law, the formation of collections and the preservation of the material past.[2]

Histories that we can easily recognise as representing endeavours close to our own were produced in the eighteenth century, but their authors rarely taught history or saw their identity as that of 'historian': David Hume, Edward Gibbon, Voltaire, David Ramsay and Giambattista Vico.[3] Such works were widely read and admired, in part because they spoke with conviction to contemporary concerns. However, they were not the products of 'research' as we understand it, which involves intensive use of primary sources, generally including manuscripts, and protocols covering footnotes and bibliography, together with consequent claims to scholarly originality. Over the nineteenth century history was widely institutionalised, in the sense of there being not only university posts but organised archives available to scholars. Only in the twentieth century has history been a staple of the higher education curriculum with all the paraphernalia of a discipline.

One effect of discipline formation is to isolate scholars within their own subject-based communities. Although it is always possible to read the books and articles produced by disciplines other than one's own, this is a different kind of activity from direct collaboration between people who have been trained in different disciplines. Encountering a discipline through reading its publications is a somewhat abstract, disembodied enterprise – it is difficult to sense its habits of mind, the distinctive qualities of its intellectual practices, and where the tensions and excitements lie. Furthermore, such reading tends to be highly selective, giving a rather distorted view of the other field. A relatively small number of authors become known outside their own areas and the reason why one rather than another gets widely taken up often remains obscure. Hence, whenever we speak of interdisciplinary work and of history's relations with other subjects, the distinction between these two forms of cross-disciplinary encounter should be borne in mind. Some now prefer to speak of 'multi-disciplinarity', which simply signals that a number of different fields of study are being deployed.

In the light of these points it is somewhat ironic that history has been a separate discipline for only a relatively short period of time. Indeed the very notion of a discipline is rather recent. In earlier times there were recognised and institutionalised fields of knowledge, such as the medieval quadrivium of arithmetic, geometry, astronomy and music, with university posts and special publications, but these were not disciplines in the modern sense, as is clear when we consider rhetoric, part of the trivium, which was more akin to a method than to a discipline, and recall that theology was hailed as the queen of the sciences. In most European languages, 'science' implied 'systematic knowledge' until the eighteenth century; there was more interest in kinds of learning than in dividing knowledge up according to its subject matter. Intense intellectual specialisation is a feature of twentieth-century societies. For most of recorded history, the scholarly study of the past has been integral to a wide range of activities, hence its separation goes against the grain. Furthermore, it is worth remembering how much of what is today widely read as history is written by those outside the university system – authors such as Claire Tomalin, Antonia Fraser, Michael Holroyd, Elizabeth Longford and Barbara Tuchman spring to mind.[4] The importance of recording, cherishing and using the past goes back a very long way indeed. It is therefore surprising that many historians have an impoverished sense of history's history. The sense of a past is central to many human endeavours – in institutions, professions and families, for example – and it is produced out of deep engagement with earlier times, which have never been the private property of 'historians'.

THEORY

This chapter focuses on relations between modern academic disciplines, and, given the space I am devoting to history's interactions with other fields, the implication is that they are extensive, complex and vital for understanding the discipline as a whole. What do we mean when we talk about relations between disciplines? We could mean a historical appreciation of how areas of study have developed, which would show how disciplinary definitions are constructed and change, and the shifting purposes for which the past is studied. As academic life has evolved, especially since the Second World War, understanding relationships between disciplines involves considerably more than this. It includes: the sharing of sources conventionally associated with a single domain; the transfer of information and insights between distinct fields; the movements of theories and concepts from one area to another; the inspiration that can come from venturing outside one's own immediate subject, when a different approach or mindset offers creative possibilities.

At first glance, the previous sentence does not contain any unusual or difficult words, yet it mentions matters which are widely misunderstood or treated carelessly. Take, for example, 'theory' – relations between disciplines and the role of theory are closely linked questions.[5] It is often said that historians are uncomfortable with theory, that they are 'mindlessly empiricist' in their tendency to search for 'facts' without possessing adequate interpretative frameworks. Hence the claim that when historians need theoretical insights they look outside their own domain, to economics or political theory, for example. The use of modernisation theory or of Habermas's ideas on the public sphere are cases in point.[6] This is an issue of major importance since it bears on the nature and status of historical knowledge and on ideas about historical method. It is therefore vital to be perfectly explicit about what we mean by 'theory'. In doing so we need to signal an issue to which we shall return in the following chapter, namely, the widespread use of the natural sciences as *the* model for reliable knowledge. Scientific procedures are still seen by some commentators as exemplifying a rationality that should be emulated by historians. This is the burden of David Stannard's critique of psychohistory, for example. The point is relevant to theory in two ways: first, the sciences, especially the physical ones, are perceived to possess intellectually powerful theories, which provide high-quality explanations; and, second, a separation between theories and facts is taken to be self-evident. In both cases misleading extrapolations are made for the practice of history. We should note how the very vocabulary we use – 'factual' and 'empirical', 'theoretical' and 'conceptual' – affirms a separation between 'raw' data and what is done with them, although the reality is altogether more complex.

I take theories to have four main characteristics. First, 'theory' implies a general account of something, which explains more than one instance of it – case studies bear on theories, but the latter are more general and abstract than the former. Second, it implies that phenomena can be explained by reference to it, with the result that these phenomena are better understood at the end than at the beginning of any inquiry. Third, it implies that new cases will be illuminated by it – in history this is not the same as prediction, since history cannot be said to predict the future.[7] But a theory of revolution might be developed, for example, in relation to the French and Russian revolutions, and then be found to be extremely useful in relation to, say, the Mexican Revolution.[8] Fourth, it implies the existence of a coherent perspective, embodied in the theory, which is able to bring together and render meaningful diverse phenomena. This is a corollary of its status as an abstract, general framework. Putting all these points together, it is apparent that 'theory' carries an aura of intellectual power.

It should now be clear why history, as it has generally been practised in the twentieth century, has not been a particularly theoretical subject. There has been a strong emphasis on providing, instance by instance, accurate and convincing accounts of what happened in the past. Much of the best history has proceeded by a kind of immersion in the sources, taking its explanatory devices out of those sources, which suggests that too crisp a separation between theories and sources is misleading and unhelpful. No empirical activity is possible without a theory (or at least elaborate presuppositions) behind it, even if these remain implicit, perhaps unconscious. All historians have ideas already in their minds when they study primary materials – models of human behaviour, established chronologies, assumptions about responsibility, notions of identity, and so on. Of course, some are convinced that they are merely gathering facts, looking at sources with a totally open mind and only recording what is there, yet they are simply wrong to believe this. Since it is rather easy to show how full historians' minds already are when they do research, the persistence of contrary beliefs requires explanation. One possible explanation is that, as professionally-based world views, disciplines generate accounts of themselves which practitioners are strongly encouraged to buy into, and that these accounts serve specific interests. The idea that history is primarily an empirical subject can be used to suggest that it taps directly into the historical record and simply gives a straightforward account of it. In this way, the truthfulness of history, its status as a discipline, and its special kind of authority, are all affirmed. Furthermore, stories about what makes disciplines special help to create boundaries between related areas of activity; distinct identities are important for cognate fields because otherwise the professional lives of practitioners and the integrity of their products would be under (perceived) threat. Once there is an infrastructure that supports disciplines, lines of demarcation between forms of intellectual authority have to be actively maintained. Frontiers between disciplines are artefacts; they are human productions doing particular jobs, even if those who create and sustain them are not fully aware of it.

We can rephrase these points in the language of ownership. Disciplines mark out territories that are 'theirs', and the resulting division of labour is designed to produce different sorts of knowledge and to prevent boundary disputes. When a scholar wants to take information or ideas from another field, it can be seen as borrowing, and, if conducted correctly, with due acknowledgement, a productive transaction has taken place. From the perspective of the other, donor field, a gift has been given. The same story can, however, be told differently with history as a kind of victim, under threat from other disciplines, which are taking it over, invading it or simply behaving as if it did not exist. Whether transfers of intellectual property are seen as gifts, theft or pillage depends on your vantage point. It would be useful if the whole idiom of knowledge as property, however appealing, could be critically scrutinised.

An alternative account eschews the property idiom and draws support from the facts that disciplines in general and history in particular are recent phenomena, and that history has been practised for centuries as integral to other endeavours. The sources that scholars draw on are not labelled with the name of a particular field of study: literature, history, sociology, and so on, but treated according to conventions. Within this framework, disciplines are recognised as constructs, the history of which is important; they are endowed, not with intrinsic, but with contingent properties. Many disciplines use materials from the past – so is there anything inherent in the materials that historians use that makes them apt for history but not for sociology, for instance? If the answer is 'no', do historians have particular things they do with their materials? In so far as the question is answered in terms of specialised skills, we must defer our discussion until chapter 7. As regards understanding these particular issues in terms of approaches or theories, they are central to our concerns here. Unfortunately, there are no clear-cut answers to these questions. The most productive way forward is to turn to specific examples. I have selected six fields – sociology, anthropology, philosophy, literary studies, archaeology and geography – that relate to the discipline of history in particularly revealing ways.

Different parts of the discipline of history have their own views and customs when it comes to affinities between fields. Many ancient historians and medievalists would put archaeology at the top of their list of cognate disciplines, and indeed the relationships between history and archaeology have been exceptionally intricate: at some points they simply merge.[9] For those concerned with the history of the environment, geography, especially new trends in historical geography, has been important. In fact, geographical approaches are becoming increasingly central for studies of colonial and post-colonial situations.[10] In what follows I shall be stressing the uses historians have made of these six domains, but we should remember that such relationships are reciprocal. Other disciplines have undergone a 'historical turn'.[11] They have their own historical concerns; after all, they emerged in eras when the study of the past was not the exclusive property of one group and they continue to draw upon their own pasts for the purposes of identity construction and legitimation.

HISTORY AND SOCIOLOGY[12]

Sociology was the first discipline after 1945 to have a major impact upon the study of history. Inevitably, sociology is no easier to define than is history.[13]

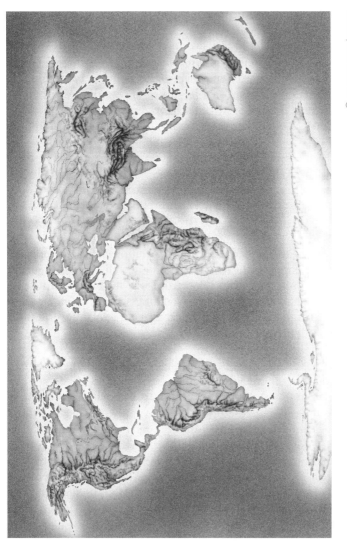

3.1 Map of the world, using a traditional projection
This is probably the image of the world that most people who read this book will have been brought up with. It is now more widely appreciated that it is based on conventions, which have become so familiar that the total package is both natural and authoritative. Maps are always laden not only with cartographic conventions but with value systems.

3.2 Map of the world, using Peters' projection
Here is a deliberate provocation to received images of the world based on a new projection system, which reflects more accurately the size of land masses. Their distribution on the page remains conventional, however. Why should Australia and New Zealand be on the right rather than the left?

By the mid-nineteenth century, a considerable body of work existed that examined society as a distinct type of phenomenon. To look at organised aggregates of people is to undertake a particular kind of analysis, and it was already recognised as such in the eighteenth century. By the end of the nineteenth century, sociology as a discipline could be said to exist and to have a number of different theoretical perspectives, which are most easily recognised by the names of the 'great men' with whom they are associated, above all Karl Marx, Herbert Spencer, Emile Durkheim and Max Weber. All of them were deeply interested in history. Thus these perspectives, as they developed over the twentieth century, were available to historians, and explicitly used by some of them. Social theory developed into a number of new avenues in the twentieth century, yet the self-conscious and explicit turn to it by groups of historians was particularly evident in the 1960s. After the war there was a marked interest, particularly in the United States, in modernisation theory, that is, in general accounts of how societies develop from an agricultural base in which there is relatively little division of labour into complex, modern industrial nation states.[14] This theory is inseparable from the context in which it was developed, namely the economic activities of the 'first world' in putting funds into so-called underdeveloped countries in order to fashion them in their own image. Thus modernisation theory combined economic, social and political concerns. Although its teleological approach, which assumes the modern west as the goal of all historical change, has been widely criticised, aspects of modernisation theory remain deeply entrenched in historical practice, in taken-for-granted terms, such as 'tradition' and 'modernity', construed as radically different social states, in 'development' itself and in '-isation' words, such as secularisation and globalisation. We should note that models of social change frequently draw upon biological accounts in general and evolutionary theories in particular, as Herbert Spencer did explicitly, and they usually assume that the bottom line of a society is its economic relations.[15] This is because material existence, catering to basic needs, is the common ground for biological as for economic survival. The continuing appeal of economic determinism is a significant point. Many comments have been made about the recent demise of Marxism – with which economic determinism is often associated – as a paradigm for historians. For those who use Marxian ideas, the claim that relations of production determine other features of a society remains central, even if it requires considerable unpacking. While it may be that the whole package we call Marxism is now wholeheartedly espoused by very few historians, many practitioners who never saw themselves in this camp are nonetheless economic determinists at heart.

If we associate the enthusiasm for sociology in the 1960s with anything it is with the concept of 'class'. When we say 'class', we are in fact referring to a whole panoply of issues that are highly charged politically.[16] Historians find it difficult to agree on definitions of class; it involves a type of social difference that combines social status, income and cultural factors, including an awareness of the dynamics between classes and of one's own class identity. In the 1960s labour relations became a central topic for sociologically informed history, together with popular protest and forms of social difference that appeared cognate to but not identical with class: above all, race and gender. The term gender was not widely used then, but only became common currency among historians in the 1980s. In France the term is still resisted as an Anglo-American imposition. But women's history underwent tremendous growth in the period, some of it prompted by an interest in showing the significance of female labour to match the attention being paid to male workers. It became crucial for feminist historians to consider whether oppressive relations between men and women were basically a form of class struggle, and to assess the adequacy of theories of class to explain the history of gender relations. These concerns are 'sociological' in that they derive from the theories and methods developed by sociologists. The discipline of sociology was never homogeneous; it contained sophisticated discussions about the use and interpretation of social variables, the analysis of social structure and the social construction of identity upon which historians drew. These discussions contained both general and specific levels of analysis, and they were frequently comparative and historical, thereby constituting a rich resource for historians working on class and on social inequalities generally. It was at this time that Eugene Genovese wrote a highly controversial Marxian account of slavery.[17] Thus a Marxian approach to society contained a number of ideas, theories and concepts that could be applied to a wide range of historical cases, as indeed Marx himself applied them.[18] In particular, the analysis of modes of production and their implications, class oppression, revolution, ideology and imperialism were taken up by historians.

The example of Marxism raises a vexed question for historians, which arises whenever they employ an already articulated theory. In sociology such a theory would be applied to a number of cases, but a sociologist would be less likely to start with the case study and then apply a mixture of theoretical devices to it, which is precisely what many historians do. Eclecticism was less prevalent in the 1960s, but nonetheless historians tend to begin with particular instances in all their complexities and then seek frameworks to help make sense of their material. When an elaborate theory is adopted in its entirety, there is a danger that it will not fit well with sources that are often patchy and uneven. The result can be a mechanistic approach to history in which two levels of analysis – theory and case study – are not adequately integrated. The lack of fit can derive from a mismatch between the language of the theory and that of the case study: for example, if the former uses class, but the latter concerns a society that deployed other terms of social distinction, such as caste. Looked at from a sociologist's perspective, there are also problems. They are more likely to look for the rigorous application of a theory, and to find eclecticism sloppy and intellectually unacceptable. The perception that applying social theory to historical work produces an overly rigid approach was one of the reasons for historians turning away, not just from sociology, but from a number of overtly theoretical orientations, and towards what is known in sociology as grounded theory. This is in fact what many historians do even if they do not describe it in this way. Grounded theory seeks to develop an apt framework out of the materials themselves and hence it is necessarily more pragmatic and flexible than adherence to a pre-existing theory. The dissatisfaction with a mechanistic use of theory also helps to explain the love affair between anthropology and history, to which we shall turn shortly. In order to understand this shift better, we can return to class and note changing attitudes to the concept among historians, which have taken them from a primarily economic understanding of class to a more cultural one. What historians have found especially appealing in anthropology is precisely its close attention to culture.[19]

In the Marxian tradition, class relations arise out of the modes of production and the social relationships they produce. While Marx himself thought about these relationships in highly sophisticated terms, it is fair to say that for much of the twentieth century class has been understood as deriving from economic structures. Because of the oppositional quality of Marxian history and of the sub-fields, such as labour history, where it found enthusiastic expression, economic inequalities and the nature of class oppression were construed as the primary phenomena for historians to explain. Marx and some of his followers, such as the literary critics Georg Lukács and Raymond Williams, were interested in the nature of class consciousness, but many historians' reading of Marx persuaded them that this was a mere product of economic forces. However, by the 1970s, it was becoming increasingly clear to historians that class consciousness was an elaborate and messy phenomenon in its own right. The more social historians dug into the subject, the more its connections with material conditions seemed intricate, even obscure. Furthermore, there was evidence, for example from eighteenth-century England, that class consciousness preceded shifts in the labour process that had hitherto been seen as primary.[20] In other words, what people in the past believed about their social relationships, the metaphors through which they were expressed and the emotional aura that surrounded them became significant historical phenomena in their own right, demanding appropriate analysis. This is precisely a cultural approach. The so-called subjective elements of class identity were given increasing attention, supposedly objective indicators less.

The notion of *reducing* one historical phenomenon to another is pertinent here – it is often invoked when theories are applied to historical materials. The criticism is oversimplification, that is, offering too limited a form of historical explanation. Briefly, the charge of reductionism involves recasting the type and level of phenomena from one that is complex to another that is less so: by implication, one too basic to be satisfying. Psychological explanations, especially psychoanalytic ones, are magnets for such criticism. They are often dismissed as simplistic, reductionist. In the shift from relations of production as determining social relations to class consciousness as a special phenomenon, *not* reducible to economics, the growing interest in culture was manifest, and cultural analysis has been strongly associated with anthropology. In fairness to Marxian traditions, we should record that throughout the twentieth century culturalist approaches were being developed, for instance by Antonio Gramsci, who has been important precisely for those historians on the left, such as E.P. Thompson, who explored the complexities of social identity and practice.[21] Other forms of cultural Marxism have come into the field through writers, such as Raymond Williams, who came from literary backgrounds.

The confidence that many sociologists possess as regards generalising about large patterns and painting big pictures is of great, and I would argue increasing, significance for historians at a time when there is a revival of interest in *longue durée* and world histories. I shall return to these types of history in chapter 8, but the influence of sociologists such as Anthony Giddens, Michael Mann and David Held, who themselves draw extensively on history in their work, who tackle the largest of themes and the most difficult of social issues, should be noted here.[22]

ANTHROPOLOGY AND CULTURE

In fact, we can discern the shift towards cultural analysis in another problem associated with class as a concept, namely the tendency to reify it, rather than to see it as always held in relationships. When we reify something we treat it, inappropriately, as an object. The whole thrust of E.P. Thompson's famous and deeply influential preface to *The Making of the English Working Class*, first published in 1963, was to affirm 'that class is a relationship, and not a thing'.[23] Yet the habit of assigning individuals to classes, as we would assign animals and plants to taxonomic pigeonholes, is deeply entrenched; it is indebted to certain styles of sociology, which examine social variables and social roles, and which can generate a rather static model of human society. For this reason, too, a cultural approach, which pays more attention to the complexities of human relationships, is appealing.

Like sociology, anthropology began to take shape in the nineteenth century. The serious study of other, exotic cultures had begun centuries earlier, and was given impulse by the waves of European exploration of other parts of the world, such as the 'discovery' of America, then of the South Seas, Australia, and so on. The experience of coexisting with another culture was common enough, and often led to detailed accounts that could be called ethnographic. Anthropology was also pursued by scholars of the Bible, by men of the church who worked outside their own cultures, by antiquarians who collected remnants of classical and medieval cultures, by lawyers mapping diverse human arrangements, and so on. Thus, in a sense, what we call anthropology is a very old intellectual concern that has long been allied with history. It draws its energy from human beings' curiosity about other, different human beings, and from the scientific impulse to map human nature, which took particularly clear shape during the Enlightenment.[24] Subsequently anthropology developed in a number of directions: it has become usual to distinguish between physical, social and cultural anthropology – the last two have closer affinities with the discipline of history than does the first. Nonetheless, archaeology and physical anthropology sometimes make common cause, and by that route the latter impinges upon the practice of history.[25]

Over the nineteenth century, anthropology became a self-conscious discipline, possessing strong links with both sociology and the biological sciences. In so far as it mapped exotic cultures, often figured as 'primitive', while historians were examining their own societies, the two fields diverged. The conditions for them coming back together were, from the historian's point of view, the recognition that there were significant similarities between superficially different societies and that the methods anthropologists had developed might be useful to them. The kinship between these two disciplines can be understood as having three dimensions: the shared content of history and anthropology, common methods and overlapping accounts of practice.

The transfer in terms of content is easy to understand: both fields analyse social phenomena. Initially the kinds of societies were seen as rather different – 'primitive' and 'civilised' – but then their similarities were increasingly recognised. Anthropologists developed a number of ideas and concepts that can be used by historians. Ritual, fetish, kinship, magic, possession, symbol, shaman and the gift relationship would all be obvious examples where, even if the concept were not exclusive to anthropology, that field endowed them with a rich significance upon which historians could draw. Sometimes a familiar historical pattern looks different, appears freshly clarified, when it is described in a new vocabulary. To see (some) popular protest in the early modern period as akin to ritual practised in, say, Africa, throws into sharp relief the purpose and significance of such behaviour. From having been seen as conflictual and disorderly, such forms of behaviour now appear to follow patterns, widely understood by contemporaries, producing positive effects for all concerned.[26] This is to recast historical phenomena so that they can be viewed afresh, since if we see forms of protest as disordered and disruptive, then a quite different set of explanations will be given to those deemed appropriate for a structured and familiar ritual. Similarly, the recognition that magic is an elaborate belief system performing a wide range of social functions, rather than unfounded, 'superstitious' ideas now known to be simply wrong, enables witchcraft, astrology and alchemy, for example, to be examined more sympathetically. There is no longer any need to stress their inherent irrationality, which becomes not just irrelevant but a mistaken and anachronistic value judgement.[27]

Anthropological approaches to gifts have been particularly important for historians. To trace gift relationships in historical cases points up the reciprocity in social relationships rather than taking the notion of 'gift' in its obvious, common-sense meaning of something freely given without expectation of exchange.[28] The anthropological cast of the term encourages historians to think about where exchanges occur and how they operate within wider networks of social relationships, whereas a non-anthropological definition takes gifts at face value. There are many further examples of historians taking terms and phrases from anthropological accounts and applying them to their own work, largely in non-exotic settings. Such transfers are possible because the two fields are concerned with similar phenomena. Yet this has been only one facet of the relationship between history and anthropology, and it does not really make sense without the anthropological mindset that many historians have found deeply inspiring. Integral to this mindset are methods that we think of as 'anthropological', and ways of imagining our own intellectual practices.

Before we turn to these matters more explicitly, we need to tackle the tricky issue of exoticism, a notion which carries considerable moral opprobrium. It arises because anthropology as a discipline was built on the study of 'exotic' cultures. The fear is that both anthropologists and historians draw upon and are implicated by unjustifiable relationships between imperialists and those they colonised. Finding something exotic can be understood as covering its exploitation with a veneer of glamour. Exoticism is a difficult topic, not just because it is inherently complex, but also because it is entangled with matters of political correctness and is, as a result, highly charged emotionally. The allure of what is palpably different is a widespread phenomenon; it does not seem to me that it is automatically wrong; it is simply a persistent feature of human relationships. However, there is no doubt that this allure takes on a particular significance when there are dramatic disparities in the power of the knowers and the known, whether these are nations, classes, races, sexes, ages, other kinds of groups or, indeed, individuals. We suspect that the dominant side constructs the weaker party as an exotic other, which can then be colonised, exploited and trivialised: exoticisation is thinly veiled domination. While there may be some truth to this, it is only a partial one, and historians need to be able to admit that they are frequently drawn to their field of study precisely because it *is* exotic, containing just such an allure for them. In other words, what is different and enticing is also to be studied, revered and idealised. Exoticising is just one way of managing the highly troubling and disruptive reactions that cross-cultural encounters provoke – reactions which are typically both positive and negative, and much more besides.

The issue of exoticism is important because it bears on both the methods and the frame of mind adopted by those who study cultures very different to their own. No one approaches such a situation with an empty mind; there is bound to be some baggage. One of the keystones of anthropological fieldwork is the simultaneous sympathetic identification and critical distance of practitioners in relation to those they are studying. The existence of baggage is not denied, and, if possible, it is put to productive use. Anthropologists are trained to be as non-judgemental as is feasible; they should painstakingly reconstruct how and why things are done and respect logics other than their own. At the same time they need to be analytical, putting pieces together so that their account makes overall sense and will be convincing to other anthropologists. In other words, they act as mediators between different worlds, seeking to do justice to the other world while speaking to their own, much as historians do. An anthropological approach, which privileges different belief and value systems from those of the observers, has enormous appeal, but it is distinctly possible that historians would not have been drawn to it without the thrill of reading about 'exotic' situations.[29] Part of the power of nuanced ethnographies is precisely the curiosity they elicit about how human beings can be so very 'other'. Such curiosity can be prurient, but it can also mobilise awe and prompt serious comparative analysis. Imagining oneself an anthropologist or a Martian can be a compelling device for viewing what is familiar with fresh eyes.

Thus, however much we may be suspicious of exoticism, it is an unavoidable feature of many disciplines, including both history and anthropology, and can be a spur to serious reflection, often of a comparative nature. Anthropology is based on such comparisons in that the payoff of long fieldwork in specific areas is a fund of insights that are compared with the findings of other practitioners. Comparisons point up both the similarities *and* the differences between societies. There have to be some likenesses for the dissimilarities to stand out and have significance. How a historian, or indeed an anthropologist, makes such comparative judgements is a complex matter, but they always require an abstract analytical framework in order to do so. For instance, a scholar already committed to the existence of shared fundamental patterns across all human societies – that is, committed to a biological approach – will be able to find common ground far more readily than one who believes in the diversity of human behaviour, in the powerful effects of local circumstances – that is, in the primacy of culture. What is like and unlike between cultures is not a given, but a product of painstaking analysis – it is negotiated by scholars, according to their own concerns and agendas, among other things.

Earlier I suggested that anthropology, in emphasising meaning rather than social description, appealed to historians because of the importance it gave to culture. This has been implicit in everything I have said about anthropology, but it is time to be more explicit. While it would be totally misleading to imply that all anthropologists are interested in culture, it would be fair to say that, as a discipline, anthropology has paid careful attention to what goes on inside people's heads. This may seem a rather bizarre definition of culture, a notoriously elusive term, but it is not a bad place to start. Culture gives priority to the ways in which our worlds are endowed with meaning.[30] This involves taking extremely seriously what people believe and why – their belief systems, world views, cognitive frameworks. Many generations of historians had found this relatively uninteresting, preferring to examine events and actions, to describe past phenomena and to seek causal explanations. It further involves looking carefully at the outward manifestations of cultural activity – objects and images, dance, myths, buildings, and so on. These had not been much studied by traditional historians for reasons to do with preconceptions about 'high' and 'low' culture. A number of areas of *high* culture, such as art, architecture, poetry and music, had long been hived off as separate, specialised areas of study, and they largely remain unintegrated into general history. These fields are respected, but not understood as central to the political, economic and social processes at the heart of mainstream history. Other areas of culture, such as glassware, jewellery, pottery, tools, clothing and body decoration, were not thought appropriate for historical study; they were not 'high' culture and were best left to archaeologists, curators, collectors and the like. Such areas commanded less respect and were seen as less intellectually demanding; they were associated with everyday life, not significant achievements, and designated 'applied' rather than 'pure' arts in a hierarchy that gave greater value to abstract and allegedly non-functional endeavours. 'Decorative' implies peripheral phenomena, which would be marginal for a field such as history that continued to emphasise political processes with big ramifications.[31]

The post-war desire to radicalise history involved taking seriously many phenomena that had previously been neglected and rejecting the frameworks that had trivialised them, which both broadened the scope of history and invited a sympathetic response to behaviour previously thought to be alien, even threatening.[32] It was thus overdetermined that culture, now more broadly defined, would become a pressing concern and that historians would turn to a field – anthropology – that seemed both more all-embracing and more respectful of its objects of study than their own. At the same time, anxieties were expressed that anthropology was complicit with imperialism and colonialism.

Thus 'culture' seems to do more justice to the full range of human experience, and only when given the inflection of *high* culture does it become narrow and exclusive. It emphasises what people make of the world, that is to say, the construction of meaning, rather than the world itself.[33] It was unavoidable that studies of cultural phenomena were suffused by worries about value judgements, their appropriateness and their political implications.

This discussion has indicated some of the tricky paths that anthropologists and historians travel when they make common cause, precisely because there is so much political heat generated by debates about how societies can and should know each other, and the purposes to which the resulting knowledge should be put. Sometimes anthropology inspires far more sympathetic and open engagements with the past, but at others it appears, somewhat ironically, to underwrite passing retrospective judgements on forebears and contemporaries for the quality of their relationships with other cultures. A related issue is orientalism – a term that has negative connotations, in that it implies fierce criticism of the ways in which eastern societies were studied by western ones. Unfortunately, this tends to foreclose discussion, rather than inviting deft analysis.[34]

HISTORY AND PHILOSOPHY

Anthropology is hardly the only discipline concerned with what goes on inside the head. Historians have turned to a number of fields and intellectual frameworks to help them make sense of the human condition. So far we have noted a number of relevant terms – ideology, consciousness, belief system and culture, for example. Some major historical traditions have focused more strictly on the *intellectual* component of mental activity – the history of ideas, of political thought and of science, to name the most obvious cases. The subject matter of all these sub-fields is inherently difficult, and sometimes requires considerable specialist knowledge. They deal with abstract thought and by virtue of that are linked with philosophy – the humanities domain most closely concerned with the nature of human cognition. Philosophy is also an academic discipline, although its reach is at once so extensive and so intellectually precise that it seems quite distinct from, say, geography or literature. The kinds of questions philosophers ask, such as 'what exists?', 'what can we know about the world?', have been posed over many centuries, not by a specialised professional cadre, but by a range of thinking people. In this sense philosophy is a long-standing and integrated activity.

History is allied with philosophy in a number of ways. First, history studies phenomena best called philosophical: for example, when it examines the scientific revolution of the seventeenth century or contract theories of society.[35] Second, since philosophy explicates thought processes, it has a great deal to say about how historians fashion arguments, the sorts of explanations they offer, their assumptions about how the past can be known, their models of causality, and so on. Indeed many historians have been deeply involved in the philosophical aspects of their field.[36] There is a third way in which history and philosophy are currently allied. Like sociology and anthropology, philosophy offers general accounts of human existence. Hegel, the early nineteenth-century German philosopher, influenced many generations of historians who conceptualised history in a Hegelian manner and searched for the development of the world spirit.[37] In this case, an entire system of thought was constructed in which human history and its study played a major role. Integral to such a system was an account of the human mind, a model of humanity that could serve as the basis and guide for historical inquiry.

All historians, without exception, employ such models, although they often do so unthinkingly. There are times, however, when they actively embrace a specific model, system or theory of human nature and apply it to their work, and generally it has come from outside history. I invoke the notion of philosophy here to draw attention to the processes whereby historians turn not so much to a defined discipline as to general accounts of humanity. Putting it this way is necessary because when historians deploy structuralism, post-structuralism, postmodernism, terms such as 'the self' and 'identity', or the ideas of authors such as Michel Foucault, Roland Barthes and Pierre Bourdieu, they are working at a level of abstraction that is best summed up by the word 'philosophy'.[38]

Let us take the case of the hugely influential French writer, the late Michel Foucault.[39] Sometimes he is described as a historian, which is seriously misleading. Foucault did detailed historical research – evident in I, Pierre Rivière (1973) – but he usually suppressed much of the historical detail when he published. He had a strong interest in psychology, psychiatry and mental health issues, partly as a result of his own experiences, but that does not make him a psychologist. Nor can he properly be described as either a sociologist or a literary critic, although he wrote both on social matters and on texts. Describing him as a philosopher draws attention to his interest in human thought, in working at a highly abstract level and in encompassing diverse phenomena in his writings. Foucault's impact upon the practice of history has been phenomenal, and it can serve as an example of the influences of 'philosophy', especially in the 1980s and 1990s.

Foucault's effects upon the practice of history have taken three main forms. First, his early book *Madness and Civilization*, first published in 1961, was written at a time of unprecedented criticism of medicalisation, especially in relation to mental illness. It outlined the ways in which categories of 'deviant' people had been separated out from their communities and enclosed in state-run institutions – for example, in seventeenth-century France. Foucault's work, by analysing the knowledge/power nexus, contributed to a widespread interest in medicalisation. More specifically, he drew historians' attention to the importance of psychiatry as a subject and provided a plausible overview of shifts in the naming and treatment of those designated mad over considerable periods of time. Many of the details of his account have been challenged by historians specialising in medicine, but it continues to hold an appeal which is not easily amenable to empirical refutation.[40]

Second, Foucault addressed the nature of human knowledge and how it has changed. In several books he charted significant shifts in science, medicine and philosophy, not in terms of great thinkers – an approach he was dismissive of, challenging the very concept of an 'author' – but in terms of 'epistemes', which are whole ways of knowing. These determine what it is possible and permissible for people to think and investigate at any given time. Epistemes are the cognitive conditions of existence under which we live. Epistemes change, although Foucault does not explain exactly how this occurs. In some brilliant analyses of events, texts and images, he showed how they embodied fundamental assumptions, and thereby appeared to offer ways into western societies that had a critical, politically radical edge. For him, what was on the surface was often not just misleading but precisely the opposite of the truth.[41]

The third area in which Foucault made an impact illustrates the point perfectly. This is the history of sexuality, which was already becoming a fashionable subject when Foucault published the first volume of his trilogy, which appeared in English in 1979. In it he argued that discourses of sexuality, from the eighteenth century onwards, recast the relationships between individuals, families, the state and related institutions, and 'experts'. This had a number of consequences: for example, 'deviant' types, such as the homosexual, were invented in what were repressive rather than permissive moves. Thus, when, in the nineteenth century, there was a growth of interest in sex and increasing numbers of people wrote about it and discussed it, this was not a sign of permissiveness but rather of how discourses serve to manage, shape and control experience. Furthermore, 'Victorian' disapproval of discussions of sexual phenomena and anxiety about 'deviance' signalled a compulsion to attend to the nature of sexuality. In the process new subjectivities, that is, fresh forms of identity and experience, were created. Later volumes drew extensively on classical sources and have been particularly controversial.[42]

What does Foucault mean by discourse? This is not an easy term to define, but we can pinpoint two significant features of it. First, it refers to cultural products, not to material conditions, so that texts become the principal sources. I use the term 'text' advisedly. The notion of discourse and work that deploys it rely heavily on the study of language. Although it is sometimes claimed that anything can be treated as a text – a political demonstration, a room, a professional association – the whole approach has been shaped by a conviction of the power of the written word and of the intellectual effectiveness of theories of language to open up its capacity to structure all human experience.[43] Second, discourse implies that there is a more or less coherent world view behind the texts, and that the ideas they express have palpable effects. The example of naming the homosexual as a permanent human type demonstrates the point, since this then became the category through which men who are erotically drawn to other men came to experience themselves and their world. According to such a classification, there are fundamentally different kinds of human beings; sexuality is not fluid but is rather an orientation over a lifetime, and homosexuality is clearly marked out as different from the norm. Hence, delineating sexual types is not an innocent scientific exercise but the exercise of power through discourse.[44] Defining otherness in contrast to oneself is precisely to exercise a form of power.

To undertake discourse analysis is to investigate the power of ideas and of the language through which they exist and in which they are expressed. Power formations are thus to be understood not in terms of elites, governments, forms of taxation, and so on, per se, but in terms of the discourses that make them possible. At first sight, 'discourse' shares some features with 'ideology', which, although widely used now by historians, came originally out of Marxian intellectual traditions.[45] Yet ideology presupposes the existence of opposing interests at any given historical moment; classes, or groups akin to classes, promote their specific interests through ideologies in which those interests are veiled. Ideologies are instruments of class or group domination; they are sites of conflict grounded in everyday experience. In contrast, Foucault's approach involves neither classes nor conflict and it certainly does not posit specific, socially rooted interests. Ideologies are best understood in terms of the material conditions in which they are forged, even if they bear exceedingly complex relationships to them. The study of discourses is not a first step, which leads the historian on to consider material life; instead, the primacy, the determining quality of discourses is asserted. Interest groups are not slogging it out, by a variety of means, for power. Rather, discourses are insinuating, and individuals and groups cannot simply adopt another position, since the structures of thought are too deeply entrenched.

Clearly both ideology and discourse are useful concepts for historians and both have their limitations. They also have their moments in history.

Scholars turn to an idea or approach when it seems apt for that time: history's relationships with other fields and their most influential authors display just such timely turns. This is all too clear in relation to Foucault. He began publishing in the late 1950s, many of his most influential books were published in the 1960s and early 1970s, and most were quickly translated into English. Yet for most of the 1970s, it was mainly historians and philosophers of science who read them in the English-speaking world. It was not until the 1980s that a veritable explosion of worldwide interest in his work occurred, led particularly by literary critics. In recent years the enthusiasm is beginning to subside. It is extremely difficult to explain how trends get started, take hold and die away. Nonetheless, they have a great deal to do with politics in its broadest sense. It is crucial to recognise that historiographical shifts in general, and the ones with which this chapter is concerned in particular, are political phenomena in two related senses. First, despite the general political conservatism of the 1980s, it was at that time that criticisms of medicine, science, technology and imperialism really gained momentum and enjoyed wide interest, not just among specialists but in the general population. It is no coincidence, for example, that environmental history, which touches on all these issues, developed at just this time, as environmental movements themselves were enjoying wide support.[46] A critical analysis of dominant discourses, one which showed their constitutive political dimensions, was appealing partly because it located the politics in the ideas themselves, and in so doing invited a language-based analysis. Scholars turn to intellectual resources from related disciplines, often outside their own field, because they seem able to illuminate their immediate preoccupations.

The second sense in which we may speak of the politics of interdisciplinary relationships is more narrowly professional. Given the organisation of academic life, new approaches are valued, especially if they claim to offer fresh insights, a radical slant and cutting-edge analysis. While traditional scholarship remains highly valued, there is always the burden of showing that it has not been done before. This accounts for many transfers between disciplines, both in terms of content and approach, because the claims to novelty seem obvious and convincing. Thus, in turning to other disciplines, historians are often maximising their own power, status and prestige. The relationships between history and literature illustrate many of these complexities.

LITERATURE AND TEXTS

Let us begin by considering our terminology. I have mentioned literary *theory* and *literature*, but what about literary *history* and literary *criticism*?[47] Often we speak of these matters in terms of the country and language of the literature, thus 'French' becomes shorthand for French literature, but does not immediately specify any particular approach to texts. Of all these terms, 'literature' is evidently the most general; it applies to any country and leaves open which orientation to writings is being adopted. Yet even such a broad and apparently neutral term raises important questions for the relationship between literature and history as disciplines – what counts as literature and hence as suitable for literary treatment, and what about aesthetic merit? Can anything written be 'literature'? Assuming the concept is still relevant, how is artistic merit to be defined? It is possible to define literature in terms of its constituent genres: such as poetry, fiction and drama. Historians may use such sources, but rarely draw upon them as their main materials. Moreover, literary genres are always blurred around the edges, and the methods used by literary critics can easily be applied to letters, newspapers and periodicals, treatises and government reports – in fact, to any kind of writing. Perhaps, then, history should be seen as a sub-field of literary studies!

Historians of literature have long been interested in the *ideas* expressed there – the work of the American scholar, the late Marjorie Hope Nicolson, being an excellent example.[48] She drew on poetry to explore scientific ideas, and in *Mountain Gloom and Mountain Glory* she charted the processes whereby mountains came to be aesthetically valued when previously they had been treated as uninteresting, even repellent excrescences. In effect, she wrote literary *history* so that it was the history of ideas. In this case, the affinities between literature and history emerge through the use of (written) sources that speak to the concerns of both. Nicolson was a literary *historian* rather than a literary *critic* because she set texts firmly in context, and although she analysed them, their formal properties were not her main concern – nor was their quality as literature.

Literary *criticism* implies close attention to texts and also a fine awareness of aesthetic issues. Literary *history* is a broad church: it does not have to put ideas at the forefront. Many works of literature have little to do with the history of ideas or shifts in mentalities. The lives of authors can be historically placed so that biographies of literary figures are 'history' and 'literature' at the same time.[49] Exceptionally well-written history is also, of course, a form of literature. It is easier to see this in the past: by any standards, Edward Gibbon and Jules Michelet were magnificent writers. These relationships between literature and history are of long standing and can be traced back to classical literary and historical writings.

However, the relationships between literature and history have recently taken on quite different qualities.[50] For instance, literary critics have become increasingly interested in texts that were previously studied by historians. This is particularly evident in relation to science, medicine and the law.[51] Sources not previously thought of as within the purview of literature have now been taken under its remit. At the same time, familiar literary texts, such as novels, have been interpreted as the carriers of broad political and ideological shifts, which may therefore be traced in them. Literature is seen not as a (passive) reflection of historical change, but as a significant (active) vehicle of it.[52] Indeed, literary approaches are profoundly shaping the contemporary practice of history. Some of the ways in which this has occurred have already been mentioned. One of the most far-reaching is the claim that anything can be treated as a text, hence critical methods are deemed to have exceptionally broad application. Texts are not transparent documents but elaborate creations, parts of discourses, and therefore implicated in the nature of power. Complex relationships between texts exist; this is known as intertextuality. Cultural power resides not in authors but in their products, rendering it misleading to name and speak of authors, since they do not, cannot, determine or control how their products are read and used. These ideas can be a real stimulus for historians, who certainly have as much to learn from literary critics as they have from practitioners of other cognate disciplines. However, the issues raised by closer relationships between literary and historical practices remain contentious; they go right to the heart of historical practice, and, as a result, historians need to be willing and able to engage with them.

In practice, many different approaches to texts are currently being adopted; historians are sometimes insufficiently attentive to the variety of approaches with which any given piece of writing may be analysed. Disciplines use each other highly selectively and in ways that are charged with significance – criticism of traditional scholarship and of political positions, claims to radicalism, and so on. It was thus inevitable that what is often called 'the linguistic turn' provoked controversy. The word 'linguistic' was used because of an indebtedness to Ferdinand de Saussure, the early twentieth-century theorist of language, who insisted on the arbitrariness of the sign.[53] Words (signs) do not possess any inherent link with what they represent, hence 'table' (the word, a signifier) is an arbitrary term for the surfaces off which we eat and on which we write (the thing, the signified). This gives language a more independent existence than is generally assumed. It also means that languages, in the sense of grammars and vocabularies and of usage, are *the* embodiments of culture, offering privileged access to the past. We cannot make claims about protests, rebellions and revolutions, then, without first understanding the terms in which protagonists experienced their lives, made criticisms and sought alternatives – a point that should be well taken by practising historians. Fundamental categories are in language rather than in the physical world. However, it follows, just as inexorably, that what can be known about the past is limited.

Accordingly, texts do not offer access to what was, only to what was said about it. For example, scholars are having to recognise that there are severe limits to what we can really know about witchcraft. The sources tell us not what happened but what witnesses and commentators *believed*.[54] The resulting conflicts between scholars are about the status of that 'it'. We shall return to this issue in chapter 4, but for now we can crudely characterise the two sides of the debate: either texts are all we have and we can only do history on that basis, or there was a material world back then, to which we can get access, and claiming otherwise is a dangerous subversion of the discipline of history. Like all polarisations, this one contains distortions, and there are a number of more nuanced positions that can be adopted. Yet mentioning this simplified polarity is useful because it points up why feelings run so high on the subject. On the one hand, there is a perceived threat to the very core of the discipline of history from literary theory. On the other, historians are thought to be making epistemological claims that cannot actually be sustained. In the middle are a wide range of interpretative strategies that historians can use, many of them associated with other disciplines. I have used literary *theory* in this context deliberately. Most literary *historians* are not particularly preoccupied with theoretical issues, while a new, distinct group has grown up within literary studies that, as the saying goes, 'does theory'. This involves considering both the nature of texts in general and issues concerning their interpretation. Setting theory apart in this manner is hardly unproblematic, since it is usually applied to and refined through specific cases, which are indispensable instruments of thought, as is the case in philosophy. It seems odd to detach theory from its lifeblood. What is called *literary* theory inevitably draws on other disciplines, above all, philosophy, in the broad sense defined above, and also more specialised domains such as linguistics and semiotics.[55]

INTERDISCIPLINARY HISTORY

I have suggested that, although we continue to recognise the existence of distinct disciplines – indeed we have no choice in the matter given the nature of academic institutions – many of the boundaries between them have been called into question through an array of processes that concern politics and fashion, certainly, as well as the generative transfer of materials, approaches and theories between fields. Yet such transfers, like the political imperatives that energise them, bring entailments, some of which I have mentioned in this chapter. History is eclectic, hence the range of its debts and the complexity of its relations with other disciplines. Sometimes these are to be understood in terms of the use of theories; indeed 'theory' can be a useful concept for clarifying relations between disciplines, yet this should not be taken to imply that in historical practice 'theory' is something special, set apart. In the business of doing history, 'theory' is a constant presence, whether acknowledged or not. And since we cannot escape it, it is better to understand, not only its role in current historical practices, but its origins, which lie in a pre-disciplinary past.

One further step we can take in thinking about history and other disciplines is to examine the notion of 'interdisciplinary history'. There is a certain ambiguity surrounding what is meant by 'interdisciplinary' – is it about exchanges between fields that remain distinct or a rather more intimate blending of domains with already blurred edges? The idea of interdisciplinary *history* is sufficiently established to have its own journal, founded in 1970 and published in the United States. Its many thematic issues have helped define the parameters of these debates. The phrase 'interdisciplinary history' implies continued allegiance to a discipline combined with openness to other perspectives. We can usefully turn to a specific example. In 1986, there was a special issue on history and art history, which appeared in book form two years later: *Art and History: Images and their Meaning*. The very title indicates something of the framework within which the book is working. For example, 'images' tends to imply two-dimensional representations, but what about three-dimensional objects? Many historians, following the inspirational work of Michael Baxandall and Svetlana Alpers, now use the term 'visual culture' to signal their interest in studying whatever a given culture throws up, rather than restricting themselves to 'Art', which implies aesthetic value judgements.[56] A further step would be to invoke 'material culture', a term to which I shall return, which implies an interdisciplinary approach to objects.[57] The 12 papers in *Art and History* largely concern images, although several do examine architectural materials. None relates to the applied or decorative arts, or to sculpture. They are diverse case studies, mainly by scholars who are *either* historians *or* art historians. Although the brief introduction makes encouraging noises about the need to draw history and art history closer together, the book remains a set of disparate studies. Interdisciplinarity in this case is a goal that remains to be fully conceptualised and brought to fulfilment.

In many countries the divisions between history and art history run deep. In the USA, by contrast, where a significant number of the major universities have large and diverse history departments, scholars (admittedly in small numbers) are employed who are equally at home in both fields.[58] And yet, even there, the vast majority of those who use art-historical evidence remain concerned with major figures, that is, with artists and architects who are within the canon. The notion of a canon, which defines who are the most important figures worthy of study and, by that token, lineages of cultural achievement, has been under attack in recent years. It was strenuously argued, for example, that in both literature and art women were largely excluded from the canon. While this was certainly true, with a few honourable exceptions that served to confirm broad assumptions about gender differences, the result of such critiques was not an overturning of the very idea of a canon, but adjustments to its membership criteria. Inevitably the value of canons in and of themselves has also been equally strenuously affirmed, largely by conservative critics.[59] In history we do not really have canons, partly because creative individuals are not at the core of the subject and partly because aesthetic quality is not a major concern of the discipline. There is a rough equivalent in the range of topics that, by common consent, form the core of the field. Thus, even if in recent years we have seen the growth of the history of sport and the history of animals, most historians would see these as extras rather than as constitutive of the subject. In these examples the subject matter has not come from other disciplines. By contrast, we might say that, in the case of 'Art with a capital A', the subject matter is already 'owned' by another field, and that it possesses a sufficient measure of internal complexity to require specialist knowledge. The specific type of internal complexity possessed by art is part of its cultural prestige. For this, as well as other reasons, many general historians would never think of trespassing into the area and are actually rather afraid of images – an alien category of evidence for those used to words, the primacy of which is constantly affirmed in academic life. Yet if we think in terms of 'visual culture' or 'material culture' instead of 'Art', the situation looks rather different, and the way is open for a more flexible blending of disciplines. Visual culture implies, for example, both that the variety of cultural forms around at a given moment should be considered and that traditional assessments of aesthetic quality need not be the primary consideration when selecting sources to study. Visual culture, like material culture, is a more *historical* category than 'Art'. Archaeology is central to the study of material culture, while it is in some respects so close to history that it becomes inseparable from it.

JUNK AND BUNK

In *Bluff Your Way in Archaeology*, Paul Bahn defined the field he has done so much to promote: 'If History if bunk, then Archaeology is junk. This bizarre subject entails seeking, retrieving and studying the abandoned, lost, broken and discarded traces left by human beings in the past. Archaeologists are therefore the precise opposite of dustmen, though they often dress like them.'[60] Three points emerge from this definition: the concern with objects, the activities clustered around finding them and the huge remit of the subject – anything left by humans could be grist to the archaeological mill. It is not surprising that ancient and medieval historians tend to be particularly close to archaeology – so close that we might say that at some points the fields simply merge. If archaeologists study the deposits of human life, there is in principle no reason why history and archaeology in general should not be intimately entwined. That they are not (yet) is perhaps worth some consideration.

As a field of study archaeology has existed for several centuries; there was intense interest in Stonehenge, a site that has acquired an exceptionally powerful aura, in the seventeenth century: 'Stonehenge in the modern world is the universal, the universally known image of the ancient past and its accomplishments, its only international rival the pyramids.'[61] Such spectacular remains exert a special magic and have long done so. Centuries ago, educated men, many of whom thought of themselves as antiquarians, examined old bits and pieces and tried to come up with explanations for them. As it studies the material remnants of the past, archaeology has had a close kinship with geology, and especially palaeontology, which examines nature's remnants, and with anthropology, often defined as the study of other cultures. Indeed in many parts of the world archaeology and anthropology are taught together. It is often thought that archaeology is mainly concerned with those periods before systematic writing began, but this is unnecessarily limiting. Certainly ancient civilisations occupy an important place in archaeology, but so do more recent societies. 'Industrial archaeology' only makes sense if material remains from any period constitute valuable evidence. So clear chronological divisions do not neatly divide history from archaeology. The emphasis on material culture does to some degree, and it should be observed that many archaeologists study huge time-spans, working with only fragmentary evidence.

I want to reflect briefly on some of the things archaeologists do and draw out their relationships with historical practice in general. Many, although by no means all, archaeologists do fieldwork. Learning how to dig and getting the practical experience of identifying and surveying sites, describing, classifying and dating finds are fundamental skills. The type of knowledge produced depends on precise understanding of where items are found and of the wider patterns of the landscape. Accordingly we might see geography and archaeology as cognate disciplines. In both cases thinking spatially is a fundamental skill, or rather, in the case of an archaeological dig, there are a number of distinct skills, manual, visual, spatial. The distribution of items in space offers vital clues concerning wider interpretation. Since many items are fragments, speculative reconstruction is required in order to produce a hypothesis about what the complete object, whether it be a vase, a statue, a weapon or a jewel, might have looked like. Further associations then need to be made, for example, with the ways in which the item was produced, used and displayed. A great deal of interpretative weight rests on such reconstructions, from which much else is often deduced – the organisation of households, gender roles, social organisation, and so on. All this is only possible if every single feature of the object, and of others like it, is analysed carefully. Archaeologists are painfully aware of the explanatory weight that the physical evidence is made to bear. And in this sense, industrial, or any type of modern archaeology differs from ancient archaeology in that there are significant amounts of supporting evidence in a range of media.

In many respects history and archaeology are inseparable; at some points they are indistinguishable. Let's take the example of numismatics, the study of coins – a quite exceptionally important type of evidence for many times and places: as metal items they have high chances of survival and as decorated items they yield up a great deal of information, some of it about art, design and symbols. Numismatics is sometimes perceived as an arcane specialist field that most people will encounter, if at all, in the coin rooms of museums. Yet it is vital for art history as well as for archaeology and history, including economic history.[62] There are parts of history, then, into which the study of coins and of other archaeological evidence is integrated and others where it would be fruitful to do so.

In this chapter we have been probing relationships between disciplines in terms of evidence, theory, habits of mind and ways of working. I am stressing types of evidence and ways of attending to them because this is where history and archaeology are most obviously related. Archaeology does not have a definable body of theory that it deploys and that history might borrow. Rather the kinship between these disciplines consists in their shared commitment to study the past with whatever sources are available. Yet the main sources of the two fields, and hence the related habits of mind, remain distinct: archaeologists overwhelmingly work with objects, that is to say that they work visually in three dimensions. Historians more often work with written materials, that is to say their worlds are verbal and more or less flat. There are different ways of thinking involved.

One of the most striking changes that has taken place over the last 20 years is the formation of the field of material culture studies in which archaeologists have taken the lead. The *Journal of Material Culture* is enormously helpful for thinking about the relationship between history and other disciplines and about what an emphasis on material culture can offer historians. Its intellectual core may be summed up by its concern with 'the relationship between artefacts and social relationships'. This is an avowedly interdisciplinary enterprise, and the statement about the aims and scope of the journal, from which I have just quoted, lists the disciplines on which it draws – anthropology, archaeology, design studies, history, human geography, museology and ethnography – and affirms its international and comparative remit. Since close visual analysis is fundamental to the field, it is notable that art history is not listed separately (presumably it is subsumed by 'design studies').

There are parts of archaeology that are closely allied with art history – the study of rock art, for example. But recent articles (many of which are historical) in the *Journal of Material Culture* do not suggest a particularly close kinship with either art history or with those parts of the discipline of history than concern themselves with material objects. Archaeology and anthropology are the dominant disciplines. There are some marvellous opportunities for collaboration here, but they will develop through specific case studies – church furnishings, domestic interiors, sugar sculpture – out of which frameworks, techniques and approaches can be refined, rather than through a transfer of theory. Thus the relationships between archaeology and material culture studies on the one hand and history on the other are indicative of the trend towards fresh forms of interdisciplinary history that have already been noted. We will see shortly how the close relationships with parts of geography manifest similar characteristics. Two further brief comments are in order. First, the remit of material culture studies is very wide indeed. It is hard to think of much that would be securely excluded. What differentiates it, then, from other fields with a generous remit? The question is designed to clarify what might be distinctive about the approach of material culture studies in order that historians can be clear about what it may have to offer them. Given its interdisciplinary aspirations, it is genuinely hard to be precise about what sets the field apart, other than a commitment to going wherever the object invites in order to explain it. Material objects are understood in the context of social relationships, rather than aesthetically and in isolation. In a sense this openness need not matter, if the term itself and the work done in its name is generative. Second, the word 'archaeology' is a powerful metaphor for the process of getting beneath the surface of things, which lies at the very heart of all intellectual endeavour. It is possible that its popularity owes something to Michel Foucault's book, *The Archaeology of Knowledge*. In this respect, 'archaeology' is like 'history' in its slippery richness, but quite unlike 'art history' or 'museology', which unambiguously refer to academic subjects.

SETTINGS AND SPACE

Geography was defined in an early twentieth-century encyclopedia as 'the exact and organized knowledge of the distribution of phenomena on the surface of the earth', a definition that reveals its alliances with the sciences on one side and with the humanities and social sciences on the other.[63] As with 'history', 'geography' refers both to a field of study and something 'out there'. One of geography's main concerns is the way in which the physical environment shapes societies, a subject of the widest possible historical significance. We might imagine a division of labour in which geography paid attention to the physical environment and history to its human consequences. In practice the disciplines overlap considerably more than this. Geography is the ultimate context within which human behaviour can be interpreted. Since the rise of environmental consciousness – itself an important historical subject – and of related fields such as ecological history, there has been an enhanced awareness not just of the importance of physical settings but of the dialectical relationships between people and their environments. That communities are vulnerable to their surroundings is obvious enough, especially in those cases where a surplus is not generated or is creamed off by elites. Accordingly, economic history and geography have been kinsfolk for some time.[64] It is hard to overstate the extent to which the material world shapes human life and in how many registers it does so at once, not just topographically but through buildings, gardens, town planning, parks, nature reserves, and so on. These are all humanly wrought phenomena, but they are nonetheless 'geographical' as well as historical. It follows that geography is also concerned with culture and psychology, an aspect of the field that has come to the fore in recent decades.[65]

When thinking about the relationships between history and other disciplines, there is a checklist of issues to be considered, and these include the types of sources, theories and conceptual frameworks and explanatory models. Geographers not only have some distinctive sources – maps, plans and photographs would be the most obvious examples – but they possess refined interpretative skills for dealing with them. Some historians use these sources too, but not to the same extent. However, when it comes to concepts, geography is rather eclectic, and to the extent it has theories, these are shared with other fields, such as climatology, economics and other social sciences.

Historical geography is in an exceptionally healthy state at the moment. It casts its net widely: travel writing, memorials, street names, patterns of disease, agricultural change, migration, gardens and islands, to take examples from recent articles in the *Journal of Historical Geography*. None of these subjects is either exclusively or obviously 'geographical', although it is evident that they invite a special concentration on spatial analysis. In the cases of travel writing and islands, for example, there is considerable interest in literary studies, which reinforces the idea that history is part of a cluster of overlapping disciplines.[66] What is particularly striking is the attention now being paid within geographical circles to the history of the field, to patterns of education, to its position alongside other intellectual domains, to the ways in which 'pioneers' are understood, indeed to how the form of knowledge we call 'geography' has been made. In other words, the multiple kinships between history and geography are coming into prominence.

BRIDGE

In this chapter we have explored the many layered relationships between the discipline of history and some of the fields with which it is closely allied. They reveal a great deal about historical practice. This is hardly surprising given the fact that the past is not divided up rationally for scholarly convenience. We impose divisions upon it in a variety of ways, all of which are expressions of our own priorities and values. What is generally called 'history' is closely connected to other scholarly practices, although the details of these connections change markedly over time and according to the historical specialism in question.

Many of the richest sources for historians are studied by cognate fields. In looking at the history of popular culture, for example, there is possibly more visual material than anything else – a visual culture perspective sees this as integral to the historical situation and proposes that it should be acknowledged and fully analysed in resulting accounts.[67] Visual culture is inclusive, by examining items accessible to the non-literate, for example. So we are not talking of 'Art' here. Historians can and should draw on diverse ways of approaching visual material, rather than simply on traditional art history. Their orientation to such material should not be connoisseurial, that is, preoccupied with attribution, value and artistic quality, but rather what we could call integrative. Nonetheless, there is always a danger of historians treating visual sources as transparent documents offering windows onto other times. Similar points apply to the possibilities and pitfalls that musical sources present to historians We will need to examine the whole concept of the document in more detail in the next chapter. Just like other sources, images, musical scores and objects possess many layers of meaning; they do not give direct access to the past, but contain their own logics, and hence require careful interpretation.

Thus, one of the advantages of separate fields is the possibility of careful reflection upon the special sources and problems of each one. Primary materials come in many different forms, and the specialist ways that have been developed, sometimes over centuries, for their interpretation demand consideration by those in other disciplines. The boundaries around disciplines may be constructions, but that does not mean they are trivial or to be ignored. Historians can learn much from other disciplines, but in order to do so they have to know something of their modus operandi, and that in turn involves appreciating their history as well as their current practices. They cannot afford to be ignorant of the issues and approaches of related areas; they need to appreciate the variety of possible relationships between disciplines. One payoff is a sharper appreciation of what is distinctive about their own.

4

The status of historical knowledge

HISTORY CHALLENGED

The whole basis upon which disciplines operate in institutions of higher education in the twentieth century lends intellectual authority to their products. What does this authority consist of? What underpins it? In what ways, if any, is historical knowledge special? One account goes something like this. Historians produce knowledge of the past, which draws its authority from a number of sources. These include the meticulous study of a wide range of primary materials, the evaluation of results by a range of experts, the provision of transparent scholarly apparatus so that claims can be checked by other scholars, specialised training in approaches and techniques, and the careful scrutiny of references and qualifications when university appointments are made. When it comes to publication, refereeing guarantees quality. The evidence historians use indicates what happened, and thus historical knowledge offers a kind of objectivity and in this respect is unlike, say, literary criticism, where a significant element of subjectivity is involved. While historians cannot predict the future, they can explain the past, which involves showing why things happened. Some areas of history, such as cliometrics, are more 'scientific' than others, and the goal of the discipline as a whole is recounting what really happened.

Over the last 25 years virtually every aspect of this account has been energetically challenged and, like most forms of knowledge, history has been subject to critical scrutiny. Earlier chapters mentioned some of the trends that have brought increased scepticism about knowledge claims in general. The critique of *historical* knowledge is especially significant for a number of reasons. A sense of history constitutes a major element of collective identity, for example, for nations, occupations, organisations and classes. Historical accounts are the base upon which the policies of governments and institutions are constructed. The past is frequently appealed to in support of current decisions, most obviously by governments, leaders and political parties, so to take away the certainties promised by history has broad ramifications. Historical knowledge is a prop for individuals as for groups. Yet, despite the fierce attacks on historians' claims to really know the past, the manipulative use of historical arguments in public life goes largely unchallenged. Unsubstantiated claims, which need to be distinguished from 'historical knowledge', are widely bandied about. In academic circles, attacks upon the status of historical knowledge have come largely from other humanities disciplines, which insist on the interested nature of all knowledge. Since historians set store by the quality of their knowledge, such attacks appear especially threatening. It is neither responsible nor right for historians to shrug and accept that it is all just a matter of opinion – if they did, what would set history apart from other fields, from journalism, from casual claims about the past? The discipline of history *is* important, precisely for the reasons I have listed, so it matters what accounts are given of the past, and there is a need to feel confident about their reliability. Mistaken claims need to be challenged.[1]

STANDARDS AND QUALITY

In this chapter I examine some of the ways in which it is possible to think about the quality of historical knowledge and the arguments that are available concerning its assessment. It will be necessary to consider the concepts – truth, objectivity, knowledge, evidence, and so on – that are an indispensable part of such reflections. But first, an observation. When assessments are made of the quality of knowledge, where do the standards for making such a judgement come from? There are two possibilities. Either the standard comes from *outside* history, from types of knowledge that are regarded as particularly secure, or it is specific to the discipline of history itself, which offers knowledge distinctive enough to generate its own standards. In the first case historians will be looking, generally nervously, at highly authoritative knowledge forms, that is, at the natural sciences. This is not a new issue: ever since producers of natural knowledge started to claim in a vigorous and coordinated fashion in the seventeenth century that they were setting new standards of reliability and truth, others have felt compelled to emulate them.[2] It is only relatively recently that more historians have claimed that the natural sciences fail to provide suitable criteria for their field.[3] There are considerable advantages to being able to assert that, in its way, history is as safe, epistemologically speaking, as science. It certainly assists in claims to prestige and to the disinterested nature of the subject, since knowledge of such high quality is deemed the very opposite of both ideology and opinion. The sciences themselves have been subjected to strong critiques, according to which their claims to authority and objectivity are flawed. Nonetheless, especially in the popular imagination, the relationship between science and truth is felt to be close, and this spills over into the general assumptions made about models of reliable knowledge. In academic circles, where many people naturally enough respect the truth claims made by scientists, there is widespread confidence in science as a paradigm of knowledge. The alternative, and one I shall argue for in this chapter, is to set standards of reliability from *within* the discipline to take account of its distinctive qualities – we do not study nature experimentally, but past human societies, over which we have no control.

TRUTH AND RELIABILITY

Even in the remarks I have just made, I have shifted the grounds of the argument somewhat from an emphasis on truth to one on reliability. We must now turn to the concept of truth and consider its relevance for the practice of history. What do we mean by truth?[4] One aspect of any answer must be the highest possible levels of accuracy and precision. Dictionary definitions of 'true' stress fact, reality, exactitude and faithfulness. There are historical phenomena, such as military manoeuvres and government procedures, where it is possible to give accounts that would satisfy most commentators in terms of their precision and accuracy. We will come to the complexities of sources as evidence shortly, but it is not particularly contentious to claim that, with careful research, narratives can be produced, of some aspects of the past, the adequacy of which can be satisfactorily judged. In this sense they may be deemed 'true'. Yet truth also carries connotations of completeness, of an account that is, by any standards, *absolutely* satisfactory. It is hard to imagine how historical writing – or indeed any other type – could fulfil such stringent criteria, which imply a distant, all-encompassing overview and tests capable of verifying its privileged status. At one level, this is simply unrealistic – how is it possible for historical work to achieve so much? At another level, it appears misguided because hubristic, aspiring to a quasi-divine omniscience that is simply not available to mortals. It is healthy to recognise the provisional nature of our knowledge. However, it does not then follow that the quality of historical knowledge is unimportant, only that the concept 'truth' does not seem terribly productive.

Similar arguments can be mounted in relation to objectivity. The very term implies impartial, disinterested perspectives, which we know to be chimeras, simply not attainable, especially in a subject where evaluation and interpretation are central skills. One problem with the term 'objectivity' is that it is too cut and dried, and hence unhelpful, because it implies the existence of vantage points that are absolutely without bias. Although we now acknowledge such vantage points to be unattainable, the commitment to weighing up and considering carefully a wide range of evidence is nonetheless a valuable one; in fact, it is central to the practice of history. The opposite of objective is subjective, which can carry pejorative connotations.[5] It implies not just one person's views, tinged with emotion, but a partial, insubstantial perspective that is not to be trusted. The common polarisation of objectivity and subjectivity is unfortunate, giving too much trust to the former and too little to the latter. It could just as well be argued that objectivity is faulty because it is cold and detached, whereas subjectivity is more warmly, honestly human. The historian's path lies somewhere in between: it combines open recognition that we are interested parties in our studies with a clear sense of how to make the resulting knowledge as judicious as possible. My stress on reliable rather than on objective, truthful knowledge is thus intended to be realistic and honest. Historians should not promise what they cannot deliver. We therefore need to be clear about what they *can* deliver.

WAYS OF KNOWING

Perhaps part of the problem concerns 'knowledge' itself. The use of a single term in relation to a wide range of disciplines does rather suggest that comparability between them exists. Instead of ranging fields on a single scale according to the quality of the knowledge they produce, it might be better to think of each one as possessing a different combination of ways of knowing. In other words, perhaps we need to think about knowledge*s*. After all, it is immediately apparent that 'knowledge' has a variety of meanings, including awareness, information, understanding, insight, explanation and wisdom, and that these involve distinct relationships between knowers and known. There is a world of difference between 'information', which makes us think of data and facts, and 'understanding', which implies a deep grasp of processes and events in the past. The latter term thus implies the capacity for abstract analysis, which the former does not. Furthermore, 'insight', 'wisdom' and 'understanding' also suggest an ability to empathise with historical actors and to build up a sense of what motivated them. It is inevitable that there should be no consensus on the desirable balance between these forms of knowledge within historical practice. Strong identification with people in the past is regarded by some as suspect, because it implies an emotional commitment that clouds the ability to make judgements, while for others it is a political necessity because it allows previously neglected viewpoints to be heard sympathetically.

It is commonplace to recognise that we know things with varying degrees of certainty. (I am not speaking here of ranking entire fields on a scale, but of pieces of information.) When it comes to human behaviour, the difficulty of achieving high levels of certainty is hardly a secret. Take the obvious example of lying. People lie rather frequently; sometimes they are aware of it, at other times not. It is quite difficult to prove conclusively that someone has lied – legal processes would be considerably easier if lying were amenable to clear demonstration.[6] All scrupulous historians realise that evidence may be deceptive and endeavour to incorporate appropriate forms of awareness into their practices. The strength of historical arguments will depend on the available evidence – its nature, quality and quantity – and hence, in thinking about the status of historical knowledge, the complexities of sources and their interpretation is a central question. I am suggesting that there is nothing particularly arcane about these points, hence my emphasis on common sense as a guide. Of course people can and must be trained to think critically, but this is to refine techniques that are actually part of everyday life. The point is perfectly obvious if we consider for a moment the ideas of reliability and trust. How do you decide whether someone or something is reliable? Consistency is clearly vital; if a person makes ten claims, all of which turn out to be corroborated by other evidence, this is a high level of consistency and reliability. Let us suppose another person has a much lower success rate and that it is necessary to choose between conflicting accounts given by these two individuals: the former will seem a much better bet. There is, of course, no guarantee that this time they are still being reliable, but it seems an inherently more plausible assumption. The more independent witnesses corroborate that account, the more reliable it will be deemed. This is why one of the central parts of the historian's craft is searching for and then evaluating a variety of accounts and diverse types of evidence.

I could have expressed this argument in terms of truth, but precisely because the term suggests a final, complete account, it is somewhat misleading, unless 'true' is always in inverted commas, which is rather irritating for readers. The significant issue is, rather, trust, which can be established in a variety of ways.[7] In the end, however, the decision whether to trust an individual, an institution, a source or a historical account depends on weighing up a number of factors and making a final judgement based on previous experience, political preferences, and so on. Such judgements, by their very nature, have an emotional component. Hence, competing accounts of the Weimar Republic, the French Revolution or the Cold War cannot simply be evaluated according to purely rational criteria. The historian's assessment of them will necessarily depend on such issues as whether they are predisposed to be critical of the Ancien Régime or sympathetic to the difficulties of the French monarchy, to see class as at the root of the political turmoil, to consider the revolution a progressive process, the harbinger of the modern order, or an eruption of unnecessary brutality. These are competing views with a strong moral component; nonetheless, each can be argued for more or less convincingly, with evidence that is more or less impressive. In making a final judgement on a historical account, the degree of trust it elicits in us is crucial.

I have just referred to evidence and also to sources as if the two were more or less the same thing, but these words do carry distinct connotations. Sources are simply 'raw' materials of whatever kind. They have the *potential* to bear on a historical problem, but it is always necessary to show precisely how they do so. To call something evidence implies that the case for its relevance has been made – evidence bears witness to an issue. In a sense evidence is a philosophical concept – if I ask for evidence of something, I have a set of logical problems in mind, to which this thing we call 'evidence' will speak. The use of evidence in legal settings may be a useful analogy. In an adversarial system each side has to provide the evidence it finds most compelling to the case in question, and the jury has to weigh it all up, just as historians do. The fact that a significant proportion of criminal convictions are found to be 'unsafe' vividly illustrates how extremely complex the whole process is. As a concept, 'evidence' draws attention to the need to demonstrate points in a manner that will be convincing to the relevant community of belief. A discipline is indeed a community of belief – assumptions about adequate knowledge are negotiated socially and, as a result, criteria of judgement emerge that vary with time, place and circumstance; accordingly, the nature and status of historical knowledge cannot be constants.

There is a further concept we can consider in relation to the reliability of history – the document. Some historians are very fond of stressing the centrality of documents in making any case about the past. What is meant by document, the noun? It means a special kind of primary source with a direct relationship to what is being studied. Certificates of birth, marriage or death, passports and visas, transcriptions of legal proceedings, letters and telegrams would all be examples. I have chosen them precisely because they seem strongly factual, especially reliable, uncontentious in their documentary status. To document means to make a record of and, by implication, to generate an authoritative, authentic account; hence one sense of 'documentary', when used of films, television programmes and photographs. In fact, such records are hardly unmediated; they necessarily pass through human agents, who select, alter and make mistakes, that is, they transform and translate. They may also deceive. Inevitably some documents are more reliable, less overtly mediated than others, but all, by their very nature, are, nonetheless, mediations. Yet, despite our *intellectual* understanding of their limitations, we continue to place special trust in some categories of documents, to have faith in sources that appear authentic. It may be that habits of wanting, even needing to believe in the possibility of true historical stories run exceedingly deep. It may also be that a pervasive scepticism about the nature of all sources goes against the grain, that it is destabilising to recognise just how little from the past can be recovered. A more critical view of what it is possible for historians to know has generated anxieties among many practitioners, and these should be viewed sympathetically. Criticism does unsettle. On the other hand, fears prompted by a critical vantage point should not be allowed to spiral into claims that the entire discipline is being threatened by sceptical approaches to knowledge. It is preferable to recognise, and calmly engage with, the complexities and tensions that much thinking about the nature of history has thrown up in the last ten years, and then to see where the genuine strengths of the discipline lie.

The epistemological complexities of history can be more sharply focused if we return to the notions 'document' and 'documentary'. I mentioned that one meaning of these words stressed reliable, solid records. But there is another, equally revealing, meaning – personal testimony. Within documentary film movements, for example, there has been an emphasis on providing an accurate record, but this is not incompatible with an equally notable point – their commitment to expressing the individual perspectives of both subjects and film-makers.[8] Indeed much documentary work sought to give voice to those, generally outside established elites, who were able to speak to the nature of daily life in a particularly compelling manner. There is a concept that joins these apparently divergent meanings – authenticity. The two meanings of 'documentary' are simply two facets of what is meant by 'authentic' – genuine and personal. Authenticity is a highly problematic category in historical practice and it is right that we offer a critique of it, noting how, even in apparently politically sophisticated work, it is not only present, but traded upon, sometimes in quite emotionally manipulative ways. Authenticity can imply truth claims that are rooted in the emotions, especially those connected with suffering, and not fully amenable to reasoned argument or critical evaluation. This was often a feature of women's history, and in oral history it is also evident. The use of slave narratives would be a further example, where we feel that an especially vibrant source has been tapped into, offering a fresh, previously marginal and emotionally powerful set of voices.[9] Similar issues arise in relation to the Holocaust.[10] I share those emotional responses even as I am aware that we need to subject them to scrutiny. Claims to authenticity are problematic because they grant privileges on emotional grounds. The first-hand testimonies of the marginal, for instance, may indeed be inspiring and fresh, but memory is a notoriously treacherous faculty. Hence it is vital to be clear about what such accounts can and cannot reveal and to avoid unthinking sentimentality.

Let us consider a specific example. During the interwar period in the United States, there was a huge growth of interest in documentary techniques, much of it sponsored and funded by the government. The activities of the Farm Security Administration in commissioning photographs of the conditions of poor white southern farmers is a case in point.[11] Indeed these poignant photographs, like John Steinbeck's novel *The Grapes of Wrath* (1939, and the widely acclaimed film, 1940), have become emblematic of the time and are frequently used by historians as 'documents'. Although not funded by the FSA, the controversial book by James Agee and Walker Evans, *Let Us Now Praise Famous Men* (1941), was part of this trend and Walker Evans's extraordinary pictures have been widely used by historians. Evans's photographs are amazing because, like Agee, he identified so strongly with the poor whites with whom they lived for several months. Furthermore, unlike some contemporary documentary photographers, Evans (he claims) did not pose his subjects, but encouraged them to pose themselves. The results are intensely moving because they seem to give, simultaneously, a noble and a bleak view of their subjects' lives. Nonetheless, we should be sceptical about what we can 'know' as a result of such documentary activities. Photographs, for instance, can be printed in many different ways, clipped, altered in size, given various titles or none, all of which affect their emotional impact. Moreover, given that they are intensely personal, what generalised insights can be derived from them is unclear. And yet they *do* convey something extremely significant at an emotional level, so much so that 'the depression' and some kinds of documentary photography have become virtually synonymous.[12]

I am suggesting that there are many ways of knowing; sometimes they become so entangled that it is difficult to be clear about the epistemological claims involved. I have evoked these diverse ways by referring to notions, such as information, insight, explanation, understanding and wisdom, that are all linked to knowledge in some way. Whereas gathering information implies collecting and organising data, wisdom implies the accumulation of human experience and the ability to discern and comprehend its main patterns.

4.1 Bud Fields and his family at home, Alabama, 1936, by Walker Evans
This poignant image neatly illustrates the pleasures and pitfalls of documentary photography. It is visually compelling partly because we recognise the family group from many pictures we have seen previously. The textures of materials and the facial expressions are gripping. But Walker Evans' photograph is also shocking in the grinding poverty it depicts and in the close to naked child. It certainly can be treated as a document, as just about anything can be, if and only if it is carefully interpreted using as wide a range as possible of related materials. It emphatically does not speak for itself – nothing does.

Disciplines vary in the value they give to these different forms of knowing. What makes the status of historical knowledge a particularly complex matter is that it is a subtle blend of all these forms. Hence, we should always be suspicious of simple formulae and blanket definitions, and accept that taste plays a part in the history we think is 'good' and 'bad'. However, just because there is an element of taste does not mean that no general criteria of judgement exist.

EVALUATING HISTORICAL WRITINGS: SOURCES
Criteria for judging the adequacy of historical writings relate to three aspects of the discipline: the use and interpretation of sources; the aptness and effectiveness of conceptual frameworks; and the quality of the writing itself. In the first case we should always run a checklist in order to assess the

ways in which sources have been used, although we need to bear in mind that 'sources' is an inherently heterogeneous category, hence the checklist has to be flexible. The most basic subdivision is between primary and secondary sources, which, although it appears simple, can be quite blurred, as we have already noted. To recap briefly, 'primary' source covers all original documents produced at the time one is studying, and the implication is that these bear direct witness to the events, people, processes, and so on, of that moment. Furthermore, 'primary' implies that it has not gone through the head and hands of another historian. A crude definition of secondary sources would be that they are the writings of other scholars, not necessarily historians, but anyone who has commented upon a historical situation, possibly using primary sources, without being a participant in it. However, a moment's reflection reveals that such definitions are too simple. What is a primary source for one project might be a secondary one for another, and vice versa. Journalism is a good example of the point – as commentary it could be considered a secondary source; it would become a primary source for those studying the history of the media. Two implications follow: the status of sources changes according to the research project in question, and the primary/secondary distinction is less important than an overall assessment of the source's relevance to a given project and of how well it is used. In both cases the mode of production of any given sources requires scrutiny. In other words, we should not fetishise 'primary' sources, but seek whatever is helpful. Having located the sources that are particularly valuable for a given project and acquired a clear sense of why, historians then find that using a variety of sources will generate more powerful insights than using only one type.

The writing of biographies neatly illustrates these points. In writing a *general* biography, if the subject published extensively, it would be essential to look at their unpublished work too, and especially at intimate records, such as letters and diaries, as well as at comments by a variety of friends, acquaintances, colleagues, relations, and so on. Yet for a study of an individual's *public image*, their reputation, journalism and other representations of them would become privileged sources; what people said and did in private would be less relevant, except in so far as it shaped public perceptions of them. An *intellectual* biography would place more emphasis on education, institutions, networks and achievements, thereby drawing upon distinctive sets of sources. A *popular* biography would be judged rather differently, and would draw on sources that recounted stories in the individual's life that made for good reading and historical 'colour'.

Judging which sources are relevant to a specific piece of research is quite an art, and often outstanding work derives from an imaginative use of sources that are at first sight oblique. So, of any piece of historical writing we need to ask what sources have been used, how they have been selected, whether they have been used in their entirety or only in part, if they have been interpreted in a plausible manner, if the result is derivative or original, and whether the limitations and specificities of sources have been taken into account. These questions immediately suggest the need for a context in which to evaluate any piece of history. How is it possible to answer these questions unless we have other pieces for comparison? Hence the use of secondary sources is as vital as primary ones. Is the author aware of relevant work by other historians? Deciding what is 'relevant' is never straightforward. Have authors taken account of recent ideas and do they acknowledge their debts both responsibly and in sufficient detail? Many of these questions are answered through the careful scrutiny of footnotes, which should be seen as just as dense and interesting as the main text.[13] Usually they indicate not just sources of information, but the author's approach, theoretical debts and intellectual lineage.

THE CHIMERA OF COMPREHENSIVENESS

It may be helpful at this point to make explicit an issue that is always lurking around the question of the use and selection of sources. There is a widespread fantasy among historians and their readers concerning comprehensiveness. Thus, if writing on an individual, the author is expected to read 'everything' about them. It is best to be blunt and state that in some (even many) cases, this is just impossible. And if we take more wide-ranging subjects, the point is even clearer. And yet the thought of having missed something generates an anxiety commonly experienced by professional historians. We want, indeed are expected, to exhibit a kind of mastery of our fields and of our chosen topics. We constantly worry about missing something. Such fears need to be probed. The goal of completeness is simply impractical, especially since, as the world of scholarship expands, there is more and more to read. Distinctions need to be made between new information and new interpretations, and between writings that are likely to change a research project and those that are not. With the development of the internet the problem has got far worse, and this is not just because of the volume of materials made available, but because it is increasingly difficult, especially for students, to evaluate their *quality*.

The only ways forward are through careful selection, through being thoughtful and open about the criteria of selection, and through traditional forms of evaluation. By 'traditional' I mean those techniques associated with the practices of scholarly footnotes, which embody quality controls that are indispensable in academic life. Unfortunately, even this is only a partial solution, since the growth in the amount published means that scholars are likely to find works in footnotes with which they are unfamiliar and it is simply not practical to check every item in every footnote one reads. In any case, the languages historians have at their command are always a limiting factor. Nonetheless, the principles hold good. They rest on making one's sources and procedures open to the scrutiny of others, and on drawing upon other work of proven quality. The goal of reading and working comprehensively is, in one sense, worthy; it implies a seriousness of purpose that helps to raise the quality of historical knowledge. But because comprehensiveness can be so hard, if not impossible, to attain, it can also become a crippling ideal. There are what could be called 'last word' books – books so comprehensive and thorough that they command special respect.[14] To produce such a volume requires a huge investment of time, which even dedicated scholars may be unable or unwilling to give. It follows that the quality of historical knowledge cannot be judged by absolute criteria, but must be evaluated in terms of the goals, selections, and so on, operative in any given piece of writing. Critics are naturally entitled to debate the wider value of these goals and of the forms of selection they dictate.

ASSESSING FRAMEWORKS

To turn to the second set of criteria for judging the adequacy of historical writings, it should be apparent that the questions around conceptual frameworks and those around sources are intertwined. Generally, the conceptual framework chosen exercises a large measure of influence over the sources used and vice versa. A harmonious fit between framework and materials is crucial. Have the key concepts in the framework been adequately explained and their use justified? It is helpful if authors explain why they have chosen one framework rather than another, and what the strengths and shortcomings of competing frameworks are. To a degree, the framework will depend on the historical genre involved, since we evaluate various types of academic writing rather differently. For instance, in the standard journal article, where there are severe constraints on length and the expectation of original research, it is necessary to launch straight in by setting up the historical problem to be addressed swiftly and deftly. Clarity of focus is paramount. The audiences for journals differ from those for books; imagined readerships shape all academic writing. Thus, the status of a piece of historical knowledge is bound up with the type of writing through which it is expressed, that is, with both genre and implied audience. If a framework is particularly distinctive and up front, then the status of the piece in which it is used will usually be linked to the esteem in which the framework itself is held. Hence a 'straight' Marxian article would now be viewed with considerably more scepticism than it would have been 20 years ago, because the framework itself is thought to be, if not exactly obsolete, at least blunted in its critical capacities. The evaluation of historical work is all too frequently coloured by reactions to what are essentially intellectual fashions. By contrast with Marxism, psychoanalysis has enjoyed a huge increase in its intellectual status over the last two decades. To be sure there are a number of forms of psychoanalytic theory, as well as highly diverse ways of applying it to the past, which should not all be lumped together, and its whole basis has been passionately criticised; nonetheless, it is widely valued. Thus, once again, it is clear that historical knowledge can only be evaluated in context.

JUDGING WRITING

The third way of judging a historical account is as writing. This may surprise readers since history students are rarely taught how to write or shown the effects of literary style on responses to academic texts. But there is absolutely no doubt that, just as dull writing turns people off, so compelling writing enhances readers' reactions. In fact it is an integral part of the knowledge itself. Two examples of these points spring to mind. The first is the capacity to generate large-scale narratives, not just to tell a complex story but to integrate considerable amounts of disparate evidence to make an overall account that is plausible and compelling. This is an extremely challenging undertaking, and, as a form of writing, the so-called 'grand narrative' has lost favour with many historians; indeed, it is thought by many to be ideologically suspect. Big stories tend to appeal more to historians, and readers, who are not narrowly academic. The late Barbara Tuchman is a good example – she twice won the prestigious Pulitzer Prize and wrote on an extraordinary range of issues. *The March of Folly. From Troy to Vietnam* (1984) explores a theme – 'the pursuit by governments of policies contrary to their own interests' – over many centuries.[15] Excellent writing and a generous canvas are a potent combination. In such writing, the literary quality, the insights it contains and the overall approach taken are closely bound together.

The second example is the ability to evoke vivid images in readers' minds, which is usually achieved through a combination of description and anecdote.[16] Fine historical writing uses detail to further understanding. Perhaps 'description' is misleading because it implies low-grade intellectual activity: simply recounting what is there. In fact, description is exceptionally telling because it selects pertinent details and thus, when done well, moves effortlessly into analysis. A brief yet vivid story or description can be an extremely effective distillation of a broader historical point. It makes what is past lively, immediate and interesting, and helps readers to build up mental pictures.

There is a range of devices, including non-literary ones, for making the past alive for readers, but their status as devices needs to be kept in the foreground. On the one hand, we have living history movements, where people dress up and re-enact behaviour characteristic of other times, and, on the other, we have lively writing that both jolts readers into fresh insights and helps them to build up a more systematic understanding of historical processes. Two completely different notions of historical knowledge are involved. These two devices tend to be aimed at different audiences, which should immediately prompt us to think, once again, about the *varied* types of historical knowledge in existence. The former is aimed more at children, whose interest in and ability to grasp abstract analysis is bound to be limited. Re-enactment, which can involve highly elaborate engagement with the past, is growing in popularity as an adult leisure activity. Nonetheless, there is a more general point to be made here about the status of historical knowledge. We communicate accounts of the past largely through the written word, and it is by these means that 'history' is judged. Yet seeing something directly is accorded special status: that is the premise of living history and of most illustrations in historical publications. Elaborate reconstructions in fiction films or TV dramas are treated similarly. Such a status is recognised (rationally) as deceptive by scholars, although the (emotional) appeal of pictures and reconstructions remains undimmed, and it is popularly assumed they afford their audiences some kind of 'knowledge'.[17] Historical knowledge, in the sense I am using it here, is *always* built up painstakingly by a number of means. Evaluating its quality involves being aware of how these processes work. So we need to recognise that while the use of rhetorical devices is integral to all communication, it is essential to discriminate between them and to assess critically each one in order to evaluate its intellectual power.

At a professional level, the quality of historical writing is absolutely central to its persuasiveness. I have already suggested that this rests in part on an ability to describe and to use well-chosen examples that evoke other worlds. For example, in a whole range of her writings, Olwen Hufton has examined the poor in early modern Europe, and the lives of women of all kinds, especially in relation to their religious and charitable activities.[18] Using her vast experience of archival materials, she draws out the most telling, pointed, poignant examples, and the quality of her writing suggests a strong ability to give a historical account from the point of view of the less privileged. These reactions are necessarily personal; just as there can be no consensus on who are the 'best' fiction writers, so there can never be complete agreement on the quality of historical writings. My hunch would be that female readers respond particularly warmly to Hufton, because her writing taps into themes with which many women identify.[19] Furthermore, and this is true of all effective historical writing, Hufton displays a strong understanding of how human beings work, which is evident in the frameworks and sources chosen, as well as in the writing itself. A historical account that makes simplistic assumptions about motivation, for example, could be technically well informed, but unable to command widespread support because it is not, on a human level, believable. There is no consensus on these matters either, and it remains a sad fact about the discipline that crudely reductive assumptions about the primacy of self-interest, in human nature and in historical explanation, continue to be produced. The contrast with a historian such as Natalie Zemon Davis could not be more marked. In her discussions of the Martin Guerre story, for example, she continually stresses the complexities of early modern imposture and of contemporary forms of identity that lay behind it. Motivation is, she acknowledges, uncertain and changeable; sometimes it must be speculated about if it is to be discussed at all. Yet, and this is a crucial point, she does not as a result throw up her hands in despair or draw back from the challenge of doing what *can* be done, that is, what the sources, our historical imaginations and the accumulated insights of the discipline permit.[20]

EXPLANATION

I fear that some professional historians may be quite impatient with the ways in which I have tackled issues about the status of historical knowledge. It might be thought, for example, that a book of this kind should produce unequivocal statements on the subject. I have argued, however, that this is not possible. Furthermore, so far I have laid no special stress on explanation as the goal of history.[21] This is partly because I have pointed up the inevitable lack of consensus on what constitutes an adequate explanation. Let's consider briefly what is generally meant by 'explanation'. Dictionary definitions suggest that it involves making phenomena intelligible, making them known and accounting for them. Historians certainly perform all these operations. They elucidate what has happened in such a way that questions asked about the past are given plausible answers and its meaning becomes clearer. In other words, explanation is a form of interpretation. Throughout *History in Practice* I am suggesting that historical interpretation is a subtle blend of diverse elements, such as the sources selected, the manner of their use, the context in which the historian works, their training, commitments and prejudices. The problem with the term 'explanation' is that it implies a more rigorous and logically exacting process than does interpretation. Explanation is, after all, a philosophical term, and philosophers who analyse forms of knowledge are interested not just in how particular disciplines explain their phenomena, but in comparing the quality and types of explanation that they offer. While these are important exercises for the philosophy of history, I am not sure that they help those new to the field. Furthermore, such discussions tend to play down two significant issues. First, there is no agreement on what constitutes a *satisfying* explanation. This is because there are different views on where the resting point in any explanation should be. The differences derive from theoretical commitments, aesthetic preferences, ideologies, beliefs, and so on. Second, the degree to which an explanation is adequate depends not just on how the original questions were framed, but on the audiences at which the answer is directed. These differences are particularly clear if we compare history books aimed at each stage of the educational process or the presentation of historical arguments in monographs with those given in museums.

Traditionally, historians have sought to explain the origins of major patterns of change and to offer causal explanations of them.[22] (Hence the popularity of exam questions which ask students to evaluate two different explanations of an event as if these were mutually exclusive.) The job of the historian, we could say, is to show *why* the Renaissance, the Chinese revolution, the collapse of the Roman Empire, and so on, occurred. I have not started with these questions because I wanted first to build up a sense of how historical accounts can be evaluated, and specifically to suggest that evaluation always happens in a context. Major elements of this context include available sources, other historical accounts, prevailing assumptions about human nature and historiographical fashion. Historiographical fashion covers a great deal, including philosophical preferences concerning evidence and explanation.

One pertinent historiographical fashion is the loss of confidence in causal explanations, in our ability to give clear answers to 'why' questions, which has taken place over the last 40 years. A number of trends account for this shift. The range of types of history undertaken has expanded hugely, which has muddied the waters when it comes to deciding where the main changes in the past occurred, that is, where to look for the most significant causes.

There is also an enhanced explanatory challenge once we accept that the paces of different types of change are varied – some political shifts can occur fast, whereas typically mentalities alter more sluggishly. We no longer imagine that causes were *either* political *or* economic *or* social, but rather see all of these at work, and find them all dependent upon, or at the very least bound up with, cultural shifts, with changes in ways of understanding and feeling about the world. In other words, conventional hierarchies of explanations no longer seem as plausible as they once did. Nor do we like the idea of invoking single causes or one type of cause, preferring to chart a wide range of factors. Hence questions like, 'Was the Russian Revolution caused more by economic than by political factors?' have come to seem rather artificial. And we are increasingly intrigued by the mental changes that go along with political and economic ones. These are, by their very nature, harder to pin down, and hence confidence in causal explanation, according to which one thing happens first and subsequently produces a clear effect that can be linked to it, has been undermined. It seems too neat and one-dimensional. There are three interrelated issues here: the difficulty in tracing clear sequences of cause and effect, especially when 'culture' is taken into account; the undermining of confidence in monocausal explanations; and the sense that different facets of a society, such as 'politics' or 'economics', are inextricably linked to one another.[23]

Two further issues may be linked with the change in climate concerning causality and history. The first concerns reductionism, a matter broached in earlier chapters. Once historians dwell on multi-factorial explanations, an emphasis on single causes appears reductionistic. It would be easy to parody historians' ever growing desire to insist on the complexity of the past, but the phenomenon is nonetheless real and must be seen in a broad intellectual context. The growth of interest in academic circles and among the general public in psychoanalysis, for example, has heightened awareness of the sheer range of human responses. As a result, the significance of the unconscious cannot be dismissed and psychological matters can be discussed in a less judgemental fashion. Furthermore, psychoanalysis itself is a 'historical' discipline. The markedly increased interest in the nature of memory and in commemoration among historians owes a great deal to the historical dimensions of psychoanalysis. Like many of its key thinkers, Freud was profoundly interested in historical study. Psychoanalysis as a field is historical in that it examines the nature and content of memory, legacies of past events, historically persistent symbols and cultural products as evidence for the structure of the unconscious.[24] One impact of postmodernism, post-structuralism and critical theory has been to insist not just on the complexity and diversity of human minds, but on their capacity to play. The point is that play is unpredictable, a force for subversion, inversion and pleasure.[25] The result is a much less tidy view of human existence, which spills over into what are considered appropriate and satisfying historical explanations.

The second issue concerning causality and history leads in precisely the same direction. I have noted several times that sources can be misleading, deceptive. The more the complexities of the 'raw' materials are acknowledged, the harder it is to generate unselfconscious confidence in crisp causal explanations. For some historians, the intricate, tricky nature of all sources is an irritation, which simply needs to be taken account of before getting on with business as usual. In their frame of mind, there is an accurate account to be had, but the obstacles have to be removed first. But for others, this trickiness is the result of how the human mind works. Human existence is not straightforward, hence any account – primary or secondary – is bound to be selective and, if you like, 'biased', even when the author is unaware of any falsification. Accordingly, the status of historical knowledge is a far more complex matter than it seems, and certainty is an elusive quality.

In fact, there are some much broader themes here, such as fraud. We may usefully distinguish a number of different aspects of fraud in relation to the practice of history. First, sources can be fabricated or adjusted in some way at the time, whether intentionally or not. This is relatively straightforward, but it should always be borne in mind. Second, sources can be produced fraudulently after the event. Probably the best-known recent example of this is the Hitler diaries, which were proved to be fraudulent after they had been 'authenticated' by a well-known historian.[26] The intention behind such a deceit is, presumably, making money. Third, processes of historical interpretation can be so extremely contentious that we reach for a word like fraud, such as duplicity. Recent debates about the 'reality' of the Holocaust exemplify the point.[27] A radical right-wing revisionist position, which casts doubt on established claims about the numbers of Jews killed, has to account for existing supporting evidence, and thereby to engage in debates about interpretation and deception. Fourth, historians have become increasingly interested in fraudulent behaviour in the past, and Natalie Davis in particular has argued that forms of imposture are historically specific and hence exceptionally rich in the historical insights they afford. But the interest goes deeper than this. Such cases involve complex legal procedures and by studying them we can reconstruct notions of evidence in *other* societies, think about *their* standards of proof and consider *their* notions of an adequate explanation. In this way historical research can be a means of reflecting, albeit indirectly, upon the practice of history. It can achieve this by keeping in the foreground of historians' minds the uncertainties of both evidence and interpretation.

SPECULATION AND BELIEF

It would be possible to recast a great deal of what I am saying by noting that historians seem to feel more comfortable now with the idea that history has a speculative dimension, which, far from being a weakness on the part of particular practitioners, is built into the subject itself. It follows that it is quite acceptable for historians to use both hypotheses and heuristic devices, that is, suppositions to think with. And perhaps this is what has made the recent interest in counterfactuals possible. This involves, as the term suggests, setting aside known outcomes, and asking about alternative scenarios

– 'what if' history. What if William the Conqueror had been defeated at the Battle of Hastings in 1066? What if Constantinople had not 'fallen' to the Turks in 1453? What if Australia had been 'discovered' at another time and by different people? What if the South had won the American Civil War? It is a game, and one that has long been played for its entertainment value. Recently, and in the hands of professional historians, it has been used as a device to sharpen historical analysis, although this enterprise is hardly ideologically innocent. It tends, for example, to affirm traditional modes of history by privileging the actions of great men and high politics.[28]

It is often easiest to be precise about a concept by considering its opposites. The key concept in this chapter has been 'historical knowledge', so it may be worth considering what is *not* taken to be historical knowledge. Three terms are relevant here: opinion, ideology and myth. 'Opinion' is used when we want to draw attention to what a particular person thinks, without any particularly strong evidentiary base to back it up. Hence, to call any bit of historical knowledge an opinion implies that it is not well grounded – a merely personal view. To call it 'ideology' is to make a somewhat different point, namely that it was driven by some prior commitment, such as a strongly held belief best understood as political, although, here too, a claim is being made about evidence. In the case of ideology, the evidence may well be there, but the charge is that it is being distorted or ignored because of the historian's deepest assumptions. The notion of myth is altogether more complex. 'Myth' suggests an invented story, a narrative devised to achieve certain ends that are usually assumed to have a strong emotional component. Sometimes we use the word myth to imply that an account has been made up, that it lacks any basis, however appealing it may appear. Once again, evidence is an issue – myths do not need evidence to generate compelling stories. Yet we also use myth in relation to history in another way. When we talk about historical myths, we are not so much contesting what happened as drawing attention to the intense affect that surrounds certain views of the past, so intense that they resist debate and modification.[29] Myths are simplified and exceptionally highly condensed accounts. In other words, historical myths are thought to be less knowledge than *belief*.

Discussing terms that might be taken as opposed to historical knowledge raises a difficulty that has been lurking in this entire chapter. I have argued that *everyone* has beliefs, ideologies and emotional investments, and that to charge a historian with doing so should hardly be seen as a damning criticism. Yet in ordinary usage, *knowledge* is rightly seen as something apart from opinion, in being grounded in the rigorous use of evidence. Is there a tension here? Indeed, is there a tension between being a professional historian who, as rationally as possible, sifts evidence and produces knowledge claims, and being a person who holds and respects profound beliefs? Put starkly and in some situations, a tension would seem to be undeniable. In practice, historians try to strike a balance, to be aware of any possible problems, to raise their own consciousness. Striking a balance and being judicious does not sound exciting, but these are the key to producing something that will count as historical knowledge without, on the one hand, making claims to certainty it cannot deliver, and, on the other, making no claims for it at all.

BRIDGE

It is not possible to make sensible statements about the status of historical knowledge without having a good understanding of how historians work, and of how the discipline and its products are shaped by their contexts. It is the purpose of this book to address, in general terms, both these issues. I argue that the practice of history is a complex and messy business and that historians are necessarily eclectic and pragmatic in their methods. Hence I have not tackled the status of historical knowledge in what could be called a philosophical manner. Indeed, I have suggested that 'truth' and 'objectivity' may not be the most helpful concepts for our purposes, and that reliability and judiciousness are more relevant. In this vein, we need to take account of the limitations both of sources and of the accounts we generate in using them. One way of taking this further is to assess the distinctive array of skills that historians deploy in their practice, which I shall do in chapter 7. But first I shall examine an issue – periodisation – that is absolutely fundamental to the practice of history, yet rarely drawn out for critical inspection. Periodisation may be defined as the carving of past times into delineated chunks, which are named and used to organise historical ideas, institutions and publications. It contains the seeds of explanation and interpretation. Our reliance on periodisation is so great that without it historical knowledge would scarcely be possible. It demands careful analysis, and in probing this theme we will observe that the manner in which periodisation is undertaken depends precisely on historians' contexts.

5

Periodisation

HISTORY AND TIME

History is the systematic study of the past, and at its heart is time. Time is a complex concept, which is most rigorously analysed by philosophers, physicists and astronomers. Historians display a more practical concern with the idea since they are interested in the effects of the passage of time on human societies. Inevitably these are extraordinarily diverse; there are no predictable patterns and the pace of change depends not only on particular circumstances, such as wars and revolutions, but on which aspect of the social formation is in question. Politics and the practice of government, for example, sometimes change extremely quickly, in days or weeks; while attitudes, styles of child-rearing and religious belief generally take far longer to alter their character. Measuring time and giving names to discrete periods are tasks basic to the discipline of history. Thus one of the most fundamental operations historians undertake is periodisation, a term we can use as a convenient shorthand for a number of time-related tasks that are rich with implicit historiographic assumptions.

The basic measures of time – hours, days, weeks, months and years – were not invented by historians. But they use them as fundamental, taken-for-granted tools, and they give them meaning by assigning additional tags to them, as Daniel Defoe did when he wrote *Journal of the Plague Year*, an account of the Great Plague of 1665 by an invented eyewitness. The practice of history is inextricably linked to ideas of time, to calendrical systems and, above all, to the metaphors through which we think about periods. Precisely because all these are part of our mental furniture, it is difficult to bring them up for conscious inspection. Here is an occasion when imagining oneself to be a Martian, or an anthropologist, can be particularly helpful. Cultivating an outsider's eye, we can ask, with deliberate naivety, what is implied by notions like 'the age of uncertainty', 'the golden age of capitalism' or, a particular favourite of mine, 'the grand century of the lady'?[1] There are *always* historical interpretations lurking in such phrases.

Ideas about periods, and the terms in which they are expressed, are largely inherited from earlier generations, and these shape the most fundamental assumptions we have, not just about how the past is to be divided up, but about its interpretation. This inheritance is unfortunate because conventionalised period terms seem to hamper fresh thinking; through periodisation particular views of history are naturalised, so that it is difficult to bring them up for critical scrutiny. Novelty is possible, however, and it stems from fresh metaphors and from new historical interpretations and events.

The events that took place on 11 September 2001 neatly illustrate a number of points about periodisation. Frequently they are simply referred to as 'nine eleven'; putting the number of the month before the day is a form of dating prevalent in North America, but not used in many other parts of the English-speaking world, which would probably say 'the eleventh of September'. What does 'nine eleven' actually refer to? It is certainly a shorthand for a number of violent and interconnected events that took place on that day in the United States. But it evokes a great deal more, including a state of affairs in which there is mutual mistrust and hostility between constituencies that are rarely defined precisely in social, geographical, religious, political or economic terms. Single terms such as 'terror' and 'Islam' are widely used to conjure up phenomena of formidable intricacy. They have acquired intense affect and, lacking careful definition, they are overused, inaccurately and manipulatively. While 'nine eleven' is a dramatic punctuation mark, most people recognise that it must be explained historically, that is to say, by antecedent events and processes. But how far back is it necessary or plausible to go? The crusades? The early twentieth century? It is a reasonable assumption that 'nine eleven', like a concept such as the cold war, now plays a prominent part in organising our sense of the recent past, despite the fact that the historical processes of which it was one manifestation have a much baggier shape and a slow pace of change. As Bernard Lewis explained in *What Went Wrong? Western Impact and Middle Eastern Response*, which was already in press at the time, and hence did not deal with 'nine eleven' directly: 'this book . . . is however related to these attacks, examining . . . what went before – the longer sequence and larger pattern of events, ideas, and attitudes that preceded and in some measure produced them.' His examination ranges over many centuries.[2]

Inevitably, then, period terms have their own complex histories and emotional auras, having been put in place at a variety of times and for diverse purposes, some openly partisan. Tracing and understanding this baggage are important parts of historical practice and should be accorded more priority than is currently the case. However, historians are not the only group that participates in the process of shaping the past. Politicians, writers, artists and film-makers, as well as institutions such as museums, are also significant players. Nonetheless, historians both reinforce and help to change the shapes of history, and they have to do so in a way that makes sense to others;

otherwise, names for periods, and the assumptions behind them, would not take hold.[3] I have noted how these names carry implicit historical approaches; they also carry subjective responses to other times. A brief example illustrates these points. To call the era between the death of Charles I in 1649 and the restoration of Charles II in 1660 'the interregnum' presents it as an interruption between two monarchs and implies both that monarchy was the normal state of affairs and that the continuity of the monarchy was, and continues to be, an important feature of British society. For most of that period Oliver Cromwell was 'reigning', even if he was not called the king. By contrast, to stress the 'Commonwealth' – England was a republic between 1649 and 1654 – draws attention to the experiments with a radically different social and political order. Making choices about period terms is not just an intellectual operation; it involves political-cum-emotional commitments and aesthetic preferences. At stake here is how the historian's imagination works. It is simply wrong to neglect the imagination and to prise it apart from the other mental operations scholars perform.

The recording of significant dates and the development of calendars are exceedingly old activities, without which neither the practice of history nor periodisation would be possible.[4] Timekeeping activities contain two facets that are in tension with one another. They have been highly interested enterprises, serving the needs of church, state, legal and administrative systems. At the same time they claim, and have been accorded, a kind of objectivity, for example, by basing time on astronomical principles, and they purport to record events dispassionately and as accurately as possible. Dates, chronology and forms of periodisation still seem to offer value-free information, but this is deceptive. The phrase 'Ming vase' and the associations between periods and colours, exploited by the manufacturers of paint, reveal how culturally dense period terms are.[5] Assumptions are built into the very recording processes themselves; historical actors introduce distinctive spins upon even quite basic chronological information – we should never forget the inventiveness of human memory; then historians and others add layer upon layer of meaning to events and eras. Historians should be sceptical about the accuracy of chronological information, aware of how units of time shape historical interpretation, often in quite arbitrary ways, and alive to the manner in which we project patterns onto the past in order to make them meaningful. All these factors affect the types of research done; for instance, by drawing scholars towards some periods and away from others, they allow some eras to appear exciting and alluring, others dull, uneventful and unappealing. This occurs because those who study the past identify with their objects of study in complex ways. The manner in which periods are thought about and represented is a central part of these processes of identification precisely because they work at a variety of emotional and intellectual levels.

DIVIDING UP THE PAST

There are a number of criteria according to which the past can be divided up, not just to produce manageable chunks, but to organise our thoughts about it, to offer readings and accounts of it. In effect we are talking about a range of taxonomic systems, which overlap and can be used in a variety of ways. We are quite familiar with such situations, readily accepting that dogs are classified differently according to context: for zoological, breeding, showing, feeding and other practical purposes – those that bite or bark and those that do not, for example. Each criterion places the emphasis in a different place and has a different use, the value of which is context-dependent. Nonetheless, we can combine these taxonomies flexibly and pragmatically when choosing a pet. The stakes in classifying the past are somewhat grander, since implicit evaluations – political, aesthetic, ideological – of whole societies are involved. Common divisions are according to rulers or dynasties, around key events or individuals, descriptively by epoch, century, decade or millennium, in terms of the type of government, and according to perceived cultural styles, moods and patterns.

Rulers and dynasties are among the most obvious and commonly used forms of division, reflecting long traditions of scholarship that place leadership in government as a key phenomenon and accord primacy to the political order. Obvious examples include Tudor, Georgian and Victorian (England); Bourbon and Napoleonic (France); Carolingian (Holy Roman Empire); Wilhelmine (Germany); and Ottoman (early modern Turkey).[6] Thus a ruler or a family of rulers can embody a period; it is as if the one who heads the state holds together disparate historical phenomena in an extension of that role. Sometimes the implications are even stronger: Mao's China, Stalin's Russia, Mussolini's Italy, Franco's Spain and Pinochet's Chile are at first sight descriptions of a particular era of a particular nation, but in fact they convey the dominance, not just of a regime, but of a highly powerful individual, over the entire society. Is it coincidental that such a formulation seems especially apt for authoritarian regimes? It is striking, then, that the use of rulers and dynasties confers a large measure of unity on a period, a unity that may exist largely at a symbolic level in the body or bodies of rulers. Not just Hitler, but small fragments associated with his person – the moustache, the salute – can evoke the entire regime in our imaginations.[7] Absolutism, and its embodiment in Louis XIV, the 'Sun King', also demonstrates the point.[8] Related notions, such as 'Viking', 'Saxon' or 'Norman', when applied to periods, carry similar connotations, and, in addition, by virtue of their association with areas such as clothing and architecture, convey the idea that a whole culture is involved since, in one of their meanings, they describe a political dominance rooted in ethnicity. It is not just rulers and dominant groups, but elected leaders who can function in this way. In the case of eighteenth-century England, we might remember a succession of powerful prime ministers who made it plausible to speak of an age of Walpole or an age of Pitt. Much later, Winston Churchill and, in the United States, President Franklin D. Roosevelt functioned in this way. Indeed the identification between Roosevelt, the Depression and the New Deal has been remarkably strong. Possibly this form of periodisation is particularly compelling when the country in question has undergone a profound transformation or crisis under someone's leadership. It reinforces a sense of the agency of special individuals and lends coherence to an era.

In mentioning these examples I do not mean to imply that they have been treated uncritically by professional historians. Nor do I want to suggest that the associations between epochs and political leaders are without foundation. I am merely offering examples of one type of periodisation, and drawing out what is implicit within it. Furthermore, we should note how many of the related adjectives (Anglo-Saxon, Louis Quinze, Napoleonic, Biedermaier, Victorian) are also terms of style. This is especially obvious in relation to houses, furniture, jewellery and clothing. While we associate 'style' with art, music, fashion and other cultural products, it is in fact an important, if largely unrecognised, part of historical practice. Style can mean what is characteristic of a given artist, that is, of an individual, but it is also used, and has been since the eighteenth century, to sum up a period and to differentiate between periods – rococo and neoclassical, for example.[9] Style and periodisation are closely related, jointly shaping the historical imagination. A particularly telling instance is 'Victorian', which is now applied beyond the boundaries of Britain or its empire to suggest visual styles of the second half of the nineteenth century. Furthermore, as is evident in the phrase 'Victorian values', it suggests a style of thinking and responding to the world.[10] Indeed, the very phrase implies a response to that style, or rather it implies two polarised responses: either approval for strong traditional moral stances, or criticism of their inappropriate use in a later period. In using a word like 'style', there may be a danger that we trivialise the effect of period terms by implying that these are merely matters of personal preference or taste. This is not my intention. On the contrary, period and style terms shape the way in which whole eras can be imagined and thought about, as the phrase 'Victorian values' reveals.

EVENTS AND PERIODS

A second important criterion for dividing up the past is key events, such as assassinations, battles, revolutions and wars. One of the most significant examples of this approach, however, is none of these – the birth of Christ. There could be no more eloquent example of how a single historical event can be made into a structuring principle and of the cultural baggage it necessarily brings with it. Since one counts backwards for eras BC and forwards for those AD, the importance of the turning point is made manifest, and every time the dating system is used, the global significance of the birth of Christ is unthinkingly asserted. There is now a certain distaste for using BC and AD, and while this is understandable, since Christianity is only one of many world religions, I am not sure that BCE (variously, before the common or Christian era) and CE really solve the problem; it simply repackages the same idea. This example raises the vexed question of whether standard, universal dating systems are really necessary or helpful. So long as conversions between systems are possible, it would seem to be most generative for historians to work within the forms of *dating* of the culture they study, although they will always be needing to rethink the forms of *periodisation* they are using, since this underpins historical interpretation.

The relationships between key dates and periodisations are intricate. The case of the Meiji restoration in Japan exemplifies the point. The restoration was announced in 1868, and is frequently taken as a major moment of transition to an era when Japan was more open to the west. Conrad Totman suggests it was 'a less transformational event than we usually envisage', and organises his book so as to bring out a multilayered approach to Japanese history.[11] The French Revolution – although, of course, only the beginning of it constitutes a clear 'event', and even that is debatable – provides a well-known example of the relationships between dramatic acts and models of periodisation. The fall of the Bastille on 14 July 1789, when a hated symbol of the Ancien Régime yielded, without much resistance, to the mob, has become a useful, emotionally apt convention for marking the inception of the 'French Revolution'. Hence we can say, metonymically, '1789', and conjure up a whole historical era. The French Revolution is important because it marks a fundamental shift in French society, recognised as such at the time. The abolition of feudalism and the transformation of subjects into citizens exemplify the point. The revolution was also taken to be symptomatic of later changes that went far beyond the boundaries of France – the modernisation of administration and warfare, for example. The French were neither the first to behead a king in recent times nor the first to try to rethink a polity anew, yet the French Revolution has special status. Thus it was natural for many generations of historians to think of this as a decisive turning point, which would help them clarify their general interpretations of European and even world history.

Historians of many different orientations could join in acknowledging its significance. Hobsbawm's *The Age of Revolution: Europe, 1789–1848*, first published in 1962, is a case in point. His concern was with the relationships between political and economic change – the phrase 'age of revolution' embraces the industrial revolution too. Palmer's *The Age of the Democratic Revolution* (1959, 1964) put a rather different spin on the era, because it sought to interpret the French and American revolutions together, and to draw out the strong affinities between the two nations in this era. So, in the national consciousness of many states, as in historians' imaginations, '1789' is an emblem, even if exactly what it is an emblem of varies dramatically. The vogue for celebrating centenaries makes the point particularly vividly – the mere fact of the celebration implies shared national and international values, while, in practice, events as controversial as the French Revolution cannot unite a people, still less the discipline of history.

Using a key event of this kind as a periodising device may be misleading. There are many phenomena that showed marked continuity across the revolutionary divide, despite its tumultuous nature. Although the prominence of health care for all citizens was high on the revolutionary agenda, medicine is arguably one example. In both science and medicine many 'bigwigs' worked throughout the period and remained more or less consistently

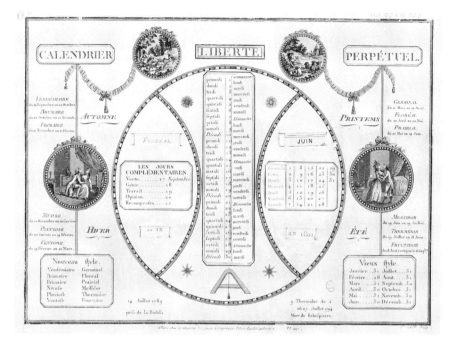

5.1 Perpetual Republican Calendar, June 1801 (coloured engraving)
During the French Revolution there were innumerable attempts to construct a fresh social, cultural and political order. The elaboration and use of new systems of measurement is a particularly telling example. The metric calendar demonstrates how far-reaching the search was for structures that carried none of the values of the Ancien Régime. To rename and reorganise time was a fundamental step indeed and it never took proper hold. Nonetheless, the attempt reveals both how ingrained and how symbolically charged the representation of time is.

prominent over a number of regimes.[12] Changes in institutional structures were more apparent than real. The invocation of Lavoisier, who was guillotined in 1793 (in fact, for his tax-collecting activities), as a *scientific* martyr fits one particular view of the revolution as a rupture, and a barbaric one at that.[13] Other accounts present significant continuities from the 1770s to the early decades of the nineteenth century. Prior commitments shape historians' claims about continuity and change. Ideally, careful forms of periodisation are made appropriate to the research task in hand. The choice of key events is value-laden, allowing very different stories to be told. It helps to know what lies behind their choice and how they are acting as symbols.

In thinking about dating and periodisation in relation to the French Revolution, three points should be made. First, although its dating is contentious and depends upon both the kind of crisis it is believed to be and the interpretation of its outcome, historians develop conventions for dealing with the difficulties. These should not cause problems so long as they are recognised as such and the rationales behind them explained. Second, the revolution was understood at the time as a special event, which would forever change the course of European and possibly even world history. It was a conscious process of collective self-fashioning and reinvention, which included, of course, the revolutionary calendar, along with metric systems of weights and measures and the cult of the supreme being.[14] Historians need to pay careful attention to deliberate rethinking about the naming and measurement of time. Third, the revolution raises vast questions about periodisation, especially on a large scale – the conceptualisation of centuries and decades. These cannot be resolved empirically, since they involve models of change in general, of revolution as a process and of the specific period. We can see this particularly clearly when we think about the use of 'modern'. For many commentators, the French Revolution was the beginning of the 'modern' era – but what does such a claim involve? We now recognise the complexities of 'modern' and 'modernity' and the manner in which our own era is implicated in their definition. One does not have to be a postmodernist to appreciate how intricate the manoeuvres around modernity are. It is vital to recognise that here we are not in the territory of research, of finding information that will clarify the matter, but of interrogating received ways of patterning, organising and imagining the past.

It should come as no surprise to discover that dramatic changes, used as historical markers, possess a mystique; perhaps they are the historical equivalent of a *rite de passage*. This was captured, for example, in *Reds* (1981), a Hollywood version of the Russian Revolution. Historians, like others, project humanoid features onto abstractions, and hence can easily imagine changes in past societies as resembling the major, symbolic transitions of an individual life course – birth, growth, maturity, death, and so on. A good example of this is the ubiquity of falls – of the Roman Empire, Troy, Constantinople. The naming, recognition and packaging of such transitions can be said to be unifying. By 'unifying' I do not mean that everyone holds the same opinion, but rather that there is a shared sense of the general significance of a particular event or process, and that it becomes an accessible point of reference, sometimes as it is happening and, more often, for later generations. As a result, these events act as organising principles within historical research.

One of the most striking instances of this phenomenon is the First World War of 1914–18, where we can see the processes I have just described occurring at four distinct levels. First, participants themselves took it to be an unprecedented phenomenon of huge significance, and I define as participants everyone who had to cope with its impact, not just those on the battlefields.[15] The people who treated shell-shock victims, for example, had to think anew about trauma, and therefore also had to think anew about the nature of the human mind.[16] Second, the management of social issues was changed decisively by the war, so that leaders of post-war societies were conscious of a major transition taking place. The Depression, on the one hand, and the widespread commitment to welfare policies, on the other, are examples of phenomena that brought fundamental changes to many geo-

graphical areas in the wake of the war. Third, historians have certainly recognised the First World War as basic to the construction of period categories, even if, inevitably, they differ on precisely what weight it should be
given. Arno Mayer, for example, suggested that it was a major watershed,
because it was only after the war that landed elites decisively lost their political power. This is only one example of how an event can be used to construct periodisations. Fourth, the war has been given significance as an
organising event through its cultural representation, both at the time and
subsequently. The current enthusiasm for books about that war, whether fictional or not, is indicative of the grip it holds on significant swathes of the
population. Poetry and poets have played a crucial role in giving the First
World War a potent cultural identity.[17]

As I shall argue in the next chapter, what is best called public history,
which includes museums, the media and historical novels, has a massive
impact upon the ways in which the past is imagined. The First World War is
an excellent example of this very point, and I am mentioning it here to show
how periodisation is involved. A more recent example, the fall of the wall
dividing West and East Berlin, could be used to make the same points; it has
become, at once, an organising principle and a symbol of a major historical
transition. Our sense of 'natural' boundaries, of discrete periods, derives not
so much from abstract analysis as from diffused understandings of where the
turning points are. And these, in turn, come from a variety of sources,
including film, poetry and art. Professional historians examine these supposedly natural boundaries from a critical standpoint, and may, as a result, want
to develop arguments that run contrary to common ideas; that, indeed, is
their job. But they too inhabit a wider world in which commitments to forms
of periodisation are woven into the fabric of everyday life. Their proposed
changes may well take hold, but it is, I believe, hard to go against the grain
when it comes to the use of major events as historical markers, since these
are constantly affirmed in arenas over which historians have no control. The
two world wars are indelibly etched on the national consciousness in most of
the countries that took part and I very much doubt that a radical revisionism, which demoted their significance, could ever take hold, even assuming
that there were strong intellectual arguments to back it up. I have spent
some time on events as period organisers because they lend themselves to
symbolisation. They can be presented as simple, discrete units, and, as a
result, they get a grip on us, fit into larger patterns and work their magic
through all the means cultures afford them.

DESCRIPTION AND PERIODISATION

I turn now to a third form of periodisation, one that is less overtly emotionally charged and more subtle in the ways it works. This is *descriptions* of a time
period, which sounds innocent, but, as is apparent from the examples
'modern' and 'early modern', they are rather slippery and contain hidden
agendas. There are many different definitions of modern history, and we
have already noted that 'modern' is a tricky term. 'Modern' has several

meanings.[18] It is often helpful to think about the opposite of such terms, of what they are standing in contrast to. The most familiar pairing until the nineteenth century was ancient and modern.[19] This is instructive, since the contrast indicated, in the seventeenth century, for example, an anxiety about whether the moderns could ever live up to the high achievements of ancient civilisations, especially those of Greece and Rome. Gradually, over the eighteenth century, anxiety gave way to confidence, so that what was recent, new, up to date, was increasingly given value. 'Modern' could then be associated with innovation, with what is palpably related to the present and to the future. Thus in advertising from the early twentieth century, 'modern' was synonymous with 'clean', 'hygienic', 'not using coal', and so on. Modern history usually carries the connotation of being closely related to the present, and, as a result, 'modern' risks carrying an implicitly Whiggish and teleological undertow. It tends to be goal directed in that it takes the present as that which is to be explained, as if this were the point towards which previous trends were leading, and it departs from the assumption that 'the winners'' standpoint is a kind of baseline.

'Modern' can also be given a rather different set of inflections. The ones I have just described are in fact relative, that is, modern is defined in relation to where one is standing now. The second way of thinking about modernity is absolute, since it seeks to specify a particular set of historical conditions that qualify as 'modern'. Needless to say, there is no consensus on what the defining characteristics of modernity are. Possibilities include: advanced capitalism; economic specialisation and high levels of the division of labour; the types of urbanisation found initially in the nineteenth century; the period since the French Revolution; unified, clearly defined, 'democratic' nation states; the development of cultural avant-gardes; post-Newtonian science; the use of steam (then electric and nuclear) power in industrial production; mass production; the discovery of the unconscious; and the legacy of the Enlightenment.[20] It is not necessary to choose between such criteria, but many commentators put the interpretative weight in a particular zone – economic, political, cultural or intellectual. Smuggled in here are notions of progress, the value given to specific areas of human achievement and causal priorities, that is, which changes are deemed to have the greatest capacity to alter human existence most profoundly.

There is an implied contrast between *early* modern and modern history. Earlier, the main distinction had been between the medieval period and modernity, where the former was construed as more static, with a slower pace of change than the latter, and also as lacking those institutions that make for modern life – printing, for example. In current historical usage, the early modern period sits between the two, its precise boundaries undefined. Early modern also implies a kind of teleology; 'society' is moving towards modernity but it is not quite there yet. The term suggests a dependence upon, a subordination to what is modern, as if it were a mere prelude, the overture to the main proceedings. When does 'medieval' end and 'early modern' begin? Is it perhaps with Columbus's encounter in 1492 with the continent now named 'America'? Or is it with Luther's act of attaching his 95 theses to the church door in Wittenberg on 1 November 1517, the symbolic initiating move of the Reformation? Could it be Copernicus's rejection of the ancient earth-centred cosmology in favour of an 'infinite universe' recognisably like the one we believe in today, published in 1543?[21] And when did the early modern period end – with the French Revolution, the Enlightenment, Newton's path-breaking work of the 1680s, the 'discovery' of Australia, the last major habitable landmass to be named, visited and charted by those who lived in Europe?[22] Again, it is not a question of right and wrong answers, but of whose vantage point is privileged, of the power of symbolic markers, and of the weight given to distinct fields of human activity. For example, from the perspective of someone concerned with human rights, the Enlightenment and the French Revolution occupy a privileged position since they forged and disseminated a discourse of rights, which has been construed as a gift to the modern world.[23] Hence the early modern period would end some time around the Enlightenment, since those we associate with this movement of ideas articulated cogent critiques of existing systems of justice and the use of torture, and actively campaigned on these issues, as in Voltaire's defence of Calas, wrongly accused of murdering his son in a situation of confessional strife.[24] And we think of these concerns as 'modern'. For an economic historian, by contrast, such arguments would not cut much ice, whereas the advent of steam power, mass production, assembly lines and rationalistic time management certainly would. 'Early modern' would then loosely characterise a transitional era, of artisanal production within both workshops and families, increasingly sophisticated trading links, including internationally, and specialised markets.[25] Yet, by their very nature, these phenomena were subject to considerable local variation; hence it becomes extremely difficult to give overall names to periods with any degree of confidence. Despite Hobsbawm's influential *The Age of Capital*, which covers 1848–75, and many other works in a similar vein, every history teacher tries to impress upon their students how difficult it is to say when capitalism began, and to assume such a statement could cover entire regions or countries.

Other innocent-sounding descriptions, such as 'pre-Columbian', 'contemporary' or 'medieval', raise similar problems. To divide the history of what is generally called Latin America into two chunks, one before Columbus arrived and the other after, is to impose a quite particular view of the past on an area.[26] The phrase 'contemporary history' is now gaining currency, but how far back does contemporary history go?[27] Are we thinking about what is within living memory? In that case, contemporary history would still include much of the twentieth century. Or is it to be taken more literally, to refer to now, our own times? This remains ambiguous. In Britain, contemporary history is sometimes traced back to 1945, which affirms the end of the Second World War as a major turning point, but at other times it means simply the 'twentieth century'. While naming a century merely by giving it a number may sound equally innocent and descriptive, in fact centuries are often used

5.2 Fifteenth-century map of the world according to Ptolemy

Maps are effective ways of reminding ourselves that the world was experienced and visualised in totally different ways at other times. Here there is no American continent.

in ways that are not simply literal. Invoking a whole century in this way is deceptive in any case, given the dramatic differences between the beginnings and ends of centuries. A phrase like 'the eighteenth century' offers only spurious coherence. In relation to British history, the phrase is sometimes taken to cover the period 1688–1815, that is, the 'long' eighteenth century, from the Glorious Revolution to the Battle of Waterloo.[28] This particular perspective is idiosyncratic and politically freighted; it is controversial even in a British context and makes no particular sense to students of other European countries. A historian of France might be inclined to have a 'short' eighteenth century, say between the death of Louis XIV in 1715 and 1789. From the perspective of the Thirteen Colonies/United States (often erroneously called simply 'America'), the shape of the eighteenth century also looks quite different, given the significance of the decisive break from the mother country in the 1770s. That is, to cast the point in more general terms, colonial periods and those of independence are *made* distinct, not just by historians, but also by historical actors. For many countries the advent of 'independence' is certainly crucial, symbolising a process widely imagined as liberating. Yet in practice, given the continuing involvement of many imperial powers with their former colonies, a single *moment* of independence may not be a really useful marker for the organisation of historical work. An event that symbolises the change may be important emotionally, yet not particularly significant economically or legally.[29]

When considering period terms, it is vital to remember that historians necessarily make choices concerning them. In the case of the eighteenth century, for example, one alternative would be 'the Enlightenment', which is used both of a movement of ideas and of the time at which it occurred. 'The Enlightenment' carries quite specific connotations in that it suggests not only intellectual changes, but, more specifically, a move towards a more secular, rationalistic and democratic world view. Specialists debate these matters, but the fact remains that associations, such as that between the Enlightenment and secularisation, are entrenched. Like all words ending in '-isation', secularisation is problematic – a point we have already noted in relation to modernisation. Part of the problem is that they appear to refer to specific periods, while in fact being extremely vague and slippery. The eighteenth century was also an era of religious revival, a phenomenon that has rarely been studied by those who see themselves primarily as students of the Enlightenment. Definitions of the Enlightenment have varied quite dramatically. In the 1960s and early 1970s, the emphasis on a 'high' Enlightenment remained, that is, a concentration upon major thinkers, such as Diderot, Rousseau and Voltaire. It was also usual to privilege France as its epitome: civilised, urbane, sophisticated. By the late 1970s, work began to be published which challenged these views, and although the temporal boundaries of the Enlightenment will always remain contentious, there is now a much broader sense of what it encompassed, in terms of geographical areas, social groups and institutions. Low life and the Enlightenment can now be placed together with some plausibility, and we can envisage a plurality of Enlightenments that were loosely related to one another.[30] This example demonstrates how notions of periodisation are bound up with both historians' other tasks and their mental maps of the past. Interpretations of the Enlightenment – the very concept gives status to intellectual innovation – including the period it covers, contain wider implications for the onset of modernity, for the boundaries between modern and early modern, and for the conceptualisation of different kinds of change, since it gives priority to ideas while construing them as influential upon social practices – statecraft, local administration, justice, education, and so on.

So far, I have discussed descriptions of periods in terms of large swathes of time, but we also have notions like the roaring twenties and swinging sixties, which are considerably more focused. So why are some *decades* seen as worthy of naming as special, others less so? Why are some seen as definable periods and others not? There are no straightforward answers to these questions, which are designed to provoke ideas about the relationships between periods and identity. This is clear in the case of the sixties, which can carry either positive or negative connotations; something about the speaker's identity is thereby revealed. The sixties is an organising idea and now we are beginning to see professional historians writing about it as an

© ALBUM/AKG-IMAGES

5.3 The Beatles, 1967
The Beatles have become inseparable from the idea of the sixties. Both 'The Beatles' and 'the sixties' possess dramatically diverse meanings.

entity.[31] As anyone who lived through that decade knows, 'the sixties' is a myth, in that it is a strategically simplified fabrication, but once in existence, we orientate ourselves with respect to it and use it for our own purposes. Such terms are capable of holding contradictory values, in this case envy, disapproval, blame, nostalgia and approval. An equally telling example is the interest in the last decades of centuries, that is, in the *fin de siècle* phenomenon.[32] Until recently, fin de siècle referred only to the 1890s and, more especially, to a cultural formation presented in terms of decadence, ennui, sexual indulgence and the critique of bourgeois society. Then, in *our* nineties, historians began to explore what seemed to be a more general phenomenon. There was indeed something special about the end of centuries, they claimed. *Fin de siècle* came to be used considerably more loosely, and not just by historians, to refer to a situation in which we found ourselves, a situation dominated by the idea of a new millennium, and by a strange mixture of fear and anticipation. It can be argued that this usage is sloppy and insufficiently historically precise, but it does illustrate how historians' identities are linked with periodisation, and how the terms of engagement with the past shift according to circumstance. In these cases it is pretty obvious that the observer's position affects their sense of periods, but the phenomenon is a general one, even if it usually occurs at rather subtle levels.

FURTHER PERIOD TERMS

A fourth way in which we can divide up the past is in terms of the type of government. I have already mentioned some examples of this mode – absolutism, the ancien régime. Another commonly used example would be Communist China or Communist Russia (actually, like 'America', 'Russia' is commonly misused). *Communist* 'Russia' differentiates it from *Tsarist* Russia. The type of regime, precisely because it changed so radically, sums up an era, although these periods are of varying length. Epithets like 'Communist' and 'Tsarist' are relatively easy to use, but they generally carry, I suspect, some pejorative connotations. Would we say, for example, *democratic* Australia or *democratic* Canada, and, if not, why not? It may well be that some forms of government are more clear-cut than others, making a label that denotes a distinctive political ideology especially attractive. Admittedly 'democracy' is a woolly concept, more an ideal than a state achieved, and there has been no single democracy party that is comparable in historical significance to the Communist Party. If it is reasonable to suggest that names go along with clearly identifiable types of government, which tend to be more authoritarian, then other types are being passed by in relative silence, perhaps taken as the norms against which 'communism', 'absolutism' and 'fascism' are judged. In the case of ancien régime, this process is perfectly clear: 'ancien' is relative to what came later, which, it is implied, was clearly better. More specifically, ancien régime carries connotations of corruption, deceit and bankruptcy – financial, social and moral. Since it implies the existence of a subsequent, new and better political order, ancien régime carries progressivist values.[33] Naming types of government, and organising historical periods around them, involves political judgements that are rendered less visible by being conventionalised.

A fifth way of discriminating between periods is in terms of cultural style, which, naturally enough, appeals rather less to political and economic historians than it does to intellectual and cultural ones.[34] Since these style terms are, as we have already noted, powerful metaphors capable of further extension, we may yet come to a time when we speak of governments as baroque or rococo, and of factories as neoclassical![35] Baroque is a stylistic category, and it is also used to describe an era of European history, although its boundaries are, not surprisingly, difficult to define. In all these forms of periodisation we are thinking about ways of meaningfully evoking a period – the use of style terms is just another case in point. 'Style' implies that there is a distinctive flavour to a period, a flavour that suffuses its main products: music, art, literature, clothes, buildings, worship, and so on. It lends a special kind of coherence to the past, not political or economic in nature, but aesthetic and emotional. This is clear in terms that are not only stylistic, such as Georgian or colonial, as used, for example, of the USA. I do not mean something narrow and connoisseurial when I say 'aesthetic'; rather I want to suggest that matters of taste, of cultural preference, of intellectual and sensual response, are, whether we like it or not, always at work when we organise our ideas of the past.[36]

My argument is that in order to manage the past it has to be classified, and that one of the most important forms of classification is periodisation. Classification puts like things together in a coherent, systematic manner. Over the centuries, historians (but not only historians) have developed comfortable, conventionalised ways of doing this, so that we barely think about them. Their function is precisely to lend to past times a sense of meaning, order and coherence. I am suggesting that although many historians would not use style terms, and certainly few would think about those they do use as such, they exemplify the unifying function of period names. They enable us to see particularly clearly how a wide range of reactions to the past is mobilised when we shape it into discrete periods – reactions that are aesthetic, emotional, political, and so on.

So far I have discussed five fairly obvious criteria according to which the past is divided up, and I have mentioned some of the issues that lie behind them. But much has not been included in the types of period names already noted. What about terms such as Reformation, pre- and post-Reformation, Counter-Reformation? These are similar to 'the Enlightenment', in that they refer to a movement and they suggest a set of themes and preoccupations as well as a specific historical period. In the case of the Reformation, there is no ambiguity at all about where the origins of change can be located. It implies a major transition – a process, not an event – in the history of European Christianity. In effect, the larger significance of Christianity, for all aspects of human existence where it was the dominant religion, is affirmed. Because these are matters of belief, where the pace of change is generally slow, piecemeal and uneven, historians accordingly stress the local variations, the very different forms Christianity took, the complex interactions between reformers and those they wished to change. As a result, the location of chronological boundaries becomes even more difficult, since the phenomenon itself is protean.[37] When did the Reformation end? Might we, to take a provocative example, want to see English Methodism in the eighteenth century as part of a *longue durée* Reformation? The possibility immediately calls into question definitions of the Enlightenment, which has rarely been seen as including religious *revival*, yet the Wesley brothers, the reluctant founders of a separate Methodist church, can also be understood as responding to and expounding Enlightenment ideas.[38] Once we begin to reflect in this way, it becomes apparent why key events, with their seeming clarity, are so appealing as ways of organising the past. Yet the discussion should also reveal how misleading they can be – satisfying symbols, yes, secure historical indicators, no. Symbols are not 'bad', indeed they are central to human existence, but they function in ways that are not necessarily conducive to deeper historical understanding. Luther's actions may indeed have been significant, and they function well as a symbol, but they are somewhat arbitrary when used to mark the beginning of a historical movement or period such as 'the Reformation'. For example, many of the theological ideas held by leading reformers derived from earlier 'heretical' movements.

Perhaps books, which also act as symbols, are more secure historical indicators. We might, for instance, want to take the publication of Descartes's *Discourse on Method* (1637) as not just a major turning point in European history, but as an apt symbol for the start of the Enlightenment, in that it was published in French, not in Latin, it gives status to mathematical and scientific arguments, and it takes the individual as the centrepiece and starting point for philosophy. To do so would affect one's interpretation of the Enlightenment, as well as of the history of philosophy; it is not inherently less arbitrary than any other symbolic initiation. To any individual a given symbol will be more or less satisfying, yet all contain both implicit agendas and a measure of arbitrariness. They are indispensable, but not to be used uncritically, however seductive they appear at first sight.

METAPHORS AND THEMES

Yet another way of delineating periods, by themes, also warrants careful reflection. Examples include 'the age of anxiety', 'the age of equipoise', 'golden age' or the 'aristocratic century'.[39] Such phrases, in fact, could be applied to many periods. The underlying principle is by now familiar: it is the desire to lend unity to a period, in this case via a combination of description and metaphor. Of course, descriptions are metaphorically charged, but these themes work in different ways. 'The age of revolution' may be considered more descriptive in that, on seeing it, the reader's mind moves to *specific* revolutions, in France and the United States, and the Industrial Revolution. 'The age of uncertainty' is rather different; it is simply a metaphor. The reader forms a vivid image, but has nothing concrete to attach it to. It does imply that other ages were more certain, and we might be able to work out that a claim is being made about a twentieth-century loss of various kinds of structures, possibly psychic, economic, social or political, that gave shape to life in earlier times.[40]

Each theme works in a somewhat different way, but here I want to draw attention to one further example, because of its exceptional historiographical interest – the Depression around the 1930s. There is something quite striking about the use of a term we have come to associate primarily with a mood to describe an era. Whatever the origins of the term, it is emotive, and it is so in a highly specific manner. It evokes the dependency of human well-being on large-scale economic trends, unexpected immiseration and the need for compassion on more than an individual or philanthropic basis. What is so extraordinary is the way these ideas mirror trends within the period itself, during which many governments and significant social groupings, especially of intellectuals, sought radical solutions to inequalities, to authoritarian regimes and to social deprivation in their own immediate surroundings.[41] Needless to say, there is no consensus on the chronological boundaries around this particular depression.[42] And since many countries experienced an economic phenomenon that was close to being global, there were marked geographical variations. In this case, periods, images of periods, self-understanding and historians' accounts are particularly closely interwoven; the underlying mechanisms are, however, quite common.[43] Many period terms derive in some way from the categories historical actors themselves used, or out of those forged by succeeding generations for their own purposes. They then become reified and take on a life of their own. In the case of the Depression, the desire to construct a record of social conditions and to develop a social critique of them, the broad concerns of the time and the enduring interest in the entire phenomenon render the whole process more transparent than usual.

My aim is this chapter has been to demonstrate that forms of periodisation are conceptually dense. In particular I have argued that the manner of naming periods contains assumptions about where historical agency lies and about what the most formative aspects of a given society are. Historians, like most people, need a sense of coherence, and although in the case of scholars this is partly for practical reasons, to make research manageable, it also serves much deeper needs. The coherence with which periods are endowed is integral to the historical explanations offered for them. The drive to find an epitome of a period, that acts to unify it, is strong, and to some degree it does not matter whether this is found in an individual, an event, a style of government or a theme. In all these cases the totality of the historian's imagination, which works through both metaphor and visual images, is engaged. Hence, it is significant what our mother tongue is, since this determines not only the precise terminology currently in use for describing periods, but their metaphorical resonances – the notions of the Enlightenment, *die Aufklärung* and *le siècle des lumières* are quite distinct. By the same token, dominant visual traditions also help to shape views of past times – the French, for example, have a more 'rococo' view of the eighteenth century than do the English!

HISTORIOGRAPHY AND PERIODISATION

Periodisation involves other historiographical issues as well, and in closing this chapter I shall mention just two of them, in order to reaffirm the importance of critical reflection upon the precise manner in which time is at the heart of historical practice. The first concerns the *amounts* of time any given piece of historical research or writing covers: what we could call its scale or compass. Deciding how long a period is to be covered is one of the historian's most important skills, and the chosen time-span should always fit with, be apt for, the kind of project envisaged. Let us take the example of *longue durée* history, an exceptionally challenging form of history to write, and found in widely read survey books, for example. The defence of taking long time-spans is perfectly clear and it relates to human rhythms, to the pace of some kinds of change, to the need to differentiate between levels and types of change, and to the distinctive qualities some eras possess. Thus there were specific preconditions for Braudel's three-volume study of *Civilization and Capitalism, 15th–18th Century*: he was primarily concerned with historical phenomena that change extremely slowly, or at least have done so at some periods. Furthermore, Braudel considered the relationships between different *levels* of change, hence a long time-span was necessary for these relationships to become clear. Braudel primarily wrote about the early modern period, and it is worth considering how well his approach would have worked for later periods.[44]

There are specific historical sub-fields, which, by their very nature, have to work across very long time-spans. The most obvious examples are demography and historical epidemiology, and some areas of economic history. Not only do the trends with which they are concerned take place slowly, but they need to be studied over long periods for their significance to become apparent. Shifts in morbidity and mortality, age of marriage, fertility and rates of illegitimacy would all be examples.[45] The nature and availability of relevant evidence tends to be patchy, and subject to marked local variations in terms of quality and survival. Hence materials need to be aggregated if anything like national, or even regional, trends are to be arrived at. Yet these are not merely practical matters, related to the accidents of record-keeping and preservation; they go right to the core of historical explanation. Judgements about how fast or how slowly phenomena change depend upon accounts of how they change at all, upon historians' understanding of the detailed mechanisms through which human beings and their environments are transformed. Hence it is imperative to ask questions, such as precisely how do attitudes and behaviours change? At what pace do they do so? How are ideas and practices transmitted from group to group, person to person, region to region? How long does such transmission typically take? These are extraordinarily challenging issues, which are too often simply ignored.

It is worth noting that many early exponents of *longue durée* history worked on mentalities, using literary and visual sources in the attempt to chart areas of human existence where the nature and pace of change are notoriously hard to reconstruct.[46] In recent years there has been a growth of interest in fine-grained, small-scale historical studies. This is related to what is sometimes called micro-history, which usually involves looking at a small community or geographical area over substantial periods of time. Such history, which uses intensively researched case studies, is based on the idea that we can get at larger patterns by looking meticulously at one or a small number of instances. While this trend in part reflects the professionalisation and specialisation of the discipline, the pressure to produce original research and constraints of time, it also speaks to the rich diversity of some local records and wider anxieties about historical explanation and, more specifically, about causal explanations to which I alluded in chapter 4. Common criticisms of the claims and methods of historians such as Philippe Ariès express just such anxieties. Rather than focusing on big shifts, micro-history explores the intricate textures of a limited area, and a sense of scale can be introduced by studying a significant length of time.

Periodisation is about managing time, the ways we imagine and conceptualise it and the amounts of it that we study in any given project. Hence its centrality for the discipline of history. At the level of individuals, both historians and those they study, time is managed by memory. Thus the second historiographical issue concerns memory.[47] The writing of history is about the transmission of memories, although the extent to which this is explicit certainly varies from field to field. Historians rely on the memories of others when it comes to sources; they require others to have conserved and to want to remember the past for their professional existence. The practice of history is, after all, a highly specialised form of commemoration. Yet we need to problematise the very notion of memory.

We could do this, for instance, through critical reflection upon the relatively new field of oral history, which relies upon the existence of memory and upon its capacity to be recorded and interpreted in a meaningful manner. Oral history has been mentioned briefly in earlier chapters; for now, we can simply remind ourselves of some key points. As it has largely been practised, oral history involves talking, generally to older people, about aspects of life that would otherwise go unstudied. Accordingly it has laid particular emphasis on the voices of those who are marginal, neglected, forgotten. It is inevitably limited in the periods it can cover, and in the types of historical issue it can address. At first sight, oral history is dependent upon what people remember accurately. However, memory is imperfect, producing 'recollections' that simply cannot be true. Hence oral historians stress the need to check material generated in this way by other means. This is a field in which scholars are creating their own sources, where the personality of the interviewer, including their unconscious, is inevitably mobilised in a special form of interaction between historians and their subjects.[48] Interviews often pick up dimensions of the past, the way people felt, which are not dependent on the literal exactitude of their memories. The practice of oral history reveals some of the complexities of memory, of historians' use of it, and the way in which assumptions about the effect of the passage of time upon human consciousness shape the writing of history. The span of a human life is inevitably the privileged unit of time in this particular field.

BRIDGE

What is remembered and the forms in which it is given expression are important historical phenomena in their own right. Since these are highly selective, they are especially important, because the processes of selection and the forms in which memories are represented are supercharged with meaning. Thus there are more general trends at work in the coupling of *History and Memory*, to use the name of an Israeli journal founded in 1988. Historians of many kinds have become interested in the nature of memory. This is because giving it *tangible* form is such an important historical phenomenon in its own right and often a genuine spur to historical activity.

The Holocaust would seem to be a particularly compelling example of more general points about history and memory. There is now an unprecedented interest in that complex amalgam of processes we have named 'the Holocaust' – it is now at a *relatively* safe distance, while some of the participants are still alive. This is by definition a temporary state. It has given impetus to many forms of historical revisionism, occurring in a context where novels, memoirs, exhibitions and films on the subject proliferate as never before. Memory, commemoration, memorialising, reinterpretation are all involved, and each is subtly different. Historians are right inside this *mêlée*. It is a *mêlée* precisely because there are a number of conflicting perspectives, and the conflicts are not only about what did or did not happen, but about how such events should be written about, who has the right to do so, whether historians should assign blame, and so on. These issues call into question the nature of historical evidence and its interpretation, the 'ownership' of the past, the validity of memory, the wider social role of the historian – especially in relation to judicial processes – and the propriety and desirability of retrospective punishment and blame. If we think that considering the effects of the passage of time is essential to the historian's work, then there can be no more tricky, important and challenging example than the myriad issues 'the Holocaust' – a reification if ever there was one – throws up. It does so precisely because historical phenomena and their representation are *not* the exclusive domain of the discipline of history. They are in the public domain, and the public is composed of numerous social, political and institutional constituencies, with conflicting interests. These are central matters for professional historians, and we can pursue them further by probing the idea of 'public history'.

6

Public history

WHAT IS PUBLIC HISTORY?

The idea of 'public history' has been used in recent decades in the United States and is now gaining ground rapidly elsewhere.[1] We should concede from the outset that 'public' is a difficult term; in this chapter I explore some of its principal aspects in relation to the practice of history. Whatever the complexities of 'public', public history is a useful phrase, in that it draws attention to phenomena relevant to the discipline of history, but too rarely discussed in undergraduate courses. This is not surprising. Universities are staffed by professional historians, and they teach what can be called 'academic' history. While the modern structures of higher education in general, and the discipline of history in particular, only came into being over the nineteenth century, they have become deeply entrenched. Professional, university-based history is a particular kind of history, although those who practise it tend to speak as if there were little else. Among other things, public history is *popular* history – it is seen or read by large numbers of people and has mostly been designed for a mass audience. For some historians, 'public history' is a central part of radical history movements, which are critical of elitist, over-professionalised history, and seek to promote politically self-conscious, community-based histories, open to all and usable in political struggles. It is true that much public history has been motivated by such concerns, but precisely because public history can be effective with wide audiences, it is, equally, a tool of establishments.[2]

The issues around public history highlight some of the ambiguities of the term 'history' itself. Remnants of the past are everywhere, but they are not necessarily seen as 'history' or understood as elements in a structured account of the past. Public history involves 'history' in many senses: the academic discipline; the dissemination and display of its findings to wide audiences using all available media; the past itself in many different forms; and a diffused awareness of that past that varies from person to person, group to group, country to country. Museums and heritage sites are prime examples of the complexities of public history.[3] Indeed, when the phrase 'public history' is used, this is what many people have in mind. Heritage broadly defined is a growth industry, and many, if not most public displays involve an element of history. Yet there are relatively few museums that proclaim themselves as being about history in the more academic sense; they are generally associated with a place, a type of object, an activity or a person, and the history is an integral part of everything they do. Perhaps there is *least* explicit, academic history in the temples of high culture, such as museums and galleries of modern art, but even there it necessarily has a presence. Displays based on themes or events – war or particular wars, revolutions and political movements, technology, childhood – are concerned with the past without necessarily declaring themselves to be offering instruction in history. Naturally, more overtly historical collections exist – the Museum of London, the Musée Historique de la Ville de Paris, the Risorgimento Museum in Bologna, for instance. Thus, although relatively few museums and kindred institutions are obviously directly connected with the (academic) discipline of history, most of them are, loosely speaking, historical and contribute to the views members of the general public hold about history.[4]

The means by which publicly displayed collections have come into being are heterogeneous. Indeed, collecting is now an important historical topic in its own right.[5] Since there are so many different kinds of museums and galleries that involve the display of history in one form or another, it is extremely helpful to have an understanding of how the objects were brought together, of the audiences who are being targeted and of the politics involved, including funding arrangements. There are great institutions, such as the Smithsonian in Washington, DC, which are hugely significant for the practice of history by virtue of their size, influence, diverse holdings and resources. It is obvious that sites set up to attract large numbers of visitors, such as Colonial Williamsburg in Virginia or Longleat in Wiltshire, are also relevant to the practice of history.[6] Just as relevant are cathedrals and churches that attract visitors, apparently narrowly focused museums, such as those of regiments, as well as the hundreds of new museums being set up to cater for what seems to be every conceivable interest and enthusiasm.

As a result, museums are an increasingly important subject for those who want to understand attitudes to the past; they have ceased to be a specialised area for museum professionals, and have become major cultural forces in their own right. They bear upon the practice of history in such subtle, diverse and far-reaching ways that it behoves historians to give them careful consideration. Precisely because of the extensive political implications of what has been called 'the heritage industry', these are matters for intense public debate.[7] Yet museums work in insidious ways. The past they present is highly refined, in the manner of manufactured foods. This renders both the original materials and the means by which they have been processed relatively invisible. My claim may sound odd, given that museums make objects

6.1 Le Salon de Musique in the Musée Jacquemart André, Paris

This magnificent nineteenth-century collection was built up by a couple with a number of historical enthusiasms, including for eighteenth-century elegance and luxury. Their house uses many forms of display to create a feel for other periods. It is now a museum, which is best seen as a display of a certain kind of nineteenth-century taste. Yet it is so visually seductive that it is easy for visitors to forget that the rooms are special kinds of inventions.

visible, and rely upon the sense of sight for their impact. Yet they display only selected objects, and these have indeed been processed – cleaned, mended, 'restored' and packaged – in a whole variety of ways. Furthermore, the elaborate ancillary materials and activities that are required for any item to be interpreted are not displayed alongside it. Museums have significant silences; their processes of selection, management, budgeting and interpretation are rarely accessible to the general public and remain unimagined by them.

The questions of silence and invisibility should serve to remind us of points raised in earlier chapters about the apparatus of scholarship and the goal of transparency, and of the importance of allowing readers access to the resources authors use. By their very nature museums cannot operate in this way and we should not expect them to do so; furthermore, there is no reason why the general public, which is not after all composed of scholars, would want the apparatus made visible. Nonetheless, it is important to be clear about the consequences of museums being major communicators to the public about the past, given their modes of display. While museums satisfy curiosity about the past, they also shape the forms such curiosity is permitted to take. They transmit ideas about that past through a variety of lenses, of which visitors are unlikely to be fully aware: they convey narratives and values as well as insights and information. Further, they often communicate a sense of the past and its meanings, about which professional historians feel profoundly uncomfortable. Two examples spring to mind. Many museums generalise about living conditions in the past, presumably in order to make it more accessible, including emotionally. This is particularly marked in relation to 'everyday life', where generalisations are particularly likely to stress the past as dirty or dangerous, or indeed as innocent and safer than today. Such claims are troubling because they are so value-laden – they touch points of vulnerability, such as fear of death, crime and disease. Museum displays also deploy more straightforward assumptions about causation than would be common among professional historians. Specifically, they allocate individual and collective responsibility more freely, given that they operate, more or less, within an idiom of heroes and villains. Displays for the public are likely to stress moral clarity and the agency of individuals. Even where named and well-known historical actors are not involved, the idioms of heroism and its flip side can, nonetheless, be deployed. These are significant matters, because there exists a widespread need to understand the past in precisely these terms, that is, in terms of achievement and blame, success and failure. The desire for clear patterns of responsibility in relation to which we can position ourselves is powerful. It gives rise to the strong emotions evident, for example, in the feelings still elicited by anything to do with Japan among those touched in some way by their prisoner-of-war camps in the 1940s. So we want to understand and respect the forms of public history found in museums, and acknowledge their influence, but equally we must be clear about their, admittedly diverse, effects on general historical consciousness, which operate at emotional levels that are hard to get a grip on. This point is all the more important because 'history' appears, in one form or another, in so many different kinds of museum.

While museums and heritage issues dominate many discussions of public history, I want to use the term more inclusively, because there are numerous forms of history that are directed at non-professional audiences and that can usefully be considered together, including documentaries, historical fiction and drama, non-specialist magazines and memorials. The motives behind such ventures are truly diverse – public history is, for me, simply a convenient umbrella term. Inevitably it includes items, such as buildings and public spaces, which serve as forms of public history, but were never intended as such. The fact is that the past is everywhere; when we are in public our senses are constantly responding to stimuli that are gorged with history, whether we are aware of it or not. This is a kind of historical back-drop that exists in virtually all societies. In some cases, however, it has become exceptionally prominent. This has been the case in many western countries over recent years, where the celebration of anniversaries of signifi-cant events for the nation and/or for humanity seems to have reached excessive proportions. By virtue of the resulting media coverage and com-mercial exploitation, they exemplify the point that the past is everywhere. The past that is everywhere frequently springs into focus when it is under threat in some way – a building designated for destruction, a park about to be developed, a square altered in some way, a memorial moved. New memor-ials also tend to be controversial. This too is the domain of public history, as David Lowenthal showed so eloquently in *The Past Is a Foreign Country* (1985). The fact that this environmental public history is mostly *out* of focus, not demanding conscious attention as a form of history, does not make it unimportant. When change is proposed it becomes clear how fundamental such features are for local and national identity; hence they require histor-ians' attention.

Public history is indeed diverse. Sometimes we are in the realm of enter-tainment, as is the case with much historical fiction, the Scarlet Pimpernel series of novels, written in the early twentieth century, being an excellent example. Set in the period of the French Revolution, and firmly on the side of the aristocracy, they have been adapted frequently for film and televi-sion.[8] Swashbuckling accounts of the past are pretty much knowing 'recon-structions' to provide their audience with a good time composed of thrills and spills plus eye-catching costumes and period effects. At other times we are in the more sober realm of education and improvement; such is the role of many museums, some television documentaries and popular publica-tions, including magazines about history. It is no coincidence that within the burgeoning museum industry a notably fast-growing sector is educational activities. Naturally it is understood that these are to be, if at all possible, pleasurable and entertaining; nonetheless, among their main concerns is conveying views of the past. Historical documentaries can be understood in a similar manner. We can appreciate the diversity of public history if we think about its less clear-cut forms, especially in the media and popular publishing. In doing so it is vital to remember that it is the past's perennial *use-fulness* in the present that underpins these phenomena.

USABLE PASTS

The idea of a usable past is hardly new, but it is probably more prominent now than it ever has been before. If the past is usable, then history is an open field that is available to be put to very different, even conflicting, ends. History as entertainment uses the past for commercial purposes. History as consciousness-raising uses the past for political ends. History as public education uses the past to inform audiences (selectively) about political and social trends. But what about organisations, such as Britain's National Trust, the widespread erection of war memorials, the maintenance of public cemeteries, and so on? What kinds of usable pasts are being deployed here? The National Trust was founded in 1895, 'to preserve places of historic interest or natural beauty permanently for the nation to enjoy' – a heritage ticket, designed to preserve what was construed as simultaneously precious, of historical importance and under threat.[9] It was, and remains, a complex and contested project, as must necessarily be the case given that they have acquired a house associated with The Beatles while promoting the grand country house. Clearly there is an educational dimension, but objects in the Trust's properties are not labelled as they would be in a museum; that is, the displays are not openly or conventionally didactic. Visitors are entering a world as close as possible to the 'original', and thereby their fantasies about the past are engaged. Yet, it hardly needs saying, the very notion of an original state is problematic. Houses evolve; there is unlikely to be one single time that they genuinely evoke, although the period of the main building plays an important part in perceptions of the whole. Displays tend to gloss over such questions, so that the main effect, from the point of view of visitors, is of unspecified historical 'authenticity'.

However, it would be a mistake, and a serious oversimplification, to present visits to country houses or palaces only in terms of 'education'. For example, visitors may have a craving for nostalgic experiences which country houses meet. Nostalgia is a longing for a past state, for something by definition unobtainable – it concerns conventionalised forms of fantasy. It is striking how, in recent times, film and television shape the specific forms such nostalgia takes. We could think of this as the *Brideshead* phenomenon, following the huge success of a television adaptation of Evelyn Waugh's 1945 novel about the English aristocracy earlier in the century, and seen in many countries.[10] Self-evidently, the country houses open to the public *now* are not at all as they *were*. As we see them today, they have been sanitised – of smells and back-breaking work, for example. So when the kitchens of large houses, often among the most popular attractions, are viewed now, they convey little or no idea of what they were like when in use. Rather they offer a special kind of fiction, which visitors agree to treat as 'history'. Ironically, since more of us are descended from servants than masters, a full recognition of the conditions in domestic service, say a hundred years ago, is potentially quite

6.2 Australian Memorial at Villers Bretonneux, Somme, Picardie, France
The distinguished architect Sir Edwin Lutyens designed many memorials to commemorate the First World War and held elaborate views on the form such memorials should take. The inscription here is taken from Ecclesiasticus and was chosen by the writer Rudyard Kipling. It may be taken as speaking to, even commanding, those left behind. Remembrance becomes a kind of universal obligation.

disturbing. Yet there is ample evidence that country houses, castles and palaces are satisfying a range of popular curiosities, which are woven into a collective sense of the past. The simple fact that there are marked *national* variations in this kind of behaviour reinforces the point. The folk museums found in most European countries, are, except in Wales, rare in Britain, where there is huge interest in the country house, while 'theme-park' history has been most extensively developed in the United States. In many, many places there is a huge appetite for the past, which needs to be understood and respected in its myriad forms. It is met by displays of 'history' and by ways of approaching the past that are not narrowly academic, but are more akin to tourism, especially in their open appeal to fantasy.

If we turn for a moment to memorials, especially war memorials and cemeteries, the matter becomes even more complex.[11] Typically, war memorials affirm the values upon which the war in question was based. This is a matter of rhetoric, of presenting a persuasive, publicly acceptable face. The complicated conditions – diplomatic, military, political – leading up to and during the conflict are hardly the main issue, which is rather giving an account that bestows honour on the instigators and the personnel involved. Memorials are built to endure but have not mainly been designed as

6.3 The Vietnam War Memorial, Washington, DC

The commemoration of recent events is particularly difficult, especially when views of them are as heated and diverse as those elicited by the Vietnam War have been. This particular war stands out because it has been so extensively discussed in the press and represented in the media. It is equally noteworthy because people across the world recoiled against the weapons deployed – napalm, for example – and the ruthless intervention of the United States government in distant territories. Yet those who died were to be mourned, those who were damaged to be consoled. War memorials have not lost their significance, even when the morality of the war in question is fiercely contested.

'history' – they become so the moment they are erected. They constitute, in fact, a public record (and a representation) of events that are of general interest. But the very nature of the record gives them a particular set of characteristics and that is why they need to be understood, like all cultural products, as representations. Like most memorials, they cannot be critical of

133

those they commemorate; they have to present a positive image, which is artfully constructed and apt for their moment of creation. What is their purpose? They celebrate events of public significance, for governments and for large swathes of the population. They pay respect to those who lost their lives in the process. They provide a location and object for mourning for those left behind, and become, in their own right, historical documents. Perhaps they also help to manage the anger of survivors and the bereaved. Furthermore, they are likely to be visually pleasing, or at least markers of some kind, and hence may be visited for 'pleasure' as well as for edification, for historical interest as well as for the expression of grief and consolation. All this is part of public history, indeed it is history *in* public.[12]

These brief examples are designed to open up the meanings of 'public', such as, 'for a mass audience', 'popular', 'non-specialist', 'of concern to an entire polity' and 'available for anyone to see'. This range of meanings that can be carried by the term 'public' and the diverse uses to which the past is put are closely related issues. 'Public' also refers more specifically to the government, to the concerns and interests of the state, which may be researched in public or state record offices. Such archives are used by numerous groups, both amateur and professional, and they contain many of the raw materials for public history, however this is defined. The *creators* of much public history tend to be drawn from small cadres with highly specific agendas, even if they claim to be acting in the name of wider groups. This is in stark contrast with what can be termed amateur history, undertaken by those who are not paid for their historical labour. Although what it produces would not usually be called public history, history as a hobby, an activity for amateurs, is an important phenomenon, usefully seen in the context of usable pasts. Local and family history, for example, are hugely popular and often practised by enthusiasts with refined skills in genealogy or charting the history of houses, for instance. Tracing origins, making lineages that serve particular purposes, are important themes in many parts of public history. Spin-offs include local exhibitions and clubs – this is very much history being used for present purposes. One important point to emerge from thinking about the nature of amateur history is the types of concern that motivate people to undertake historical hobbies – remember that 'amateur' originally meant 'doing something for love', not 'lacking in skill', as is sometimes supposed. The difference between professional and amateur historians is probably not as clear-cut as the former think. Furthermore, it may be worth recalling that many historical bestsellers are by people who write, outside the university system, for money. Hence what constitutes a professional historian, a historical writer or an amateur historian is somewhat fluid, as reflection upon public history demonstrates.

GENRES AND AUDIENCES
However they are to be defined, professional and amateur historians tend to work within different historical genres. By 'genre' I mean a recognisable type of representation, whether in the form of words, displays, pictures or

film, that is governed by literary, artistic or institutional conventions, such as the novel, the monograph, the diorama or the local history lecture. Inevitably there are huge variations within genres, and their conventions are far from static, but the concept is nonetheless a useful one. Genres are historically specific. Indeed, genre is a notion of central importance for understanding public history, and vice versa. Because genres always involve elements of convention, they are recognised, often intuitively, by audiences and readers. There are certain expectations on both sides that are, in effect, informal rules of engagement. Historical fiction is a genre with many subgenres, including historical romances. Readers of these expect closure, romantic resolution between hero and heroine, especially in ones written by popular novelists such as Georgette Heyer, who, writing between the 1920s and the 1970s, specialised in eighteenth- and early nineteenth-century England.[13] Other sorts of historical novels may culminate in an adventure successfully completed or the death of the hero(ine). These are narrative types and they deploy easily recognised topoi. I want to insist on the importance of genre (and other literary conventions) for any understanding of the practice of history. All writings have a generic context, and being aware of the point enables one to evaluate any given piece more effectively. Recognising genres and analysing instances of them depends precisely on understanding conventions and their implications. This is particularly important in thinking about *public* history. Public history uses a wide variety of genres, which differ from those of the academic discipline – a fact that shapes the content of the type of history we are designating 'public'.[14] If we can identify and reflect upon this generic range, the whole phenomenon, including the means by which publics develop their sense of the past, can be appreciated more fully.[15]

One thing is certain, the audiences for history are wide, diverse and in places extremely well informed. Thus 'public', which covers so much, is elusive and ambiguous, but nonetheless useful. One historical account, which has become hugely influential, by Jürgen Habermas, the German sociologist and philosopher, charts the development of a so-called 'public sphere' over the eighteenth century.[16] 'Sphere' here is a metaphor, which unfortunately carries the misleading connotation of watertight areas. Many historians refer, rather unselfconsciously, to a gendered distinction between the public (male) and the private or domestic (female) spheres, which is also supposed to have developed over the eighteenth century in concert with the economic and social shifts summed up in the phrase 'the Industrial Revolution', and with a political conservatism about female roles in the wake of the American and French revolutions.[17] Habermas's approach is rather different, in that it focuses on the generation of 'public opinion' – a concept and a set of practices – and on arenas for debate within which matters of wide interest could be discussed in a liberal and tolerant fashion. Emblematic of this shift is the development of newspapers, which Habermas finds particularly marked in eighteenth-century England. We might note with interest that public museums developed in Europe at this very time – the

British Museum, for instance.[18] Although the growth of print culture was gradual over the sixteenth and seventeenth centuries, and certainly subject to considerable local variation, the eighteenth century does mark a significant turning point in relation to the history of communications, of audiences and of the idea of 'the public'.[19] Benedict Anderson summarised the point particularly eloquently in his influential book *Imagined Communities* (1991). His purpose was to identify the preconditions for a modern sense of nationhood, in the development of which citizens all over a nation reading simultaneously the same or similar news, played, he claims, a significant part. He was concerned with mechanisms through which what is essentially an abstract idea – 'nationhood' – can be communicated to large numbers of people. Part and parcel of this idea was a sense of their nation's history, shared by a significant proportion of the population, and incorporated into their lives and identities. So the concept and practices of 'the public' are themselves historical phenomena, and, more specifically, what I am calling public history has been bound up with nation formation for nearly three centuries. Tracing the uses that governments, professions and other interested parties make of 'the public sphere' and of the past, and charting the ways in which the results have become part of each society's imaginary, helps to explain the origins and current importance of public history.

I am suggesting that Anderson provides a helpful model for understanding the development of the phenomenon 'public history'. People from far-flung places encounter historical displays and publications that are relevant to them, and through which they construct their identity. Political structures, such as nations and their administrative infrastructures, mediate the processes involved, which are thereby value-laden. These days the public can visit museums, use internet sites and see films that have similar effects. They use what they read and see in other bits of their lives, they become parts of imagined communities, often through the nation which, Anderson suggested, exists in part through having a shared, publicly available history. Memorials to leaders and to events of symbolic importance are, like dynasties of rulers, visible signs of a nation's shared history, even if that past has been subject to the equivalent of creative accountancy. While education systems put in place the building blocks of collective identity, it is further shaped and sustained, occasionally radically altered, by public history. It follows that one of the most important insights the phenomenon of public history affords is that collective understanding of the past is imbibed by *all* the senses, and worked upon in the imagination.

In discussing 'public history' I have in mind three principal issues – the non-academic audiences for history, the general cultural uses of the past and specific displays that relate to history broadly defined. 'Public', then, indicates a wider interest and participation in history than simply professional historians and specialised publications. The past is essentially open-ended, and accounts of it are public property, available for numerous uses. Recognising this should help historians to see their own activities in a wider perspective and to raise broad questions about the practice of history. In particular, it should be possible to focus more clearly on those issues that are central to public history, but that are frequently neglected in professional practice. I shall briefly pursue one of these, which has elicited widespread interest: who, if anyone, *owns* the past? Raising the question involves thinking less about the raw materials of history – although ownership of these is certainly a matter of some significance – than about who is entitled to represent the past authoritatively. I understand this to be a political issue, so it is important to be clear about the ways in which this is so.

PUBLIC HISTORY AND POLITICS

We should remember that the state, which in many countries plays a major role in funding institutions such as archives and museums, lies at the very heart of public history. Public history is a political matter in that the 'displays' that make up public history contain and promote particular interests. They depart from specific vantage points, although the precise nature of these varies from case to case. These are indeed political matters; they concern alignments and representations of power. For example, understanding the role of the state in funding, and of elites in shaping, historical displays, is a vital part of examining public history. The representation of political winners and losers, whether these are classes, religious alliances, political factions or ethnic groupings, is an obvious example. Furthermore, much public history in museums is sponsored by businesses, who are thereby giving their names to exhibits, and when it comes to displays concerning the history of food production or nuclear power in which the related industries have a hand, then there are complex political forces to contend with.

There is a related and looser sense in which public history is political in that it weaves moral discourses around objects displayed. We are familiar with the idea that history is composed of narratives. For most people, historians tell stories, not in the sense that they make things up, but in the sense that their accounts of the past are structured and gain plausibility in the same manner as other narratives. We are equally familiar with the idea that historical stories are morally charged. Everyone can laugh at *1066 and All That*, the comic account of British history, or the Asterix stories, cartoon strips about Roman Gaul, because they recognise that judgements about, for example, kings, political leaders and whole nations being 'good' or 'bad' are absolutely everywhere, including among professional historians.[20] This should come as no surprise, and I am certainly not suggesting that historians either can or should refrain from moral discussions altogether. The point about history that reaches wider audiences is that the moral judgements can be crude, implicit or concealed, making them (sometimes) hard to discern and to be held up for critical inspection by those not 'in the know'.

The political nature of history for the public becomes exceptionally clear when there are fierce controversies, as there were over the plans to put the *Enola Gay*, the aeroplane that dropped the bomb on Hiroshima, on display at the National Air and Space Museum in Washington, DC in 1995, 50 years after

6.4 A page from *Asterix in Spain*
History reaches the public in many forms. In the case of Asterix cartoons, the past is a source of fun and especially of wordplay; readers are expected to have some familiarity not only with the Roman world, but also with literary representations of it. Note here the reference to Shakespeare's *Julius Caesar*.

the end of the Second World War. Its proposed mode of presentation caused an uproar, especially among veterans. The resulting controversies have been extensively documented and debated, providing an exceptional range of insights into public history in the United States.[21] This was a political matter in that it revolved around how objects associated with one of the most highly charged events of the twentieth century should be presented to the public, the

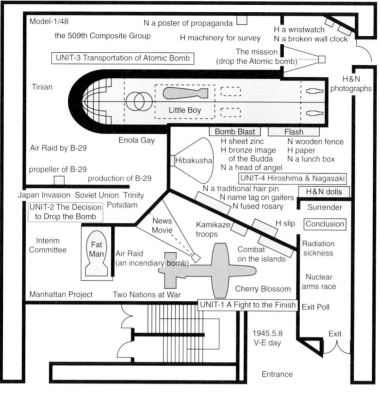

Model-1/48   N a poster of propaganda   H a wristwatch
    the 509th Composite Group   H machinery for survey   N a broken wall clock

UNIT-3 Transportation of Atomic Bomb   The mission
(drop the Atomic bomb)

Tinian   H&N photographs

Little Boy

Bomb Blast   Flash
Enola Gay   H sheet zinc   N wooden fence
Air Raid by B-29   H bronze image   H paper
    Hibakusha   of the Budda   N a lunch box
propeller of B-29   N a head of angel
    production of B-29   UNIT-4 Hiroshima & Nagasaki
Japan Invasion Soviet Union Trinity   N a traditional hair pin   H&N dolls
UNIT-2 The Decision   Potsdam   N name tag on gaiters
to Drop the Bomb   N fused rosary   Surrender
    News   Movie   Kamikaze   H slip   Conclusion
Interim   troops
Committee   Fat   Radiation sickness
  Man   Air Raid   Combat
(an incendiary bomb)   on the islands
    Nuclear arms race
Manhattan Project   Two Nations at War   Cherry Blossom
UNIT-1 A Fight to the Finish   Exit Poll

1945.5.8
V-E day   Exit

Entrance

Key: H = loan from Hiroshima Peace Memorial Museum
     N = loan from Nagasaki International Culture Hall

6.5 Proposed (and abandoned) exhibition layout for 'The Last Act: The Atomic Bomb and the End of World War II' (1995)

Since 1945 the world has had to live with nuclear power, but has found no easy ways either of coming to terms with the bombs dropped on Japan or with the integration of nuclear energy into everyday life. Telling the story of how this particular form of energy was developed, used at the end of the Second World War and deployed subsequently, inevitably provokes violent reactions; there can be no neutral, purely factual account. Any version of the story will be controversial because it will contain both implicit and explicit assumptions about politics broadly defined. There is nothing unique about this issue, but the polarised responses are particularly dramatic, as the Smithsonian Institution's National Air and Space Museum discovered when they tried to mount an exhibition built around the *Enola Gay*.

balance between commemoration and historical interpretation, and the soundness of received accounts that the bombs 'saved' lives in the end. Many people now think that the Allies were simply wrong to drop the bombs on Japan and that their motives for doing so were decidedly mixed. For others the Allies were right, and the event may legitimately be celebrated. It is impossible to present these issues 'neutrally', and it could be argued that it is improper to do so, given the huge destruction of civilian life and the long-term effects

6.6 Pages from the *Past Times* catalogue

These pages are from the catalogue of a successful company that sells goods related to the past in its chain of shops and by mail order. Note the associations between periods and styles.

of the bombs. Yet publicly funded institutions are subject to a range of forces and constraints, which have nothing to do with academic history. A critical analytical view of the end of the war proved threatening both to veterans and to the United States government.

Other institutions besides governments and museums are involved in public history, however, which remains a loosely political issue even in its more commercial forms. History is part of many industries that sell the past in one form or another. Reproduction clothes, jewellery, furniture and decorative objects in effect present views of particular historical periods to the general public, thereby creating and maintaining an image of distinct eras – the eighteenth century was elegant, the nineteenth ornate, the twentieth streamlined, and so on – based on notions of style. This may sound innocuous, such clear fictions that they are hardly significant, but, as I argued earlier, aesthetic responses are a powerful force in shaping attitudes to the past. Although there appear to be no political elements here, it is vital to remember what dramatic forms of selection are involved. To see the eighteenth century in terms of elegance, for instance, depends on giving priority to aristocratic lifestyles and to their cultural hegemony. It further depends upon particular readings of the ancien régime, which buy into the ideologies of the time.[22] The huge growth of retailing in museums, for example, selling items related to the collection, has greatly contributed to this trend.

Another significant element in public history is the *commissioning* of books by commercial enterprises, such as those designed to celebrate a business's history, that is, to construct a particular kind of public face for it. The whole question of commissioned histories has become a rather vexed one. Professional associations and political organisations, like departments of government and other organisations, frequently buy in the services of historians, who become dependants, losing a measure of intellectual freedom. Such relationships are never unproblematic. One major issue is whether historians are given unfettered access to the relevant archives and allowed to make what they will of them, or whether they will be expected to write a history that is constrained from the very beginning by the restricted materials to which they have been given access. Then there is the question of interpretation: are commissioned historians able to pass whatever judgements they think fit, or is the account to be written in order to show the company or organisation in a good light? I have stated the issue rather crudely and, no doubt, in practice it is less clear-cut than this. But it is as well to be aware of the possible pitfalls – he who pays the piper . . . Although some commissioned histories are written mainly for other historians, and thereby contribute, for example, to the growing field of business history, they also have wider publics. Potential audiences include those who work for or support the commissioning body. Here, the writing of history is being used for purposes determined by the commissioners, making tensions between commemoration and analysis almost inevitable.[23]

The difficulties of commissioned histories remind us of a theme that runs throughout this book and that is especially important for public history. It is generally accepted that historical accounts are, unavoidably, implicitly moralising. Some historical accounts are commissioned specifically to make the subject look good, precisely because history is deemed to have moral authority and people with power try to make themselves, and those with whom they identify, appear worthy of respect by these means. This is a particularly important issue in the case of biographies, which, for living or recently dead subjects, are often commissioned by families, colleagues and friends. Readers may be surprised that I mention biography in the context of public history, yet as one of the most popular and enduring of historical genres, biographies bring history to a broad public and are themselves widely discussed. They make an interesting comparison with official, commissioned histories. It is worth remembering that *un*authorised biographies can cause a fantastic stir. How a life is publicly valued *is* significant – the actions of prominent figures and their interpretation are morally charged.[24] The reputations of major historical actors are of public concern. Since many biographers need special permission to use private papers, their relationships with the guardians of those papers is vital. Let us be clear that the issue is rarely that of 'the truth'. Families may know things about relatives but still prefer biographers not to publicise them – indeed, this is sometimes a condition of granting access to papers. The biographer who agreed to such terms would not so much be distorting the past, as this phrase is generally used, as deftly omitting material that is in some way problematic. Selection is a central historical skill, and its evaluation is exceptionally tricky, since much of it is rendered invisible in the final account. When the sources are not in the public domain evaluation is even harder. The presentation of historical figures in a positive light is not as simple as it might appear. To write a convincing biography the author needs a certain measure of sympathy with their subject, and they are likely to identify more or less strongly with that person – this is true of all historical projects. A few biographies are written out of dislike, disapproval or hatred, but they are relatively rare.[25] If family members are still alive, the historian may get close to them too, and inevitably emotional bonds are set up. Unconsciously, then, historians tell their stories in particular ways that could be seen as 'flattering', but are not necessarily intentionally so. All such accounts are necessarily selective. Naturally a historical training involves raising one's consciousness about such matters, but the unconscious is a powerful force, never completely mastered.

In the very process of writing a biography, the historian's responses to and evaluations of their subject are expressed. Readers, who already think in terms of praise and blame, of innocence and guilt, will pick this up. All historical accounts contain moral judgements, either implicit or explicit. History written for a general public is, by its very nature, likely to bring such judgements into prominence. In other words, although all historical activities raise questions about morals, responsibility and ethics, public history does so with special urgency. This is partly because public historical discourses tend to be condensed and simplified, bringing out such issues in a pristine form. Biographies make the point particularly clearly, but they are hardly the only genre of historical writing where we run across debates about the moral judgements of historians – debates that are at once about the emotional and political dimensions of history. The content of (much) public history – wars, genocide, dictators, diasporas, religious persecution, ethnic cleansing, national and international crises, for instance – places moral issues in the foreground. Moral and political dimensions are inseparable.

WHO OWNS THE PAST?

I have described the past as 'public property', which brings us back to the question of who owns the past.[26] Property and ownership are potent metaphors. I am less interested in the issues around public access to historical sources, although these are important matters, than in the investment in and identification with aspects of the past, which, somehow, make them our own. The notion that the past is public property can be used to stress the openness of the past, its availability for diverse purposes. But its implications need to be followed through. For example, the past is routinely deployed for openly manipulative ends. The claim all too commonly made by racist groups that their country began to decline with increasing rates of immigration would be a case in point. This claim depends upon people believing a specific, highly interested account of two past trends ('decline' and 'immigration'), positing a causal relationship between them and drawing a political inference from it. To say that the past is public property certainly implies that there will be diverse, competing accounts; hence developing a critical perspective upon them is essential. Yet, beyond personal preference, it remains unclear how, in the case of public history, competing accounts are to be evaluated. Both historical sources and the ability to construct historical accounts cease to be the exclusive domain of a professional cadre, and the ubiquity of history is affirmed.

'Public property' implies thinking about the past in the idiom of ownership. In order to pursue these matters further, two preliminary points need to be made. First, in drawing attention to the language of ownership I am not implying approval of it. Rather I am spelling out common assumptions and encouraging critical reflection upon them. Second, if history is popular because people identify with aspects of it, then the question of ownership is bound to come up one way or another. Ownership is not only an exceptionally powerful metaphor, it is totally bound up with identity – this has *not* been true always and everywhere, but it definitely is here and now.[27]

A familiar example, women's history, makes the point.[28] During and as a result of 1960s' feminism, a distinctive brand of historical heroine was sought and celebrated. The notion of role models began to be widely used at that time. Women *readers* of history were encouraged to identify with women *makers* of history through the *writers* of history, and to applaud, and emulate, past achievements, which embraced all women. In this sense, women's history was not just *about* women, but *for* women, to use in their own lives. And for some it was 'our' history, that is, a story with special relevance for one group – women – who were its rightful possessors. Who was part of that 'our'?

Black women were quick to point out that a false inclusiveness had been implied by generalisations about women in the past, and the extent to which there are common threads in female experience across classes and races at a given time and place remains a contested issue. Some of the pioneers of women's history in the 1970s were men, and this gave rise to considerable comment – they were muscling in on the act, 'using' women for their own career ends, since this was a trendy new field. All this implies assumptions about relationships between subjects and interpreters of history most familiarly expressed in the language of ownership. To say 'my' or 'our' history is to evoke the past of a group with which the speaker is strongly identified. It is essential to remember, however, that each speaker is likely to have a number of possible identities; in practice, it is never self-evident which one is dominant. Histories, especially popular ones, find multiple identities difficult to negotiate, often because political imperatives dictate that *one* should be paramount. There are those who would say that only women can write women's history, because only they can know the subject from the inside. While I happen to think this argument is fallacious – it has to assume that woman is a timeless category – it is not hard to feel its emotional tug, and for 'women' we could substitute a number of ethnic, racial, religious or social categories.

I wish to draw attention both to the assumptions about the practice of history upon which arguments about who may practise what we could call identity history draw, and to their implications for history presented to the public.[29] In fact, these arguments about identity history are quite widely believed in, especially in the United States, where it is commonly assumed that black history should be written and taught by black people, Jewish history by Jews, and so on. Similar questions are raised about museums and exhibitions – should a non-Jew, for instance, be appointed director of a Jewish museum? For the case in favour of such restrictions to be plausible, two conditions have to obtain. First, the insider point really has to work. There has to be some privileged insight that is afforded by belonging to the category in question. However, it is unclear just how this privilege works, especially for historians interested in much earlier times: can enough continuity across centuries reasonably be assumed to make the insider argument plausible? What kind of continuity is involved? Second, a political assertion has to be made, so that even if the historian has no privileged insights, it would somehow be wrong for them to study a group unless they were part of it. An ethical-cum-political argument would be required about who is entitled to study the past and by virtue of what characteristics.

All historians, whatever their professional status, have ethical obligations – to be humane, accurate, self-aware and judicious, for instance – but these are mobilised in the actual practice of history and not by virtue of those aspects of the historian's person, parentage, sex, skin colour, over which they have no control. Indeed the best historians excel precisely because they can understand conditions that are *not* part of their own immediate experience. This capacity is central to the historian's imagination. My position is consistent with one aspect of public history that I am presenting in this chapter. The past is everywhere, it is constantly being used and re-presented, and ideally should not be appropriated by special interests. Yet my position is in manifest tension with another aspect of public history to which I have also drawn attention. Public history, by and large, is interested history, and the closer it is to the state and its concerns, or indeed to any powerful faction with a strong identity and plentiful resources, the more insistent those interests are likely to be. Displays concerning the history of empire, which are invariably controversial, are an excellent example of the point. This is precisely why those who are alienated from dominant interests have developed oppositional strategies to bring their histories into the public eye. This has resulted, in the museums and heritage world at least, in a proliferation of museums representing the concerns of different groups. Curators within what could be called establishment museums are working extremely hard to present divergent views within their institutions. There is a vital distinction to be made between the urgent need for oppositional public history, and assessments of who is best qualified to carry it out. To locate those qualifications in the race, gender, class or religious background of the individual historian is dangerous. It misplaces historical authority by putting it in biological or social attributes, rather than where it should be – in carefully acquired skills and experience.

MORAL JUDGEMENTS

One theme that has been running through this chapter is the importance of public history for any understanding of general attitudes towards the past and of beliefs about history among communities. The centrality of public history has two facets. First, public history reaches mass audiences; its capacity to penetrate into everyday life is formidable. In the way I have defined it, 'public history' includes many phenomena, including television and fiction. My hunch is that these two forms of culture have done more than anything else to shape popular historical mentalities. It follows that professional historians need to understand them and appreciate their complex effects. Second, in mobilising potent feelings that can loosely be described as 'moral', public history works with the emotions. There are thus powerful investments in a significant proportion of historical accounts. Some events in the human past are disproportionately dense in these respects. I want to explore these questions a little further, while insisting that they are not unique to *public* history; it just throws them into sharper relief.

The twentieth and twenty-first centuries have witnessed – and we are currently witnessing – a number of events that appear so terrible we flounder in the face of them. It is unclear to me whether they are completely without precedent in human history, and in any case the intellectual challenge they present would not be lessened if precedents could be found.[30] Their terribleness consists partly in their proximity to us, which has less to do with how recent they are than with their *sensual* immediacy through film, television and fiction, as well as through radio, newspapers and oral transmission. Although the Holocaust and the dropping of the bombs on Hiroshima and Nagasaki are extreme in their horror, the responses they elicit have a lot to tell us about public history, and hence about the practice of history in general.

In memorials to the millions who died in the 1930s and 1940s, and in museums on related subjects, a limited number of quotations are repeatedly used. They concern the importance of remembering in order to learn from the past, and in particular they stress that those who forget the past are destined to repeat it.[31] Indeed, for many people this would be one of the most important goals of public history: we remember in order to learn. But what precisely can be learnt? What are the lessons of history and how are they to be applied to other times and places? Are there clear, unambiguous inferences to be drawn from past events that can be transformed into recipes for doing it better? We should note that 'doing it better' would necessarily involve an entire society, so historians would somehow have to become politically effective conduits between past and future. It is certainly a problem that historians draw extremely diverse conclusions from the materials they study. The notion of 'lessons from history' is so glibly invoked that its complexities are often missed. These are extraordinarily difficult questions, and people easily misunderstand each other because feelings about them run so high. The result is a desire for simple answers and for clear moral polarities. One of the most important insights historians can bring to wider audiences is that there are no such things, however clear-cut the moral issues appear. Saying this is emphatically not the same as claiming that the historians can or should be neutral.

At the heart of these difficulties lie guilt and blame. Obviously historians evaluate the competing claims of historical actors; they piece together accounts of how decisions and actions were taken, and they form ideas about responsibility. Once responsibility is assigned, it is a tiny step into the territory of guilt and blame. The need to find culprits for terrible deeds is deep-rooted: it is emotionally satisfying to have hate-figures; it brings clarity and simplicity, and, most important of all, it clears others of blame. There will always be prior emotional preferences about where blame should lie. I believe it is impossible to explain fully where those prior commitments come from, but historical controversies bear witness to them. For example, in recent years, as events in Germany that led up to the Second World War have been re-evaluated (and how far back do you go in explaining the rise of Fascism?), there have been huge public debates about the role of the German population as a whole. To what extent did they know what was going on? If they did know and were complicit or even willing participants, what kind of responsibility do they bear? Whose fault was the Holocaust?[32]

These questions spawn another set. If responsibility is successfully assigned, what follows? Should the perpetrators make reparations, and if so, how? Is literal or symbolic compensation being sought, or both? Will justice be achieved by saying 'sorry', as demanded by those who suffered in Japanese prisoner-of-war camps; by returning property, which is being asked of museums and banks who hold Jewish possessions; or by paying compensation, a fairly frequent request to governments, banks and businesses? Should aged Nazis be prosecuted so long after the relevant events took place, and, if found guilty, punished? What punishments are appropriate – imprisonment, execution, public shame? Naturally the intensity of these debates is fuelled by many of the participants still being alive, while the practical consequences of prosecutions are hardly straightforward. It is possible to reflect upon many of the questions just posed in an abstract manner; more concrete responses have to be based on national and international law. Legal cases demand extensive historical evidence. Furthermore, each case, each issue, must be seen in context, its particularities examined. This is, at least in part, the historian's province, a point which explains why many of the protagonists in the ongoing consequences of the Holocaust are employing historians to undertake archival work. Much of the sorting out involves trying to determine who knew what and when, because only then can responsibility, blame and guilt be assigned in a more secure manner. The Holocaust and its aftermath involve historians in a number of ways: historians are doing research upon which judgements are based; they participate in wider debates about what happened and why; they bear responsibility, especially to survivors, for accounts that go out in the name of history. Historians are thoroughly implicated, then, in the history that reaches the public. It follows that they carry special responsibilities by virtue of the stakes in historical accuracy and the moral authority that the discipline of history enjoys. But what counts as authoritative 'history' here is just what is at issue. Not all accounts of the horrors of the 1930s and 1940s are equally authoritative. Popular discourse, which is rather unreflexive about moral polarities, and scholarly history need each other, yet they march to different beats.

It is widely known that there are revisionist historians around who believe that a distorted view of, for example, Nazi concentration camps has been disseminated in order to exaggerate the suffering of the Jews. This is anti-Semitic history and its existence reinforces many of the points raised earlier in the chapter. If the past is open, available, usable, public property, what is to stop revisionist historians, such as David Irving, telling stories that could be regarded as deeply malicious, unethical and completely irresponsible, especially when they claim to have evidence to back them up?[33] In earlier chapters I argued that the apparatus of scholarship, and the ability to scrutinise other historians' sources, methods and arguments, are the solution. In the context of public history and debates about the Holocaust, this response might appear naive and inadequate. It does so precisely because public discourse is not scholarly discourse. Given that many people do not possess the materials or the tools to evaluate radically different accounts of a morally charged event, they will turn to their emotions for guidance. It is in the interest of many groups to present the past in simplified moralistic and didactic terms, which play upon intense feelings. The problem is that feelings are not always a very good guide because, by their very nature, they make people uncritical. Since there is never unanimity on matters of the heart, who is to say whether one person's emotions are 'better' or more justified than another's?

At this point we have reached the hub of concerns about relativism.[34] A simple definition of relativism would be 'the rejection of absolute standards of judgement'. In the eyes of critics, however, the term implies a repudiation of any standards at all, a lack of discrimination in seeing everything as equally acceptable. However tricky or emotive a subject, 'relativism' sums up a cluster of concerns that historians have to consider. On the one hand, it has been part of educational philosophy for some time that different opinions are to be respected; seeing the world through the eyes of diverse groups has come to be preferred over passing judgements based only on our own perspective. The recent growth of interest in environmental history is a striking example of this trend. Changes to the management of natural resources are no longer seen in terms of necessary and inevitable economic progress, but from the vantage points of natives, poor labourers, and so on. This example further illustrates the close relationships between politics, public policy and the practice of history, given the rise of environmental movements over the same period.[35] Many recent trends in the discipline depend on this orientation towards other ways of life and belief systems, which is partly due to the huge influence of anthropology.

On the other hand, we have been encouraged to respect (some types of) interested history. Committed history puts one particular perspective and may not be terribly sympathetic to other, competing ones. This rather different form of relativism sanctions value judgements, usually so long as they are on the 'right' side. For example, it was only relatively recently that left-leaning historians have turned with some confidence and pleasure to writing about the history of the aristocracy. While there are diverse ways in which the history of the aristocracy can be approached, the 1960s and 1970s witnessed a surge of interest in less privileged groups. Since then the ideological climate has shifted and the rich materials left by aristocrats have exercised an allure over historians, who are approaching their research with the agendas of social and cultural history in mind.[36]

There are a number of possible responses to the resulting dilemmas. One could say that all history departs from a specific viewpoint, so that identifications and preferences are inevitable, they are not objectionable in themselves so long as they are avowed, and the scholarly apparatus is in clear view. However, this works better in scholarly than in public history. Or, one could say that the positions taken should depend upon the situation studied. This implies that historians need to be open and flexible, rather than coming to research with fixed ideas. For example, the assertion that history should, on principle, be written from the servants' rather than the masters' viewpoint, could be criticised as too abstract, ungrounded in the materials. It seems that many servants exploited their masters, for instance through blackmail, while in other cases masters exploited their servants, for example sexually.[37] Indeed, even in a single household the situation might vary, so that to take *one* position as *the* starting point fails to do justice to the historical complexities. Thus it could be argued that the framework should always be grounded in the historical problem it is designed to elucidate, and not in abstract positions.

Yet another response to the complexities of relativism in relation to public history might be to attempt to change the terms in which history is debated in public, so that the genuine ambiguities can be acknowledged and more generally appreciated. But does this mean that a historian has the right to publish a book 'sympathetic' to Hitler – to take an extreme case?[38] I feel the answer must be yes, *so long as* they abide by the rules for the responsible use of evidence and for the production of an authoritative historical account. They should also declare the nature of their commitment to their approach, and justify it on *intellectual* rather than political or emotional grounds. It needs to be made clear that analysing something is not the same as approving of it, a mistake that is all too commonly made. In any case, the censorship of historical publications is inherently undesirable, and diversity of opinion is healthy, so long as the results can be critically evaluated, in *both* scholarly *and* public history.

BRIDGE

The moral commitments of historians and the nature of their human values need to be made explicit whenever possible and tempered by evidence that is open to scrutiny.[39] But because of their professional obligations, historians must be willing to mount arguments about their commitments and values rather than just asserting them, and to explain more openly to a wider public the processes through which historical judgements are reached. As I have argued, public history raises exceptionally complex issues upon which all historians must reflect. We cannot dismiss public history as 'mere' popularisation, entertainment or propaganda. We need to develop coherent positions on the relationships between academic history, the media, institutions such as museums, and popular culture. One way in which this can be done is by addressing the misleading notion of lessons from history. The study of the past is indeed inspiring and instructive, but it is not a fount of clear, unambiguous lessons or recipes. Rather it is an arena for contemplation and thought. Certainly the past is the context for the present, but it does not, by that token, generate simple instructions. Historians do well when they raise awkward questions and unsettle received views. To imagine that the general public could not appreciate these points is patronising, and they should, at the very least, be given alternatives to tabloid history. My vision of a world where scholarly and public history work more closely together depends not only on collaboration between constituencies too often kept apart, but also upon the widest possible dissemination of the skills and insights that historians possess. These are too often veiled in public history. The array of skills that is the foundation of the historian's craft is the subject of the next chapter.

7

Historians' skills

WHAT ARE SKILLS?

'Skills' sounds like something basic, a starting point, the tools that enable their possessor to get on and do more interesting things. Hence it may seem odd that I have left this topic until close to the end of the book. In the present chapter I want to examine the skills that historians can reasonably be expected to have, and to assess whether they are in any way distinctive – does a particular combination of skills help to define the discipline of history? The key point about such skills, whether they are definitive of the discipline or not, is that they are built up over time, as one practises as a historian. They are not mechanical, like the skills required to operate machinery, change a plug, and so on. These can be taught, and then the pupil can go off and exercise them right away, without the need for change unless the technology itself alters. Historians' skills are completely different; they are developed and refined over a lifetime, becoming an integral part of the person. They are enhanced by the ability to write well and to grasp the complexity of situations. Naturally there is much that can be taught, but there is a great deal else that relates to more subtle human qualities, which are not so amenable to direct instruction.

The issues around skills are less straightforward than they might appear. For example, they reflect notions about a discipline's priorities, and about its proper relationship with cognate fields. As a result, they are a site of conflict. Skills have come into new prominence in recent years, partly because in many countries higher education policies are laying particular emphasis on 'transferable skills', which can be used in a variety of contexts. In some ways this is positive, since being a historian involves diverse skills, which can indeed be extremely useful in a variety of settings. Hence the study of history can be presented as having general value. However, the political emphasis on transferable skills does also tend to emphasise what could be described as a mechanistic approach to learning – a model that is unsuited to historical work, and that can give the misleading impression that there are finite things to learn. As a concept, transferable skills give more weight to the similarities than to the differences between disciplines. For many people, historians are those who have acquired a lot of *information* about the past, so how does this fit in with the idea of skills?

At first sight, the term 'skills' implies techniques that can be applied generally; hence it appears to be more about methods than about content. The point is reinforced when we add the word 'transferable'. Although I will attempt in the rest of this chapter to specify and evaluate the specific skills historians need, I want to state at the outset that it is unhelpful to draw too firm a distinction between skills and the materials to which they are applied. Historians' skills are refined through use, that is, through their application to concrete historical problems. In this way a fund of knowledge and experience is built up, and it is meaningless to divide it into techniques and substance, since the two are blended through constant interaction. Let us be clear that knowing lots of historical facts without any sense of how to use and interpret them is pointless – perhaps the most common lay assumption about what characterises a professional historian is that they know lots of facts, and especially dates. I would suggest that in reality the important skills lie in tracking down information and knowing how to deploy it thoughtfully rather than in remembering it.

I am arguing against a polarity between skills and substance because I see these two aspects of the historian's craft developing together in mutual dependency. Skills need to be applied to something, and that something, which has a number of facets, helps in refining skills. The *substance* of history is important because it provides concrete information through which to construct historical arguments. It is a source of comparisons without which no case study can be interpreted, it suggests the broad patterns of change within which specific phenomena need to be seen, and it offers insights into the fundamental structures of human societies. So having a sense of the main contours of at least bits of the past is absolutely vital. I am emphasising experience as a blend of knowledge and skills. It is hard to generalise about such matters, but there is a 'feel' that comes from familiarity with a subject, even if it is unwise to romanticise or idealise it.

TYPES OF SKILLS

A number of skills are fundamental to historical work, most of which are used in other humanities and social science disciplines. We can divide these skills into three types. The first can be called technical skills, such as palaeography and diplomatic, cliometrics and prosopography, and I shall discuss these fairly briefly. The second could be called source-based skills, and they relate to the finding and evaluating of sources, whether primary or secondary, *once* a historical problem has been identified. The third are interpretative skills, in which I include the ability to construct a plausible argument. These three types of skill are inseparable, and are being treated here under distinct headings simply for clarity of exposition. I will take each type in turn, but first I want to draw attention to perhaps the most important skill of all – identifying and shaping a historical problem. This does not fit neatly into any of the three categories; it is even more fundamental than they are, and without it no decent history can be produced.

A historical problem is not simply a topic, a piece of the past. Studying something just because it is there leads to unfocused, empirically driven accounts. Of course, it is very tempting to turn to a place, a person, an institution or an archive and study them because no one has done so before. But the results tend to be intellectually unsatisfying. The way into any historical work – whether undergraduate essays or the most advanced research – must be through a question, a puzzle, a conundrum, an anomaly, a surprise, a hypothesis. These can take many different forms, but most often they involve some kind of comparison, which provides a context for the question. Historical work is based on the idea that there is an issue requiring explanation; it therefore depends upon existing explanations. Thus comparison is at the heart of historical practice. Historians constantly compare sources, case studies, secondary accounts and theories – it would be impossible to develop a historical problem without making comparisons, and, in comparative history, the method is made the explicit centrepiece of the field.[1]

Historians ask many different kinds of questions, and why they do so follows from what I have already said. Questions are shaped mainly by scholarly traditions and by the concerns historians find around them. Thus fields build up their own traditions and by that very process spawn questions; these questions are less in the sources than in the minds of those who study them. Let me give a couple of examples. First, the history of Norwich, a city that was for several centuries the most heavily populated in the country after London. By the eighteenth century, patterns of regional development were changing decisively with the growth of Bristol and Liverpool as ports, and Birmingham and Manchester as industrial centres. Nowadays Norwich is an attractive provincial city with a Norman castle and a medieval cathedral, but is, in a number of respects, 'out on a limb', a fact reflected in the limited transport links in and out of Norfolk. This situation prompts a historian to ask a number of questions. Why was Norwich so important before? What caused its relative decline? How is the importance of urban areas best measured? What effects have these changes had on the city and on the region in which it is located? Even an elementary answer depends on the understanding of long-term economic trends, including types of industry and agriculture, patterns of trade, including overseas, and the distribution of wealth. Norwich needs to be put in a context, in fact in many contexts, to answer these questions, and the production of historically sophisticated answers depends on comparisons between Norwich and Norfolk and other *comparable* areas. Areas would be comparable if they shared some features – cathedral cities with agricultural hinterlands, for example – while differing in others – such as patterns of population growth. Hence the choice of cases for comparison is highly significant, because it will weight the research in certain directions simply by virtue of which features are shared and which are not. Indeed questions about Norwich only arise because there are accumulated ideas and explanations of urban and regional development across Europe to draw upon. Furthermore, we might want to set up the historical problem quite differently, by questioning whether the analysis should be primarily economic, and considering other possibly relevant dimensions, such as the institution of the church, local elites, and religious practice. Of course, these all have economic dimensions, just as economic questions have social, political and cultural ones.[2] The important point is that there are a number of ways of thinking about an issue, such as regional decline, and that selecting and formulating a problem also involves making choices about the sorts of answers one wants, and expects, to find. Historians' choices are shaped by existing work and by their views on regional development. Setting up a problem for historical research thus involves subtle skills; these choices always possess a comparative dimension.

We might consider another, more tricky example, namely the history of illegitimacy, a relatively new subject for historians. Its trickiness resides in two of its aspects – it is an extremely emotive and topical subject, and it is amenable to quantitative treatment. Although largely studied by demographers, illegitimacy would not arise as a topic without legal structures governing marriage and inheritance, and without administrative procedures for recording such matters. So how does one formulate historical questions about illegitimacy? These might be prompted, for example, by perceptions that its incidence has changed markedly. Changes, especially increases, are perceived to be problematic, particularly for social welfare provision. Indeed the history of illegitimacy has direct relevance for current debates, and the terms in which current debates are being conducted can therefore affect the way in which historical inquiries are set up. It is to be hoped that, conversely, historical work might inform current discussions. The association between single parenthood (mainly mothers) and poverty has become a major area of concern because in welfare states these are pressing matters for public policy. Links between infanticide and illegitimacy have attracted the attention of historians, since it seems that unmarried mothers were more likely to kill their children than married women were.[3] Furthermore, illegitimacy bears on the status of marriage and thereby on the maintenance of social order. Attempts during the French Revolution to abolish bastardy as a legal category suggest how much had been invested in legitimacy in the Ancien Régime.[4] Closely connected was a much more permissive notion of marriage and divorce, which was rather short-lived.[5] This example reveals how politically significant marriage and the legal status of children can be. Many societies stigmatised the women who bore children out of wedlock; hence the phenomenon of illegitimacy raises questions about the position of women and responses to female sexuality. In some cases tremendous moral pressure and severe punishments were brought to bear upon 'bastard bearers'.[6] There must be complex historical forces at work because there have been societies with a high average age of marriage, low illegitimacy rates and no mechanical forms of contraception. Hence far from being 'natural', sexual behaviour varies markedly, being bound up with a wide range of historical conditions.

Illegitimacy continues to be an emotive subject, frequently mentioned as an indicator of social trends, but just what do figures about illegitimacy indicate? Answers offered have included: changes in family structure, decreasing social control, increasing economic independence of women, enhanced mobility, which allowed men to escape their responsibilities, and changing moral frameworks.[7] So formulating a historical question about illegitimacy is challenging precisely because the topic is so morally freighted. And the fact that it is amenable to quantitative analysis compounds the problem. Is it appropriate or meaningful to study such a topic quantitatively? Are the sources reliable enough to justify the exercise? How long a time-span is needed to reveal significant trends? Might a quantitative study give a false sense of precision and allow the results to be used in a misleading manner by policymakers? In order to place illegitimacy figures in context, what sort of comparisons are appropriate across time and place? Is it reasonable, when a topic is so *culturally* complex, to use case studies that are disparate temporally and geographically? The list of questions illustrates the difficulties surrounding research on this topic. This example reveals some of the diverse and complex issues that are packed into the formulation of a historical problem.

TECHNICAL SKILLS

One thing is crystal clear: when it comes to formulating a problem, we depend hugely on the work of other historians. For a problem to be a really good, juicy one, a researcher needs the sources, the time, the framework and a sense of how their project fits into larger patterns of scholarship. They also need an acute sense of whether any special technical skills will be required. I used the example of illegitimacy above in order to suggest that what I am calling technical skills relate to the entire way in which a historical problem is conceptualised. A quantitative study of illegitimacy requires a sound and critical understanding of demographic methods. In this sense skills and framework are inseparable. While I will not discuss technical skills at length, it is worth giving them careful consideration, because they are more integral to the practice of history than may be apparent. In carving out a historical problem for study it is essential to consider and then evaluate the range of ways of approaching it that the sources permit. Thus, to return to illegitimacy, it would be possible to think about the topic in terms of the history of the family and of attitudes of female sexuality, which is in effect to recast it as an issue in social and cultural history. 'The family' is exceptionally hard to define, because it embraces so many historical phenomena.[8] Some of the concerns of demography relate to family phenomena, especially through the study of birth and death rates, and marriage patterns. Demographers also use tax, poor relief and census records to reconstruct households in past times.[9] Yet household composition and 'the family' are hardly the same, since family members are not necessarily co-resident, and the numbers of children, age at marriage, and so on, do not necessarily shed light on the *quality* of personal relationships. There is a gap between demographic patterns and cultural ones – one cannot be extrapolated from the other – and therefore historians need to be clear about what their chosen techniques can or cannot reveal. So the techniques of demography may have to be mastered for some kinds of historical research to be pursued, but they also have to be evaluated, and the decision to deploy them brings entailments with it.

It would be unfortunate if readers supposed that demography was the principal part of history in which quantitative methods are used. Measurement is, as Roderick Floud pointed out some time ago, everywhere in the practice of history: 'the measurable areas may help us in our interpretation of the immeasurable'.[10] It would be impossible to provide a brief summary of where quantitative issues come up within the discipline, but two general points, which reinforce the ones already made about technical skills, are in order. First, statistical methods involve aggregates; they bring together sets of data that are processed according to standardised procedures. This is significant, not just because the methods are transparent, but because it becomes necessary to think about collective phenomena. When, for example, information about individuals is brought together under categories such as occupation, income, marital status, class and age, historians need to reflect upon the historical meanings of those very categories. There are issues concerning groups that can only be rigorously studied using quantitative methods, which will, if used well, become integral to the conceptual framework being deployed. Second, quantitative methods have their own history. It is helpful if those who deploy them understand their origins. Such insights reveal why and how phenomena are measured and the assumptions and values that are built into the process, all of which should raise historians' awareness of their own procedures. Studies of the *history* of statistics are thus warmly to be welcomed.[11]

If we are interested in skills that assist us in analysing collectivities, then prosopography, the study of collective biographies, should be mentioned. Its origins lie in the piecing together of fragments of information that ancient historians undertook in order to overcome the dearth of more complete sources. More recently the technique has been taken up by historians who study communities that are relatively easy to define. By 'community', I do not just mean people living in the same location, but those voluntarily associating together or linked in some significant way, that is, groups likely to have values and aspirations in common. It is no coincidence that historians of science have been drawn to the technique, since organisations of like-minded men [*sic*] – scientific and medical societies, for instance – can be approached fruitfully in this way. The aim is not so much to select variables and treat them according to rigorous quantitative techniques, as to discern patterns, for example, in religious affiliation or social background, that will promote deeper historical understanding.[12]

7.1 Signatures deciding Louis XVI's fate (1793)

There is something inexplicably exciting about seeing a document so directly associated with a dramatic historical turning point. The fact that it is relatively easy to read and that it contains the signatures of several famous historical figures adds to the thrill. The human drama to which this document bears witness is immediately apparent.

Other technical skills may be more straightforward: they are principally palaeography, diplomatic and languages. Although we think of palaeography as principally concerned with handwriting, the whole array of issues connected with the authenticity of documents comes within its remit. Historians who work on periods prior to the late nineteenth century have to become comfortable with styles of handwriting, which vary markedly with space and time. Sometimes this is principally a matter of familiarity, so that getting plenty of practice is the prime requirement. At others special instruction may be required for handwriting in Gothic script or in secretary hand, for instance. Many important medieval documents are available in printed editions, but the ability, at postgraduate level and beyond, to go back to the originals is essential. In fact, for medievalists much more than deciphering handwriting is involved, since every aspect of a document has the potential to yield up rich insights, including the ink, parchment and paper. The complexity of manuscript illuminations is well known, although the historical insights they afford are matters of debate. Of particular importance are the formulae according to which documents were drawn up; the ability to recognise them and spot variations that may be significant is therefore a fundamental skill for those working on the Middle Ages. Hence an appreciation of the complexities involved in editing manuscripts, whatever period they come from, is important. Indeed, since the medieval period saw a profound transition 'from memory to written record', the nature and role of those documents that became part of everyday life over the thirteenth century are the way into broader social questions.[13]

The arguments for working in other languages, despite the availability of some primary sources in printed translations, are similar: historians need to engage with *all* aspects of their original sources.[14] These technical skills involve thinking more deeply about the period under scrutiny and about how records were generated at that time. I am totally against mystifying archives and original documents.[15] Nonetheless, experience of working with such materials is indispensable. One advantage is the total range of sensory experiences available to historians, which raises overall levels of historical awareness – format, style and size of handwriting can all help build up a picture of the past. It is necessary to go back to originals in any case, since it is always possible that mistakes have been introduced in transcription and translation. There is no substitute for reading sources in their original language. Each language has its own flavour deriving from its grammar, the history and size of its vocabulary, and its historical traditions. Picking up these resonances is an important part of historical work. Thus we can reaffirm that apparently technical tools relate to the whole way in which sources are approached.

The skills required to construct footnotes are also, to a degree, technical ones. But this example illustrates yet again how intertwined a historian's various types of skill are. Footnotes naturally require accuracy; the idea behind them is the transparency of scholarship. But it remains a challenge to translate this into concrete terms. Clearly not everything can be footnoted

– that would be cumbersome – so selection is required. It is generally agreed that all direct quotations require footnotes of sufficient detail that any reader would be able to consult the original, although popular works frequently dispense with such supports altogether. There is also consensus that the writer's intellectual debts should be acknowledged. Furthermore, footnotes should give a sense of other work in the field, as well as substantiating the broad approach taken in a specific piece of writing. All these tasks, except giving details of quotations, involve selection – anything else would be impractical. So although footnotes require a certain technical competence, they also involve judicious selection and rhetorical skills: footnotes help to convince readers of arguments, and hence are an important part of historians' persuasive strategies.

I have suggested that groups of people working in an academic field can usefully be thought of as communities of belief. The purpose of putting it this way has been to highlight the centrality of the social context within which intellectual work is done. The peer group is audience and judge. Footnotes are a significant element within the system of communication between members of a peer group, a field, a community of belief. Two points follow from this. Footnotes reveal lineages, alliances, lines of power within a field, and it is best to be aware of this. In this respect, footnotes are not neutral pieces of information, but social signals. If people feel their work should have been acknowledged in a publication but is not, they can take serious offence. Thus footnotes are also tools of diplomacy. The second point is closely connected. When similar materials are used by different fields and sub-fields, their manner of footnoting is likely to be correspondingly distinct. Earlier I mentioned the history of the family, which nicely illustrates the point about footnotes. Let us take the example of widowhood, which can be studied in a variety of ways – demographically; using legal records, especially wills; economically, in terms of poverty and poor relief; culturally, using representations of widows in literature, art, music, and so on; or through case studies of particular families.[16] These approaches, even if they use material from the same place and time, will produce writings with very different footnotes. This is not just because they will emphasise different sources and different traditions of scholarship, but because their implied audiences are different. They may also display different assumptions about evidence and about what constitutes a convincing argument. Hence the whole way in which they make their writings persuasive is likely to be different too. This point is particularly important because of the trend towards interdisciplinary history. Bringing together sources and perspectives from different disciplines poses a number of challenges. These include technical ones, some of which I shall discuss shortly. Footnotes are a challenging issue for interdisciplinary work because they are means for establishing convincing arguments when you are talking to and drawing upon a number of scholarly communities. Many of those now publishing historical work have been trained in other fields – literary studies, for example – and they are likely to establish their points in their own ways, drawing on work that is literary in orientation, and on conceptual frameworks rooted in literary theory.

While it is often assumed that historical research starts with the sources, I have argued that many tasks need to be performed before one even gets to the primary sources, because some context within which to place them is required. It is unhelpful to think about historical research in terms of a simple sequence of tasks that should be performed in a given order. In fact, historians constantly move between the main types of activity they perform, namely, engaging with the sources, delineating a problem, setting it in broad contexts, developing a framework and constructing arguments in written form. This is a more dialectical way of imagining historical work. Unfortunately, it does not fit particularly well with the norms implicit in the practices of grant-giving bodies, which are based on an idealised view of scientific research, according to which one proceeds in a logical sequence from initial questions to research with sources and then to written-up conclusions. Many historians return time and time again to their sources, finding different things in them at each return journey and using them to illuminate a range of problems. The idea that you can 'gut' a source, take away what you want and then move on, seems to me to promote an overly mechanistic view of the subject, and to lessen the complexities of the interpretative process that engaging with the sources necessarily involves.

SOURCE-BASED SKILLS

The nature of the source-based skills that historians use can be described quite briefly, although their execution is by no means straightforward. It is necessary to identify the relevant sources, to read them accurately and critically, to evaluate them and then to integrate them into a historical account. This last step forms the transition into interpretative skills. Deciding which are 'relevant' sources is rarely straightforward, and often it is a question of thinking laterally, even of finding oblique sources that provide unexpected insights into a problem. Making judgements about the value of sources cannot be done in a vacuum. Sources need to be compared with one another, and their value will depend on the research project in question. Sources have no *absolute* value, however enchanting they may be. Every time a source is examined, a set of questions runs through the historian's head – who, what, why, where, when, how . . . ? Asking these basic questions has two purposes – to understand the source as a *text* and to reconstruct the circumstances of its generation. Every text used by a historian can be analysed somewhat in the manner of a literary critic. The vast majority of the 'raw' materials historians use have been knowingly made by people, who leave behind them, unknowingly, traces of both themselves and their circumstances. The purpose of close, critical reading is to reveal as much as possible, to allow a source to yield up its riches. Of course, the manifest content has to be clearly understood, but so do any hidden agendas. In the case of written sources, the precise language used has to be probed, along with sentence constructions and the organisation of the whole text. Thus an awareness of metaphor, for instance, including historically specific resonances, is an important part of the historian's toolkit. It is important not so much for its own sake as because it enables the reader to think laterally, to move in their imagination from text to text and from texts to contexts. Reconstructing the circumstances of a given source's production requires great skill. Careful textual analysis is necessary but by no means sufficient for doing so. The source's maker, their situation, including the pressures and structural constraints upon them, all need to be considered. Legal historians, for example, have been assiduous in pointing out that court records need to be critically assessed in just this way. All one's knowledge of a specific historical situation is mobilised in setting the source in its context of production, which has to be done in order to appreciate both its fruitfulness and its limitations for a particular project. These skills come from practice, from constantly checking and comparing different sources, and from familiarity with the particular historical situation that gave birth to them. In this way, yet again, we see that skills and content are closely connected.

Most sources are, as I have already emphasised, mediations, the products of complex minds, composed of conscious and unconscious dimensions. No sources are transparent records of a past situation, not even archaeological fragments. So historians need to be able to imagine the kinds of mediations at work in any given artefact, and I have suggested some of the means – textual and contextual – by which they do so. The problem is that there are a number of different possible approaches here, some of which are simply incompatible: there is no one 'historical method', just as there is no single method of textual analysis. The differences stem from fundamental assumptions, for example, about human nature. The language I have used and the examples I have given – metaphor, unconscious, mediation, and so on – already indicate a particular view (one I happen to think is well grounded), but many historians feel uncomfortable with talk of the unconscious, a situation which exposes profound disagreements about human nature and its study which cannot be resolved. It is essential to be open about these disagreements and to chart the exact ways in which they affect historical work. Taking notice and critically evaluating are *skills*, whereas claims about human nature are *beliefs*. Thus we can agree that an ability to analyse texts and objects critically is a fundamental historical skill, but may fail to agree on precisely what the analysis should consist of, or on what its founding assumptions should be. Are human beings the same at all times and places or not? Is self-interest their main motivating factor? Do historians need to think about the unconscious? On the answers to such questions will depend the detailed manner in which sources are interpreted. Skills and world views are intimately entwined, but by no means identical.

INTERPRETATION AND SKILL

If this seems complicated, questions of interpretation are yet more so, although again it is possible to summarise the skills required fairly briefly.[17] They include: using historical materials and ideas in a coherent argument, showing their significance, especially in the light of other accounts, making convincing, plausible claims based upon research findings, and employing concepts, theories and frameworks appropriately. These are dependent on other skills: clear, logical and evocative writing, critical reading, making connections and the ability to see patterns and links, that is, to think laterally, integrating different kinds of materials. These are complex and subtle skills, and in so far as they can be taught, it is by the power of positive and negative examples. Yet interpretation is largely a matter of taste, and I use the word 'taste' advisedly to indicate that personal preferences are involved. These can be explained partly by the interpreter's training, politics and past experience, and they need not be completely idiosyncratic – a preference for a certain style of history can be shared by a number of people. The skills required for generating compelling historical interpretations are intricate and cannot be presented in terms of formulae. It does not follow, however, that they are mysterious. What follows is that they are embedded in the practice of history, not set apart from it, and can best be evaluated through results.

Perhaps the idea that there exists *a* historical method, along the lines of scientific method, is appealing because it appears to simplify questions of interpretation. Indeed the very notion of a method emphasises the gathering rather than the interpretation of materials. As we know, 'scientific method' is something of a fiction, since there are many methods used in the production of the kind of knowledge called 'science'. And so there are in history. It seems implausible, in any case, that a field as complex and diverse as history could have one unifying method. I would argue that the most important act historians perform is that of writing, because it is through writing that their disparate ideas are integrated into a single whole. Historical ideas, accounts and claims are apprehended by others via the written, and to a lesser extent the spoken, word. Writing is the foremost act of interpretation. As we saw in chapter 6, a sense of the past may be communicated by many means, yet *within* the discipline of history texts are the principal means of communication. It is curious then that the practice of history has been identified much more with the archive than with its results: with a privileged repository of sources rather than with historical interpretation in written form. This displacement requires careful consideration.[18]

THE CULT OF THE ARCHIVE

There is no doubt that there is a considerable cult of the archive among many historians. It is where one cuts one's teeth, develops identifications with the 'raw' materials, lodges claims to originality and, to a degree, inhabits another world. What is implied by invoking this notion of 'the archive'? It certainly involves the authority of collections of unpublished sources, which are imagined as closer to their originating situations, that is, less mediated, when they are in an archive. 'The archive' implies a kind of intimacy with particular aspects of the past that are more personal, individual, private, and hence worth looking at precisely because they concern 'real life'. There are, in fact, many different kinds of archives, and it will be worth tracking changes in attitudes in the next few years as more and more public archives are making records available on the internet. The love letters of a famous person, the confidential minutes of high-level political meetings, witness statements to a court, all share the qualities I have described, despite being distinct types of sources and typically located in distinct types of organisation. Many archives bear witness to the manner in which major areas of administration functioned and interacted with their constituencies. In these contexts quite separate social groupings come together – colonial administration would be an excellent example – and touch each other at pressure points, such as death, crime, political insurrection, dire poverty, and so on. Furthermore, much archival material can be understood in terms of stories. This is especially true of legal records, and hence they seem to offer a seduction into past worlds. Such narratives are recognisable types, they follow the patterns of contemporary fictional work, and hence they are particularly appealing. The use of familiar, attractive narratives becomes an issue for historians if, in writing up their research, they seek to trade on or reconstruct stories uncritically. However delicious, they should not be glamorised or used as substitutes for analysis. The entrancing stories in the archives are quite distinct from the historical arguments in which they will be deployed. Evidently there are many different kinds of archives: local, regional and national, personal, institutional, and so on; using them requires a wide range of skills and of background knowledge, above all about the processes that led to the generation, selection and cataloguing of their materials. Until recently, 'the archive' implied materials not looked at by anyone else or only by a few – the very idea nurtures historians' fantasies about their privileged access to the past.

I have presented the archive as enjoying a special place in the practice of history. In itself this is neither bad nor good, it is simply a feature of current historical practice. Naturally, like all other aspects of that practice, it needs to be held up for critical, yet sympathetic inspection. These complexities of the archive have clear implications for historians' skills. As I have already said, it is an absolutely basic skill to reconstruct the means by which materials were originally produced and have come into archives. We need to know how the archive has been managed and classified, whether items have been lost, destroyed or altered. Just as crucial is an insight into one's own responses to the material – the skill, if you like, of self-analysis. At another conceptual level altogether, there needs to be a critique of how and why historical achievement is still understood as being derived from the supposed quality of the primary sources. I have argued that this draws our attention away from interpretation and towards 'research', away from the historian's mind and towards historical actors and past states. While this move may be salutary in that it forces historians to engage deeply with other worlds, to recognise their difference, it may just be that it is also safer. If so much rests on the sources, we shift responsibility away from historians and towards their materials. I am not denying the myriad delights of archival sources, but I am giving priority to what is done with them by historians.

Historical achievement, then, derives from the manner in which sources are handled; it is not located in the sources themselves, however enchanting these may be. The skill of finding unusual, little-known or previously neglected sources is certainly valuable, and it reinforces my point, since the accomplishment is the historian's. I am stressing writing as a major historical skill because that is how achievement has to be judged. The transition from primary sources to historical account involves many steps, and is not a simple journey from document to book or journal article – typically there is much doubling back, many twists and unexpected turns. The quality of the resulting narrative, itself a composite, is what counts. Inevitably there are many different ways in which the final result is arrived at. The writer's choice of the theoretical framework, given that there are so many possibilities, is an obvious example – and this further reminds us that skills inform every part of historical practice. A less obvious example would be the selection of historical genres. I have laid great emphasis on the skills required to delineate a historical problem, but this is not independent of the genres through which it is given expression. It is vital to choose the right genre for the problem and vice versa. A journal article can only cope with certain kinds of problems: the genre has strict word limits and fairly rigid conventions and demands an exceptionally clear focus. In a book, by contrast, which requires distinctive writing skills, such as the ability to sustain a conceptual or narrative thread, it is possible to explore issues that are more ramifying and wide-ranging, possessed of different facets. Choosing a genre and using it well also involves decisions about the level of detail required, and where it should be located – in the main text or in the footnotes. We cannot legislate about such matters, since so many variables are involved. The way forward is to bear these issues in mind every single time we read a historical account. It is less a matter of having a formal checklist than of understanding the implications of the seemingly mundane elements that make up published historical work. The skills involved are inferred, backwards as it were, by comparing a range of practices and evaluating their effectiveness. Such an evaluation must take into account the chosen genre and its aptness, and place the work in the context of other similar accounts. We could summarise these points about the centrality of writing in historical practice by stating that all historical texts need the power to convince others. This is the art of rhetoric, which is an important historical skill, or rather a blend of skills, and is not to be understood pejoratively.

SKILLS AND NON-TEXTUAL SOURCES

So far, this chapter has presented historians as both users and producers of *texts*, but what about other kinds of sources and the skills needed to use them? Non-textual sources include items of visual and material culture, such as seals, maps, photographs, drawings, prints, paintings, jewellery, costume, tools and machines, archaeological remains, buildings, town plans, films – indeed any artefact. They also include music – compositions, libretti, performances, instruments, stage designs for operas, and so on. Non-textual sources tend to elicit one of two responses from general historians, and both are unproductive. According to the first, they require very special, almost arcane skills. As a result such sources are mystified and their differences from texts reinforced. In fact we can approach them in a *similar* manner, by thinking about the technical, the source-based and the interpretative skills required. According to the second response, visual sources are privileged as transparent windows onto past times rather than artful constructions in their own right, which implies that no skills at all are required in their use!

I want to pursue a little further the suggestion that non-textual sources are similar but not identical to textual ones, by taking the example of the skills required for the use of visual materials. Thinking about technical skills first, prints provide a useful example, and they are especially popular among historians.[19] It is emphatically not necessary to be a connoisseur of prints to use them in historical work, but it is essential to be able to identify the type of print – engraving, etching, mezzotint, lithograph, and so on – and to have some understanding of its mode of production, its cost and likely audiences. These are relatively 'technical' issues, which form the basis for any work with such sources. The source-based skills would take these points further in a given historical context. For example, the print makers and sellers should be considered: where did they practise, did they work with particular artists, what were their political affiliations, how does their output compare with that of others? Prints are rarely studied independently of other types of evidence; hence another set of source-based questions would place prints into the context of other comparable sources on related *themes* – fashion excesses, politics, scandals, for example. Whereas a traditional art historian might be especially interested in prints that were the creations of a master, such as Hokusai, Dürer or Rembrandt, a historian will want to integrate prints with a wide range of other materials and to evaluate their status as historical evidence. This involves moving away from the print itself and into its context. Historians will still need to pay careful attention to the visual conventions of artistic genres and to the way in which any given image is working. The print becomes a form of evidence only by meticulous analysis, just like any other document, and the distinctive kinds of mediation it represents must be taken account of.

When it comes to interpretation, historians are well advised to read and engage with accounts given by those with an art-historical training.[20] Disciplines, as we know, have their own habits of mind, so a degree of 'translation' is certainly involved. Nonetheless, the procedures are not so very different from the interpretative ones required in all historical work – a clearly shaped argument, the apt use of visual 'quotation', a well-chosen framework, a good fit between materials, arguments and conclusions. So, non-textual sources have distinctive logics and conditions of existence and they have been interpreted in particular ways by other disciplines, which have their own scholarly traditions. The principles behind the skills needed to use them well are the same as those applied to texts. The problem comes when we use unfamiliar materials and want to endow them with a special status. I

7.2 US marines planting the flag on Iwo Jima, February 1945; taken by Joe Rosenthal for Associated Press
This photograph has become extremely well known. Its powerful composition is both pleasing and dramatic. This evocative image looks spontaneous; it suggests triumph. Viewers place special faith in photographs, especially those designated 'documentary', and we tell ourselves that the camera never lies. Yet this is demonstrably false. So what trust can be placed in a photograph? Can it be treated as reliable evidence?

have already referred to one of the most problematic examples, namely, what could be called reflection or window history. This is the surprisingly widespread claim that (some) art offers a window onto past worlds, so that by looking at it historians can see directly what it was like then. Or, to put it differently, art reflects life. This is not what working historians assume about written sources, which are indeed recognised as mediations. Art is a mediation too, but of a distinctive kind. Historians writing illustrated books often fail to recognise this point. The pictures become decorative add-ons: they are not integrated into historical arguments, but are treated as unproblematic illustrations of insights arrived at by conventional means. The images are not contextualised in the way any written source would be. This is a kind of double standard and has rightly been criticised, for example, by Michael Baxandall in his *Painting and Experience in Fifteenth Century Italy*, a beautifully conceptualised and highly accessible discussion of what pictures are, and are not, evidence of.[21]

I want to insist on the need to treat images, or indeed any item of visual culture, critically. This is necessary because they have repeatedly been used unthinkingly by general historians to evoke a mood or emotion and attach it to a specific time and place, to encourage readers to identify with particular categories of historical actor and to convey 'authenticity'. All of these are at work in the use historians make of documentary photography, of Hogarth's oeuvre, of Dutch genre painting and of Victorian domestic scenes, to give some obvious examples. These are manipulative and *un*skilful uses of non-textual sources, precisely because the procedures I am discussing in this chapter have not been followed. I want to insist equally vigorously on the advantages to be gained from acquiring the skills needed to use non-textual sources. A wider range of evidence will provide richer insights. An argument will be stronger if it can be shown to apply to a larger number of examples. A theme will be understood better if we can trace more of its modulations and variations. Each type of source affords its own kinds of insight. People in the past did not experience the world in the compartments into which sources are conventionally divided; still less did they think in terms of divisions between kinds of history, such as economic and political. Many of the skills demanded by non-textual sources are in any case part of everyday life. In scholarly contexts they need to be brought up for conscious inspection and deliberately refined, and, if approached in this spirit, they can only add to a historian's strengths.

Admittedly, historians' use of some types of musical evidence demands skills with a high technical component. One problem with music is that to the extent it may be said to be representational at all, it is so in a quite different sense from, say, figurative art. This accounts for the fact that it is much easier for historians to use music with an accompanying text than 'abstract' music, much easier for them to approach the subject via patronage, institutions and performances than through scores. However, with the right skills these limitations can be overcome, and in general similar arguments apply to the case of music as to other non-textual sources – all carry historical traces if we know how to capture them.[22] The goal is a balance between respecting the logics of different media, while integrating them into historical arguments, not leaving them as decorative extras. If done well the result is a more holistic view of the past, and a greater awareness of the critical skills needed to use, evaluate and integrate any type of source. Using materials that are seen as the property of other disciplines raises questions that are best described as political, and I shall come to them shortly. But first I want to trace out the implications of my arguments for the teaching of history.

TEACHING HISTORY

The pedagogical implications of my arguments about skills are totally straightforward and can be stated succinctly. There are core skills that every historian needs, and the main one is critical reading – the ability to dismantle any piece of writing as fully and rigorously as possible, no matter when or how it was produced. The purpose behind critical reading is certainly not to treat texts in isolation, but to develop the basic analytical tools that will reveal their composition and mode of production. The result will be an understanding of the skeleton of a given piece of writing, as well as of its outward appearance, its core assumptions, its use of evidence, metaphor and footnotes. In order to apply this particular skill to secondary sources, students benefit from having a familiarity with what I have called scholarly traditions. They need to be able to navigate around their discipline, to have a sense of its history, the main changes it has undergone, the important journals in the field, influential approaches and relations with neighbouring domains. Navigation involves not just recognising signposts, but the capacity to evaluate the main contours of a field and current trends within it. Historians depend on their ability to write, and hence need to be taught about authorial skills. They also require plenty of historical cases through which to develop a sense of patterns, and these should be cases of different types – focused case studies, large-scale surveys, thematic courses, source-based studies, and so on. These cases will form a repertoire, a fund, resources to think through and with. It follows, then, that an undergraduate course which allows students to specialise in nineteenth- and twentieth-century Europe or the history of their own country, for example, is providing an overly narrow education. I know of no history department that teaches its students to write. Some teach 'historiography', in the form of 'philosophy of history', 'methods and approaches' or focus on recent critiques of the discipline, about all of which students tend to be sceptical.

The key to a good history education is to marry a wide variety of substantive courses with skills-based ones, which should include what I have called 'navigating the field'. Ideally, skills, in the way I have presented them here, would be fully integrated into *all* historical teaching. The advantage of naming and drawing attention to them is that awareness of their significance is thereby raised, so that they can be practised and refined quite explicitly. Styles of teaching should also encourage students to take notes effectively and to develop their oral and aural techniques, since these reinforce the other central skills – selection, evaluation and argumentation. None of this is possible if students cannot undertake critical analysis, which is the foundation of all scholarly work in the humanities. This is not an end in itself, but a way of opening up wider intellectual perspectives.

Professions reproduce themselves through teaching their skills and transmitting their knowledge to others. As a result, what constitutes the core skills and the way in which they should be transmitted become political issues within the profession, because they affirm views of the discipline in which those who seek dominance have huge stakes. They are also political in a wider sense, by virtue of the phenomenon of public history, from which it is both impossible and wrong for academic historians to disengage themselves. There is little consensus today about how to teach history at university level, and there has been a noticeable move away from the idea that curricula should have a core and towards a modular, 'supermarket' approach that offers students what they want, like and find relevant. And since historians differ greatly in their attitudes to related disciplines and to what defines 'history' – both of which are significant issues in shaping the curriculum – no consensus about a core can be arrived at by these means. Unfortunately, claims that there *is* a core to the subject are widely perceived as old-fashioned, even reactionary. They seem fundamentalist and are often associated by their critics with an interest in reasserting the centrality of traditional forms of history, such as 'high' political history. My argument in this *chapter* has been that there is a core – an assemblage of skills and substance. We can think of it in terms of a portfolio of skills, which are learnt most effectively through being applied to a wide range of historical situations. My argument in this *book* has been that this core has an ethical dimension, since historians have obligations to their sources, their readers, the past and the public at large.

Some of the most heated debates about the history curriculum concern the nature and range of topics covered. Since I advocate giving students a variety of historical fare, I consider an emphasis on world history, on going beyond the history of one's own nation, to be healthy. This is not because nation-based history is *ipso facto* 'bad'; everything depends on how it is presented. It has been subjected to savage criticism as a vehicle for promoting conservative and elitist values, for marginalising minority voices, and for providing self-justifying teleological narratives that pre-empt political dissent. It is possible and indeed desirable to teach a nation's history in a critical fashion. The same arguments apply to larger geographical areas. 'Europe', like 'the west' and 'the east', is an invention: the very idea has become and continues to be central in shaping identities and practices. Hence the history of Europe needs to be taught critically and with these points in mind. It does not follow that, because these types of history carry baggage, they should not be taught. They should be for two reasons. First, being able to locate oneself and one's own community or communities historically is intrinsically important. It builds on people's own experience, as much radical history advocates. It is therefore a vehicle through which a great deal can be learnt, for example, about patterns of identification (involving religion, the workplace, the family, and so on); about the methods and sources best suited to this specific type of history; and about the past of an immediately available situation. Second, it illustrates the different analytical *levels* of which historical work is composed. To study the history of a town or an ethnic group, a nation, a continent, and then to think in terms of world history is to move through analytically distinct levels, which are complementary to one another, not mutually exclusive. This is the repertoire point – historians need the *range* of levels precisely because it illustrates different types of historical problem. It would be entirely wrong to think of some of these levels as 'better' than others. Here is the point about contexts in another guise. Historians need to see their chosen level or levels in the light of others: regions have national settings, continents global ones, and so on. Obviously levels do not only concern geographical scale, they also involve types of generality (individuals, families, villages, occupations, classes, political parties), and the point about contexts holds for these cases too.

Throughout the book I have strenuously resisted the idea that some forms of history are better or worse than others and suggested that such terms should be applied instead to the quality of the historical knowledge. I raise these moral terms because that is how, in the light of debates about political correctness, these matters have come to be considered, so that using the suffix '-centric' is a criticism on both political and moral grounds. Thus, it is often said that much history teaching, including in the United States, is 'Eurocentric', which is to say that it privileges a European perspective on the world. Such a criticism has bite if one viewpoint is presented as unquestionable when other viewpoints are potentially relevant but actually neglected, and if Europe is, inappropriately, taken in isolation from other parts of the world. I am sceptical about whether there is *a* single European point of view, in which case, if such a thing were claimed to exist, that would be wrong because it would be a distorting simplification. The problem is that once a notion such as 'Eurocentrism' or 'orientalism' exists, it gets bandied about rather freely, becoming an unthinking term of criticism, and thus pre-empts critical thinking. As I suggested earlier, effective teaching about 'Europe' would subject the very term to scrutiny, ask what work it does, ponder the implications of distinctions between Eastern and Western Europe, think about relationships between regions both within and outside 'Europe' and hence eschew a single viewpoint. The eastern borders of 'Europe' have long been problematic – where does Europe end and Asia begin, and what is at stake in where the line is drawn? Such an approach draws creatively upon what students already know about Europe, whether a little or a lot. Since every historian comes from a particular background, it is necessary to build upon it, not pretend it does not exist. Thus world history is always and inevitably written from particular standpoints because it cannot be otherwise. Yet by consciously varying the level of focus, it is possible to raise one's awareness about what is taken for granted, to imagine other ways of cutting the historical cake, and to enhance intellectual flexibility.

SKILLS AND THE DISCIPLINE OF HISTORY

The discipline of history has been subjected to a number of critiques, especially over the last 20 years. In the course of this book I have alluded to many of them. They are important in relation to skills, because they contain implications for the manner in which the discipline should be taught as well as practised. Many, if not most, of these critiques have their roots in intellectual paradigms that are outside the discipline as this is customarily defined. As a result, some historians feel attacked from outside. Yet recent commentaries on the field have brought to historians' attention hitherto unfamiliar perspectives and insisted on their relevance for contemporary historical practice. If, for instance, history is simply one type of narrative, whose claims to intellectual authority are fragile because based on stories that serve particular, limited interests, then claims about the distinctiveness of the discipline are correspondingly fragile, and there are important consequences for its pedagogy. So now, I want finally to turn to the question of how the discipline of history may be distinctive.

Taken individually, none of the skills I have described defines the discipline of history. If we put them all together, and think of them as closely related to substance, we may get closer. It is vital to remember that there can be no firm boundaries around 'history' – there are no watertight definitions for any humanities or social science discipline, and the boundaries have definitely become more permeable in recent years. It is possible to think of the discipline as a capacious umbrella – people choose to come under it, and to call what they do 'history', and others can agree or not as the case may be. These matters are in any case socially negotiated. 'History' has never been and cannot be a stable category. Those who shelter there have a sense of being 'a historian'; they construct a professional identity around the label. It may be possible to get slightly closer to what is distinctive about 'history' if we think about the assemblage of skills involved. It is not possible to define history simply as the study of the past, because other disciplines do that too. While they share some features, archaeology and history remain different fields. Furthermore, there is contemporary history, a fast-growing area – the very name suggests that past and present are brought together in its practice. Nonetheless, for the most part history is concerned with a past for which there are extensive written records, and with accounting for continuities as well as changes.

It is possible to be a little more specific. For example, we can say what history is *not*. History does not involve one specific category of human activity or production, such as music, dance, dress, leisure, procreation, literature or travel. Specialised sub-branches have a narrower focus, but these are only fully *historical* if they set such activities in a broader context. However hard it is to define, context is a central concept for the practice of history. Historians study human nature in operation. They do not observe this directly as anthropologists, sociologists and psychologists have the chance to do, but mediated through sources. They are interested in both the abstract and the concrete features of past societies, and in the connections between them. They want to make statements of a fairly high level of generality about the past, to speak of phenomena that encompass many of its facets. General trends are always illustrated in particular instances, which, reciprocally, contribute to the delineation of broad features – history involves intricate dialogues between the specific and the general. Any given text, image, activity or experience is set in context*s* – the plural is important since historians typically consider a range of contexts, including those in which their sources were produced, received and used, and those in which complex phenomena take place and are given meaning. Customarily such contexts involve structural elements, that is, the systems through which a given society functions – the production and distribution of wealth and of power, forms of social difference, collective identities, institutions, administration, governance, and so on. While undertaking these operations, evaluation, reasoning and judgement are exercised – all of which depend upon carefully, knowingly honed skills.

A wide range of historical explanations results, but they carry the features I have just described, with certain variations, according to the type of history in question. So it would be possible to say that history is simply what historians do, which helps to recognise the huge diversity of practice. It would follow that skills were anything people who call themselves historians deploy in their work. Yet this is too bland. The rather abstract account I have just given of what may be distinctive about the discipline indicates some of its specific habits of mind, and we can be a bit more precise by examining some of the ways in which history is *unlike* related disciplines.

There is no single concept around which the discipline of history is organised in the way that sociology is predicated upon the concept 'society' or anthropology upon 'man'. Similarly, there is no set of master theories or of founding fathers, in the way that sociologists and anthropologists can turn to Durkheim and Spencer, Marx, Mauss and Malinowski. There were great and influential historians in the past, but their legacy was much looser, and their writings are relatively neglected, except by specialists. Whereas sociology students still read Weber, for instance, to familiarise themselves with his ideas and assess their usefulness, no comparable figures exist in history. Sociologists and anthropologists are expected to know the gist of the theories upon which their fields have been constructed in a way that no history student would be expected to do for the great historical writings of the nineteenth and early twentieth centuries. The field has become more theoretical over recent years, but this difference remains: there do not exist in history a limited number of thinkers, about whose status as founding fathers practitioners – whatever their theoretical predilections – agree. In other words, history is inherently an eclectic discipline and the skills it requires are correspondingly diverse.[23] And therein lie its strengths. Eclecticism is sometimes treated as a dirty word. At the very least it sounds untidy – just so: if historians treat the past in too tidy a manner they lose a great deal. Hence the discipline is rightly pragmatic, including in its sources and methods and the skills these demand. It is precisely the ability to embrace complexities while making sense of them, and to think flexibly about diverse phenomena at distinct analytical levels, that characterises historians' purchase on the past.

There is not a single category of sources that is privileged within the discipline either. If art historians cease to pay attention to works of art, musicologists to music, or literary specialists to texts, then they lose something quite central to their fields. We can grant the point while recognising the diversity of the sources within the category 'music', 'art' or 'literature'. Nonetheless, those categories are important, as is evident from the forms of identification they produce. Starting with a work of art is very different from starting with a revolution. It is irrelevant whether one *likes* the work in question or not: it provides a point of departure that issues from the consciousness of one or more human beings; it has been designed for specific purposes; it has been treated, whether by markets or by audiences, in quite particular ways. None of this obtains when it comes to coups, famines, religious orders, hospitals, and so on. Distinct types of scholarship can be brought together in creative ways, but this does not lessen their distinctness. It is obvious, but true, that interdiscplinarity is predicated on disciplinarity.

BRIDGE

I have argued that being a historian involves the self-aware development of a wide range of skills. Since the nature of historical practice is deeply, intricately informed by the immediate context, historians are also critical observers of the worlds they inhabit. This role demands skills too, among them the ability to discern and evaluate trends, not only in history and related disciplines, but in publishing, government policy, museums, as well as in local, regional, national and world politics. In the final chapter, I discuss a small number of recent trends that stand out to me, and I suggest some of the ways in which practising historians might consider them.

8

Trends

WHY TRENDS MATTER

In this chapter I shall examine some of the recent trends that seem to have developed most markedly over the last five years. No attempt is made to predict the areas of or approaches to history that will come to the fore in the future. This is partly because events themselves are unpredictable and it is so often they that endow particular subjects or approaches with resonance. I was going to say 'world events' in order to point up the way in which the dramas of politics shape historical practice. It is undeniable – to take the most obvious example – that the events of 11 September 2001 changed attitudes to and interest in terrorism, Islam and the Middle East.[1] Some of their effects have been profoundly troubling for professional historians. Gross generalisations about 'Islam' and 'global terrorism', which are evoked as if these were easy terms to define, with the capacity to explain a great deal, are a striking example. There are also opportunities here: indeed this is a classic instance of both the huge potential of public history to make a fundamental contribution to politics and policies, and of the terrible costs of ignorance of the belief systems and past histories of huge parts of the world.[2] It should be a matter of universal concern that the numbers of historians able to speak the necessary languages, with first-hand experience of the relevant geographical areas, and with the time and inclination to explain hugely complex phenomena, seem inadequate. It is vital that such historical understanding exists in the most powerful countries in the world, in their governments and media specifically, in the countries that are major players in the Middle East, in areas that speak the languages in which war is waged.

Clearly big events affect the practice of history, but so do many other phenomena, including the personal experiences of those who study and engage with the past. In earlier chapters the impact of movements such as feminism and gay rights upon historical research has been noted. To these we might add anti-abortion and animal rights campaigns, for example. Such movements have a distinctive profile. They draw attention to issues in a dramatic, often highly emotive way. They touch participants in an intimate and immediate manner. When taking part in protests, people express a commitment to a cause, they experience powerful feelings, and they conceptualise the struggles with which they are involved. These movements combine abstract ideas, such as 'rights', with potent emotional reactions. They frequently prompt intellectual analysis, including historical inquiries.

There are other ways in which trends come about. We might invoke here 'fashion' and 'taste' – terms that describe trends rather than explain them. Nonetheless, they are useful for thinking about the nature of historical practice. Many historians want to work on topics or to use approaches that are manifestly up to date, that grab people's attention through being new and original. Originality is difficult to define – by its very nature scholarship is built on foundations laid by others. In academic life, originality is prized as it is in cultural activities such as film-making, music and the writing of fiction. Yet audiences need to be receptive, and once an idea takes hold and becomes fashionable, others follow, creating trends, certainly, but by that very token raising questions about originality and modishness. So these ideas, fashion and taste, suggest preferences, even *mere* preferences, which is simply to say that something is around and people latch on to it. There are three distinct issues here: how originality is assessed; how trends get established; and how they find receptive audiences. We need to look critically at historical fashions, and especially at their commercial dimensions. At the same time, they respond to emotional needs, even as they help to create them. Since historical trends do not occur in isolation, it is always worth exploring the ways in which the broad context shapes scholarship.

One way in which trends are established is by reaction against existing assumptions, styles of research, current orthodoxies. The profound urge that children have to contradict their parents has academic equivalents, and it takes many forms in the discipline of history. What in a family setting is called rebellion, petulance, grumpiness and just plain growing up, is styled 'revisionism' in academic settings, and one form it takes is finding errors, misinterpretations and omissions in existing work. Simply dismissing it as passé is another. Attacking the world view implicit in authoritative work is yet another. Partly this stems from the impulse to stand out, to be seen to be doing something different, new and important, which is integral to building a career. Trends in all academic fields come about in similar ways, and that would be reason enough for historians to pay attention to them. Historical trends, however, are particularly closely tied up with public affairs – the intimate connections between modern history, international relations, the study of politics and world affairs reveal as much. Historical work has public consequences and draws considerable energy from contemporary preoccupations. It is a situation that obliges historians to be especially scrupulous. The explicit use of historical claims and ideas in public life is increasing.

Historical trends, then, are as much about broad debates, global changes and climates of opinion as they are about current academic fads.

Trends are also about cutting the historical cake in new, inventive ways. A method of slicing that has not been tried before has its merits; it will result in fresh shapes and juxtapositions. In writing *Falcon*, about the fastest animals that have ever lived, Helen Macdonald drew on sources of many kinds, times and countries, to explore the 'light [this extraordinary bird sheds] . . . on the cultures through which it has flown'. By putting together myth, poetry, zoology, ecology, military history, diaries, children's literature, film and newspapers from many centuries, she carves out a new and illuminating interdisciplinary history. Few animals have carried this type of significance, but enough to generate a series that really does open up fresh perspectives.[3]

PAST WARS, PRESENT EXCITEMENTS

Maybe it is because of the current war-torn state of the world that I have become curious about the field of military history – to the surprise of many historians, an increasingly popular and prominent area, including among the young. This is evident in television programmes, in the wide range of titles available in bookshops and also in successful blockbuster films, academic publications and tourism. Here is a case through which the relationships between professional, public and amateur history can be examined. It is by no means straightforward what 'military history' includes, and specialists make distinctions between war and warfare, between war studies, strategic studies, the history of military thought, international relations and military history. War studies, like its more fragile sister, peace studies, is an interdisciplinary field, in which history and historians participate along with scholars from other social science and humanities fields. I am using the term 'military history' as broadly as possible to include the historical study of all aspects of war and warfare. 'Military' immediately suggests armies, and indeed there is considerable interest in armies as institutions and in their most prominent and best-remembered participants – great leaders, brave soldiers and inventive strategists. Military history is far more than this: it examines battles, wars and the nature and impact of warfare more generally, along with the structures that sustain them. It invites reflection on the different types of history – economic, political and social, most obviously. Since it also touches upon the history of science, medicine and technology, oral history, contemporary history, comparative history and many more subfields, its methodological significance for the discipline is hardly in doubt. In other words, warfare touches every aspect of the societies involved, their economic and technological capacities, their political structures, especially the state apparatus, their education, training and professional organisation, their social forms, their national, regional, ethnic, class and gender identities, their cultural products. Thus it is arguable that military history lies or should lie at the very centre of historical practice.

For many years, however, there has been a perception that it was set apart, the domain either of old-fashioned historians preoccupied with the state, foreign policy and diplomacy, or of (male) enthusiasts who were keen on war and weapons, on the minute details of battles, campaigns, uniform, guns, and so on. There are stereotypes, often unhelpful or inaccurate ones, associated with historical specialisms, because their object of study or the manner in which it is pursued raises difficult issues or mobilises prejudices. The high levels of specialisation in academic research, manifest in the continuing proliferation of journals, lessen the chance of prejudices being challenged by exposure to exponents of historical styles very different from one's own. For this very reason a broad basic historical education is essential – arguably it should include some consideration of military history, given the importance of war as a historical phenomenon. By the same token we can argue for the vital role that thematic conferences that cut across specialisms can and should play in bringing historians together. So while fields such as military history should not be seen as zones for aficionados, the pace at which new organisations and books series, as well as journals, are proliferating, fragments a discipline that thrives on eclecticism, intellectual promiscuity, and breaking down the prejudices that exist about its constituent parts, their intellectual status and their fashion rating.

However, it must be admitted that military history is still considerably more appealing to men than to women, and if recent letters to the *Journal of Military History* are anything to go by, there remains some truth to the perception that there are many enthusiasts, 'old soldiers' and buffs in the field.[4] Yet the articles and book reviews suggest both a rigorous, broad and generous intellectual remit and a huge chronological range, from the classical world to the present day. A closer look reveals some of the complexities of the field. Letters, like articles and reviews, frequently concern the status of personal testimonies, always a contentious form of evidence; but they become particularly controversial when witnesses are stakeholders in historical accounts, are still alive or recently deceased, and when the central issues – such as national humiliation and pride, imperialism, communism, the legitimacy of invasion, assigning responsibility for mistakes and rewards for success – are still being debated fervently.

They are debated in part because there never can be settled accounts, but also because current conflicts reawaken deep anxieties and encourage comparisons with earlier episodes, many of which remain highly charged. The point is reinforced by the twentieth-century proliferation of civil wars, which, by their very nature, are exceptionally divisive, and the significance of which is marked by a new journal devoted to that theme. The precondition for such a development is certainly the timeliness of bringing the study of diverse civil wars together. Just as important is the implied claim that 'civil wars' is a coherent category, based on the existence of common features of particular civil wars across time and place. The majority of articles concern the last hundred years, although there was no shortage of civil wars in earlier eras. Furthermore, the inaugural editorial concedes that 'civil war' is hard to define.[5] Since civil wars are a significant contemporary phenomenon in which a number of constituencies, policymakers and governments, as well as academics, have an

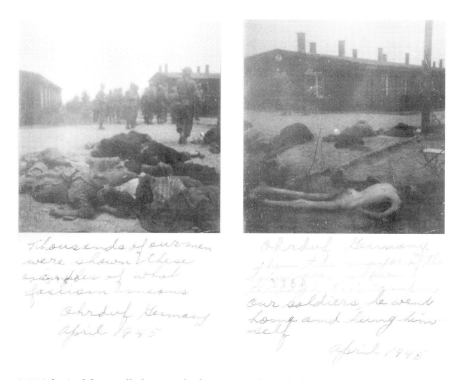

*Thousands of our men
were shown these
examples of what
fascism means
Ohrduf Germany
april 1945*

*Ohrduf Germany,
[...] the [...] of the
[...]
our soldiers he went
home and hung him-
self
april 1945*

8.1 I inherited five small photographs from my mother, which, I was told, had been sent to her by an American soldier. I have selected two and include his inscriptions on the back; they convey something of the drive to bear witness to events of profound significance, which lies at the heart of 'history'. Images associated with the Second World War, and especially with concentration camps, continue to elicit powerful and complex responses. The continuing fascination with that war is noteworthy, yet the historical insights such pictures afford are not at all obvious.

interest, this new journal shows how current conflicts help to shape historical practice, including, in this case, models of periodisation.

Living witnesses to violent conflict increasingly want to speak out, to tell their individual stories, to have their words both believed and respected as reliable historical evidence. The media give value to first-hand accounts, while historians are always presented with the difficulties of evaluating them and of working out how to integrate them into larger interpretations. Media reporting not only gives a voice to survivors, but also to actors' relatives, who want to visit significant sites and connect the big events of history with more intimate narratives. The publics for military history are indeed extensive. One context for a refreshed interest in military history is tourism. Visits to battlegrounds – battlefield hikes – and concentration camps seem to have increased and become common especially for school pupils – perhaps a man-ifestation of the belief in lessons from history.[6] The numbers of museums associated with war, imperial activities, recent conflicts and, especially, with the Holocaust is growing. In other words, war is not only a grim, ever-present reality in an era of 24/7 news, but a thriving leisure industry. As a result, both popular and academic history are affected.

Military history also touches the raw historiographical nerve of economic and technological determinism. How changes in the nature of warfare come about is no longer seen as self-evidently led by new materials, techniques, weapons, and so on. Indeed, explaining the intricate relationships between social organisation, political structures and foreign policy, the roles of science and technology, of military thinking and situations 'on the ground' demands all the historian's skills. Intellectually ambitious forms of military history, which have decades of scholarship to draw on, may well change the ways in which other historians think, by showing the capacity of wars and armies to shed light on all of history. These subjects are inseparable from other developments, while the new military history tackles tough methodological and interpretative issues in a rigorous way.

For those outside the academy, military history looks a bit different – less abstract analysis and more a way of engaging with the legacy of particular sites, which are often supercharged with significance. It is undeniable that being in the very place where significant events occurred – extermination camps, escapes from notorious places of detention or battlefields – can trigger powerful emotional effects. What remains to be worked out is exactly how these assist historical understanding, which necessarily involves processing, while critically assessing, large amounts of diverse evidence. It is especially difficult to analyse the pull of being in the actual place where a momentous historical event took place when, as is often the case, there is little to be seen. The role of interpretation centres at historical sites is worth mentioning – how are decisions made about which sites require them and, once made, about what they contain? Can battle sites be said to speak for themselves?[7] Perhaps it is significant that it is the remnants of human beings – for example, the glasses, shoes and hair displayed in some concentration camps – that produce especially intense responses. In their ordinary everyday familiarity, these items enable onlookers to imagine their owners in a state of exceptional suffering. Even without such objects as prompts, it is possible that being able to say 'I was there', to share the experience with others and to show photographic evidence, is such an accepted part of everyday life now, and so securely enshrined in patterns of leisure and in their associated commercial forms, that it is utterly taken for granted. New types of imagined communities are formed in the process. It may be that such visits have become routine within families and schools; the sense that they are historically useful, totally ingrained and all too rarely analysed. It may be that a vicarious thrill, analogous to that experienced in reading or watching films about notorious murders, is integral – albeit difficult to acknowledge – to being in a place where terrible violence and unspeakable suffering occurred. Naturally, going to a war site is only one aspect of the growth of popular interest in military history, but it is a significant part. Since there has been a rise in academic interest at the same time, there is clearly a complex phenomenon to be explained.[8]

REGRETS AND RESPONSIBILITIES

The fascination with war is directly connected with two other trends. The first is the curiosity about extremes of violence and cruelty. Admittedly, countries differ in the degree to which their mass media reinforce morbid curiosity. But the desire to know about human extremes, hardship, triumph over the elements, as well as cruelty and torture, the horrors of war and the anatomy of power in past societies shows no sign of diminishing. Students remain fascinated by Hitler, Stalin and Mussolini and their regimes. Television programmes, books and articles about concentration camps are legion. Historical interests in authoritarianism and violence need to be put in the context of general attitudes towards these phenomena. The fascination may be as much with how responsibility for dreadful acts is assigned and explained as with the acts themselves. Thus it may be worth noting that the popularity of biography remains high, and while a relatively small number of the lives recounted involve tyranny or violence, associating such phenomena with individuals renders them not only more accessible, but also offers the possibility of explaining how they came about through the agency of named people. This would be consistent with all the talk about attributing blame and responsibility for past acts that is a fallout of the living presence of wars.

Thus the second trend is the demands of victims and their representatives that perpetrators say sorry, by recognising and taking responsibility for past actions that were 'wrong' and, in some cases, making amends, for example, by restoring property taken 'illegitimately' or paying compensation. Discourses of apology seem to be more prominent than five years ago and scholarly interest in the phenomenon is increasing.[9] Yet not all war-torn countries or sufferers make such demands. These discourses do not exist, for example, in Vietnam, where a pragmatic approach dominates, enabling former oppressors to be seen as valuable trading partners. It is precisely because the saying sorry phenomenon is not universal that it demands the careful, critical attention of historians, and should not be seen as obvious or natural.

I connect it to war because it is generally in this context that demands for apologies come up, the debates about slavery in the United States being a notable exception. Often victims' organisations are pressing governments or their heads to admit guilt retrospectively. In the well-publicised trials of war criminals, blame is attributed to individuals. This is a formidably complex phenomenon, involving intricate assumptions about the responsibilities of individuals, institutions and states, and also about war itself. I put two words in so-called scare quotes above to indicate that the moral judgements involved in such cases are rarely uncontested or straightforward, however intuitively horrendous the acts in question are perceived to be. They do not imply that atrocities are to be condoned, but they do signal that occupying moral high grounds can be more problematic than appears at first sight.

'Apology' is a shorthand – it is worth remembering the range of concepts that come up here: restitution, repentance, reconciliation, redress, renunciation, regret, responsibility, recompense, and many more. While it is easy to see that apologising has considerable symbolic value – it acknowledges wrongs done and assigns both blame and responsibility to either groups or individuals, which is what victims often desire – it does raise a number of major issues. The distinction between blame and responsibility is worth making. 'Responsibility' implies an analysis of cause and effect. 'Blame' implies that too, plus an emotional charge – righteousness on one side, guilt on the other. It further implies that once blame has been assigned, the other party *should* feel guilt and behave accordingly, for example, accepting their guilt and, if appropriate, offering compensation. By contrast, the statement, 'I am responsible', does not necessarily imply any of this.

Assigning responsibility rests in the end on an authoritative account of what happened, that is, the process presupposes prior, well-grounded historical analysis, which commands the support of both sides. For example, drawing a clear line capable of generating widespread assent between normal, acceptable treatment of prisoners of war and their misuse is extremely difficult, yet without it there is unlikely to be a resolution of the claims by those prisoners against their captors. It is a ghastly but undeniable fact that one side's abuse can be construed by the other as business as usual. The following questions are worth posing: Is it the job of historians to assign retrospective responsibility? How are secure distinctions to be made between individual, collective and institutional responsibility? What arguments can legitimately be used if historians do decide to make judgements about responsibility? Is it morally defensible for historians to engage in a process that may lead to imprisonment, confiscation of property or the death penalty? There will be many who respond to these questions by simply affirming historians' active involvement in these complex issues, in the elucidation of which they use all their special skills. I cannot feel so sure, and wonder whether there can be a general position on such matters rather than a case-by-case assessment. Nonetheless, it is valuable to reflect upon historical responsibilities in broad terms because it helps sharpen the understanding of agency, both with respect to those in the past and to historians themselves. It reveals the moral complexities that historical practice necessarily generates. Unfortunately, these are frequently either disregarded or deemed less significant for those who work on earlier eras. These are matters for all historians, even if those who work on recent times see them in their starkest, most troubling forms. When historians observe the activities of pressure groups, law courts, governments and the media in response to requests for apologies, they can test out and refine ideas about responsibility, which are themselves historical phenomena. These are always emotive matters, too often debated in the heroes and villains idiom.

A pertinent example is the recent book by Daniel Goldhagen on the role of the Catholic Church during the Nazi period, a topic on which there was an extensive pre-existing literature. *A Moral Reckoning* has provoked impassioned responses. Goldhagen not only wants to assign blame and responsibility to the Church and, specifically, to Pope Pius XII, for both their anti-Semitism and their moral cowardice in failing to stand up against

Hitler, but he wants to find ways in which past wrongs can be redressed. There are a number of issues here: the quality of his historical analysis; the inferences he draws from it concerning misdeeds; the remedies proposed and their anticipated effects. None of these is straightforward. It may appear persuasive that institutions with long and more or less continuous histories should accept responsibilities for past acts, even when those directly involved are long dead. But in fact there is a problem here, noted elsewhere in the book, about the continuity of historical categories. In any case, the categories themselves are of different kinds – it is not self-evidently appropriate to treat individuals, groups, governments, leaders, and so on, in identical ways. Whereas it appears implausible to claim that present-day men are somehow responsible for acts now perceived as wrongs done by their ancestors to women, it may be more convincing to claim that in the case of governments and churches there are chains of institutional responsibility across generations. Furthermore, it is a considerable challenge to demonstrate the precise nature of the wrongs, especially when the accusation concerns moral *failings*, such as *not* speaking out on behalf of a persecuted group – one of Goldhagen's claims against the Catholic Church. There would seem to be another problem lurking here, that of identification. Goldhagen identifies, and in complex ways, with the Jews he claims were not protected by the Catholic Church; he demands justice now, and thereby casts himself as a vindicator, a deeply interested party.[10] These patterns of identification and attempted vindication are widespread; they come up, for example, in discussions of the legacy of slavery and also in the writing of the history of the many groups that have been legally, socially or politically disadvantaged in the past.[11] Thus some women may indeed demand justice retrospectively for individuals and sub-groups with whom they have a strong identification, and may express these sentiments in the form of historical writing. It is possible to frame these claims in terms of abstract moral arguments, such as absolute rights for justice. But in such cases the applicability of modern notions of universal rights to past times has to be demonstrated. Yet behind demands to say sorry for past acts lie intense emotional energies, including rage and fury, in the face of which abstract reasoning and historical analysis appear misplaced.

An equally pertinent, but analytically distinct, example is the recent case brought against Deborah Lipstadt and Penguin Books by David Irving, in which a leading historian of modern Germany, Richard Evans, was called in as an expert witness for the defence, an experience about which he has written most movingly. Lipstadt had argued, in print, that Irving distorted the historical record. David Irving lost the case, and Evans is as robust in his condemnation of Irving's conduct as he is of his history – Irving is exposed 'as a manipulator of historical documents and a Holocaust denier'. The issue here certainly was about responsibilities for past actions, but the trial was occasioned by one historian's claims about the fatal inadequacies of another published account. Evans dedicates the book to the victims of the Holocaust: 'seeing the camp survivors on the public benches in court was a daily reminder of the human significance of what we were discussing'.[12] This was not directly about saying sorry, but it was about the accountability of historians in an area where retrospectively assigning responsibility correctly was of the utmost importance. It illustrates a point I make elsewhere about historians being privileged witnesses to what happened in the past; hence the requirement that their accounts be as sound as humanly possible.

These two trends, and the current prominence of military history, prompt a further thought. War and violence are, so far as it is possible to know, found in all societies. Increasingly it is understood as a rule-bound phenomenon, which prompts protests if it is perceived that the rules have been violated. It is undeniable not only that clear-cut precepts and the actual processes of war sit uneasily together, but also that the status of international law and the relevant codes of conduct are hotly contested. It is as if all the attention that is being paid to the misdemeanours and their rectification helps to make war more tolerable. Given the historical record, it may be worth examining why there is such widespread surprise about the atrocities of war and about the persistent flouting of conventions, which may not even be recognised by all the warring parties. If there were an opening for lessons from history, this would be it.

GLOBALISATION

If there is a drive to assign historical culpability, there is also a drive to invoke impersonal forces such as 'globalisation'.[13] The term itself may be morally charged, indeed it is sometimes meant to convey opprobrium towards the impact of the United States upon world affairs. The phrase 'anti-globalisation protester', widely used in the media, suggests ready recognition of the term 'globalisation' itself, and of its emotive, politicised connotations. 'Globalisation' evokes large-scale, even overwhelming processes that threaten to engulf individuals, families, communities and regions. Concepts that end in 'isation', such as modernisation and secularisation, convey the idea of a multiplicity of inexorable forces, almost beyond human control. They have often formed the main subject of what is sometimes sneeringly called grand narrative history, and they are present, if without acknowledgement, in much history writing. Evidently such terms possess an appeal that is both wide and deep; they provide accessible accounts and reinforce commonly held assumptions, although their vantage point and the interests they serve are frequently veiled. It is entirely appropriate that historians attend to large-scale forces, both social and natural, that they conceptualise the paces of the diverse changes they bring. The '-isation' words, however, are frequently used quite loosely and as if they are capable, by their mere invocation, of explaining large historical shifts. They are also implicitly teleological; the core of the word is the end point of the process to which it refers. They are difficult to define precisely, which possibly constitutes part of their appeal. They are used by a number of different disciplines, such as law, education, international relations and economics, acquiring specific inflections in the process, and are also ripe for interdisciplinary analysis. Rather than possessing self-evident

8.2 A Coca-Cola truck at the Jucatan Market in Guatemala

explanatory power, such notions describe an array of processes, partly by evoking widely shared perceptions.

In the case of 'globalisation', such perceptions are triggered by the aware-ness of apparent sameness and direct contact, by uniformities where before, allegedly, there were diversities, by the instantaneousness of both news and personal communication. The idea that there is 'one world' conveys some kind of connectedness, immediacy, and the belief that there is cultural benefit to be derived from globalisation. That brand names, usually Coca-Cola or McDonald's, are used to criticise these processes is telling. They serve as familiar markers, as well as emotive symbols; they combine easy recogni-tion – that, after all, is what branding is about – with a ready if often facile understanding of global corporations and changing patterns of consump-tion. The job of historians is to disaggregate these terms, to set them into a wider, long-term context and subject them to critical scrutiny. It is fairly obvious, for example, that alongside 'globalisation' there are marked trends towards localisation and regionalisation, the protection of minority lan-guages, the cultivation of local traditions of food production and, perhaps most ironically, the use of worldwide communication networks to preserve, protect and celebrate the diversity of what is now known as 'world music'.[14]

183

Currently, 'globalisation' is something of a buzz word, hence in urgent need of critical scrutiny. David Reynolds's robust remark that 'globalization is cold war victor's history conceptualized in a wider frame' is a useful reminder of the care such terms demand.[15] Current debates about globalisation are not only important historical phenomena in their own right, they are also part of the setting in which historical frameworks and forms of analysis are forged – they seep into mindsets. Recent ambitious attempts to write world histories, of which Reynolds's magisterial *One World Divisible* is an example, are both part of this context and important commentaries upon it.

'Globalisation' refers to the processes whereby parts of the world become more connected to and have increased impact upon one another. It is widely assumed that inequality is constitutive of such relationships, that the impact has mostly gone one way, from a domineering 'west' to other parts of the world, that uniformities have somehow been imposed illegitimately. The manifestations of such connectedness are varied, including trade, investment, communication, travel, international law, shared technologies, institutions with a worldwide remit. Underlying these interdependencies are not just more or less tangible exchanges of people, objects and, especially, technologies, but concepts such as rights, justice, democracy and heritage, as well as shifts of taste and fashion that make products originally made in one part of the world alluring in another. Underlying many such connections is the profit motive. Globalisation also claims attention because included in its remit is environmental change, much of which is attributable to human agency. We might link threats from pollution, for example, not just to the increasing use of the internal combustion engine, but to the geographical spread of industrial manufacturing. It has long been evident that events in one part of the world can have an impact on distant environments. Historians of the environment make an important contribution by charting the patterns and causes of major shifts in the 'natural' world, as demographers and historical geographers do in demonstrating how climate change has an impact on populations.

Historians are valuable participants in debates about globalisation. They can take both the long view and the broad, comparative view. While we might plausibly claim that in some recognisable form 'globalisation' was taking place in the sixteenth century in the wake of the voyages of 'discovery', those who work on earlier periods, including archaeologists, will offer yet larger vistas, so that the movements of people, goods and ideas long before the crusades are also taken into account. In answering the question, 'Is globalization a new phenomenon?', Steger starts with 10,000 BCE![16] One result of taking a wide view is an enhanced capacity to identify when, where and how the really decisive shifts occurred, to conceptualise more precisely the nature and pace of different types of change. It is always important to be able to scrutinise claims about novelty made in the media, politics and in other fields, and to give them historical substance as appropriate, thereby demonstrating how a historical perspective generates more plausible explanations and better understanding of broad patterns of change.

WRITING WORLD HISTORIES

Given the currency that notions of globalisation now have, it is hardly surprising that the popularity of world history would appear to have increased over the last five years. This is to judge not only by reference books and re-editions of earlier works, such as John Roberts's *History of the World*, now in its fourth revised edition as *The New Penguin History of the World*, but by the appearance of important new works that are global in their remit.[17] The best of these are seeking to think afresh about many of the historiographical issues mentioned in this book, such as periodisation, agents of change, the pace at which shifts of distinct kinds occur, the appropriate concepts and models, and the nature of evidence. Jerry Brotton's *The Renaissance Bazaar* is part of a trend towards seeing the Renaissance, a period frequently perceived as paradigmatically European, as a global phenomenon, which had material objects at its core.[18] It does not, however, aspire to be a history of the world during the fifteenth and sixteenth centuries.

An outstanding example of the world history genre is *The Birth of the Modern World 1780–1914* by C.A. Bayly. Many claims have been put forward for when the 'birth' of the modern world occurred, which is now more often imagined as a suite of protracted labours than as a single dramatic eruption. Any new contender is necessarily redefining his terms – and we know 'modern', for instance, is notoriously elusive. He is also rethinking the issues around periodisation, while grappling with the range of patterns and paces of change in all the areas the globe comprises. He also has some negative tasks, in that received ideas of cause and effect – change was something some bits of the world imposed on other bits – have to be dismantled, a point which is closely linked to the tendency to see many profound changes as economically and technologically driven. Shifting entrenched preconceptions is challenging enough, but new ways of seeing have to be put in their place. Doing so involves an array of intellectual operations in rethinking types of historical explanation, periodisation and the impact of postmodernism, as well as in mastering and then transforming the basic materials, while selecting the most apt and persuasive examples. It is arresting for a Europeanist to be shown how the revolutions of 1848 are best seen in a world context. It is telling that the illustrations in Bayly's volume insist on the distinctiveness of his enterprise. It is not just that they are so diverse geographically and that many will be unfamiliar to a lot of readers, and hence capable of pulling them up short, it is that they are intimately interwoven with one of the main themes of the book – changes in 'bodily practices', which he uses to demonstrate 'the rise of global *uniformities*'. 'Uniformity', Bayly insists, is to be distinguished from homogeneity, defining it as 'adjusting practice to create similarities on a larger scale', and using changes in dress to illustrate the point. In drawing our attention early on in the book to the significance of bodily deportment and dress, he sets up a framework through which many of the illustrations can be viewed. At the same time he is in conversation with others who are using notions of globalisation.[19]

8.3 Pyramid of the Niches, El Tajin, Mexico

This pyramid, part of a UNESCO World Heritage Site, is considered a masterpiece of ancient Mexican and American architecture. The building itself, with its elaborate carved reliefs, is understood to be full of astronomical and symbolic significance. El Tajin was an important centre from the early 9th to the early 13th centuries. This important archaeological site is now much visited. Even a cursory internet search reveals many first-hand accounts of visits. A number of trends are made evident here, such as a dramatically-growing curiosity about cultures, places and periods that were previously little known, and the enthusiasm for travel as well as for communicating the resulting experiences on the internet.

Writing world histories is not new. It may be useful to distinguish between those, by Reynolds and Bayly, for example, that aim for geographical width, over a relatively limited time-span, and those like John Roberts's, which adds chronological depth and aims for 'total' coverage. To take a period of 134 years is already a mammoth task; Bayly makes a convincing case for this being a genuine historical period, a kind of long nineteenth century. Whatever their remit, world histories are exceptionally challenging to write. They neatly represent contemporary preoccupations with big patterns in human history and with the ways in which the connections between different parts of the world may be understood. There is a certain poignancy in the search for affinities and discernable patterns, in the attempt to find the threads that link disparate peoples, times and cultures together. While they may indeed be revealed by historical analysis, the instability of those links is inescapable.

WEBS OF AFFINITY

Arguably it is the internet that has made the biggest single contribution to the sense that all parts of the world are linked, although it is vital to remember that access to it varies hugely even within a single region, let alone across the globe. It has dramatically transformed the speed with which information in diverse forms can be transmitted, and in this sense it facilitates communication, and thereby fuels a need for it, just as mobile phones have created both enhanced desires and possibilities for conversation. Assessing the impact of the World Wide Web upon the practice of history, however, is difficult and may even be premature.[20]

Nonetheless, since significant amounts of funding and energy are being expended on mobilising information technology in the service of history, both public and academic, some reflection upon its impact is called for. We may chart that impact in three ways: storage, manipulation and visibility. The historical information now available through websites is vast, I would say unimaginable. It is not just the proliferation of specific websites, but the ways in which they are linked and the sophistication of the search engines that act as portals to many sites that is significant. Most people who use computers are familiar with one specific engine, Google, and use the name as a verb to refer to the process of doing internet searches. For historians, it is particularly significant that specialist sites and portals are growing apace, especially in the English-speaking world. At its most basic, a vast amount of material is now stored in an electronic form and may be accessed, sometimes at a cost, by anyone with the necessary equipment and skills. The internet enables a lot of material in all media to be stored electronically and made available to users. This means, for example, that texts, manuscripts, publications and electronically generated materials, that would otherwise be difficult to obtain, can be downloaded relatively easily. While this is handy, even democratising in allowing more people access to sources, by itself it hardly possesses the capacity to change radically the ways in which professional historians work. There is still a strong and quite proper drive on the part of researchers to work with original materials whenever possible. The electronic alternative can only be as good as the quality of the work that goes into preparing, storing and cataloguing the originals. Since it is not always possible to make an informed judgement as to that quality, the user is epistemologically vulnerable. Even the use of electronically stored materials, then, is far from straightforward. It may fuel an uncritical hunger for 'information' as if it were unmediated, and thereby diminish the sense that the core of historical practice is engaged, critical evaluation, whether of sources or of arguments, giving rein to an all too common conception that history is about hoovering up 'facts'. There are dramatic changes around access – that is, in the numbers and kinds of people who can see historical materials in electronic form.

The capacity to manipulate materials electronically is more significant for historical research and is not in itself novel. What the internet permits, in principle, is customised manipulation from any networked computer – the practice, including charging for access to sites, is somewhat more complex. This too depends on preparing and treating the materials in particular ways that may not be evident to users. Even a very simple operation such as keyword searching depends on decisions about which specific terms are to be searchable – and on the quality of the tagging – on the general criteria developed for significance. The more variables there are, the more elaborate the built-in assumptions will be. Some of these issues are evident in the design of websites. The word 'design' here is covering quite distinct phenomena: the look of the thing, the ease of use and the way the invisible structures have been set up – the cognitive skeleton of the database. There is no doubt that the capacity to look at large data sets, to think about aggregates, makes certain kinds of work easier, less back-breaking. Record linkage, where distinct sets of documents are linked up electronically, to enable, for example, a name, whether of a person or a place, in one set to be associated with the same name in other sets, may have far-reaching consequences for historical practice. When it is possible to work with groups, members of an occupation, for example, new, unforeseen patterns may emerge which could not have been detected without information technology. While it remains unclear whether any of the fundamental research approaches have altered, this is an important and exciting part of the discipline to which engaged and critical consideration should be given by all historians.

There are some insidious ways in which the internet revolution bears indirectly on historical scholarship. Earlier in the book I alluded to the anxieties about mastery and completeness that many historians experience. The internet feeds those anxieties in quite unhelpful ways. It encourages fantasies of being able to do truly exhaustive research, of access to 100 per cent of the relevant bibliography, of controlling vast data sets while concealing many of the built-in problems. The most effective remedy – indeed, perhaps the only one – is a wider understanding of information technology itself. Some departments of history offer training in this area, which is quite distinct from the word-processing functions of computers, but many do not. Since these are excellent ways of refining logical reasoning skills, it is to be regretted that, like economic history and demography, history and computing is often seen as a specialist domain dominated by enthusiasts.

The key problem associated with the internet that touches historians, indeed all those who seek material that has a quality tag attached to it, has already been mentioned. Anyone, more or less, can set up a website, and hence it is vital to acquire some information about the processes through which the site has been funded and generated, the nature of the editorial controls in place and the interests it serves. This is not always easy to do, although it should normally be possible to work out who owns a site and whether any particular line is being taken in it. Even 'techies' concede that the authority with which the internet is sometimes endowed is worrying.

I used the term visibility above in order to draw attention to the virtual reality dimension of the internet, an area of particular significance for historians, who are enabled to see, in colour, materials that are rare, inaccessible or should not be handled, to compare versions of the same object, picture or text on screen, which may be impossible to do with the real things. Recent work on the Shahnama, the Persian Book of Kings, written by the poet Firdausi of Tus, exemplifies the point. Scholars will be able to see and compare the hundreds of illustrated manuscripts produced over many centuries and held in private and public repositories across the world.[21] Even so, the image on the monitor and the original are manifestly different phenomena. For example, it is hard to generate a sense of scale or of textures from images on a screen, whereas when confronted by an object we apprehend its dimensions and textures almost without con- sciously reflecting upon them. Again, the internet permits a certain kind of access to vast swathes of the past, which were previously available to very few or that must remain restricted for conservation reasons – some rock art falls into the latter category, for example. Yet this access, this deceptive truth to reality, comes at a cost, which needs to be carefully considered in each case.

Dramatic as these developments have been in terms of the availability of historical materials and opinions, it remains unclear in 2005 precisely how the internet will radically transform, if at all, the nature of historical schol- arship. It can easily be conceded that it already has altered modes of learn- ing and teaching, access to original sources and to information. It also makes usable types of documents that would otherwise be incredibly pains- taking and time-consuming to study in large numbers, such as the records of court proceedings. Yet the value of the end product still depends on someone undertaking the painstaking and time-consuming tasks involved in scanning, preparing and indexing the materials, and on the quality of the editorial input and on researchers asking historically informed questions and then interpreting the results in an equally historically informed manner. Using the internet demands precisely the array of skills and the stance of critical scepticism outlined in chapter 7.

One area where the internet is making an immediate impact is genealogy. In Britain and the United States the passion for tracing family histories has been growing for some time, and has done so exponentially in recent years. If records of births, marriages and deaths, census returns and wills are made more freely available, removing the need for visits to archives, then the floodgates are opened to yet wider participation in what is genuinely amateur history. Such love-inspired research derives from curiosity about origins, family stories and identities, as well as about social and geographi- cal mobility, and manifests itself in diverse ways, including historical fiction.[22] In societies where there exist elaborate public discourses about migration, whether inwards or outwards, popular enthusiasm for historical research that helps provide accounts of when, how and why people move, marry, take up jobs, and so on, is one way in which difficult, complex matters are negotiated. Thus what might seem at first sight to be a history of private life, nurtured by the most intimate of relationships, is in fact closely allied with public history. There is no doubt that the history of migration now has

8.4 This unusual and intriguing example of rock art, an anthropomorph and an abstract image reminiscent of the double helix, comes from Paidahuen, Aconcagua Valley, Chile. Produced by pecking the rock surface with a harder implement, such marks are difficult to interpret; they suggest some of the explanatory challenges archaeologists encounter. The photograph was taken by members of the Rock-Art of Chile Project at the University of Cambridge.

an even higher profile than it did five years ago, that the fallout from zones of conflict, not only in the Middle East but in Eastern Europe, Africa and Asia, has redrawn attention to religious divisions, to the nature of diasporas, to forced migrations, and so on. By these means, amateur history leads naturally into larger social issues. While the study of family migrations may be supported by establishments for just this reason – it permits a relatively safe, personalised exploration of potentially explosive political issues – that does not diminish its value. Indeed it may be that such micro-historical under-standings help to transform wider attitudes.

As migration becomes more contentious politically – it is arguably the most intractable issue in many countries – it comes to the fore historically. These trends, together with the ever more pervasive claims about lessons from history, reinforce the move towards modern and contemporary history, where there is a blending of fields – such as war studies, international rela-tions, area studies and history – and types of discourse – such as historical analysis, political commentary and prophesying. Yet the excitement about and participation in medieval history is healthier than ever (see p. 196, n. 3), and the glamour of archaeology is increasing. What prompts historical curi-osity and how might new technologies play a role in historical trends? People in general, not just scholars, want to know how things came to be, and their motivations are generally a jumble of nosiness, intellectual puzzle-ment, anxiety, fear, anger, desire, ambition, love, hatred, pride, disappoint-ment . . . Curiosity about what appears 'other' remains intense, and can be mobilised by many factors, including time, place, culture or religion. Those interested in distant times sometimes speak of their mystique as a way of explaining why they study them, why they feel a special affinity to them. Undoubtedly the internet has a capacity to nurture users' connections with distant times and places, but it does not do so in isolation.

The technological phenomenon is accompanied by a striking vogue for thinking about networks and for using webs and nets as metaphors: lan-guages of affinity are timely ideas that have immediate resonance.[23] Interest in them is encouraged by 24/7 news, by the exponential growth in the scale of tourism, especially using air travel, as well as by what we can call the recon-structive turn, which is fed by television documentaries, by the many forms of re-enactment and living history that are practised, by anything that pur-ports to show the past as it really was. In a world of virtual realities, of block-buster films that use computer-generated imagery, the lure of reconstruction grows. If the effort required for such reconstruction is heroic, as it arguably is in archaeology, then public interest will be piqued.

Although not directly connected with the internet, talk about lessons from history has grown. A majority of students, when asked to explain their interest in the subject, cites the capacity to learn from the past. Books are now appearing that proclaim the point. In advertising a book about the South Sea Bubble (1720), allegedly 'The first crash', Princeton University Press claims it 'throws light on the current debate about investor rationality by re-examining the story . . . from the standpoint of investors and commen-tators during and preceding the fateful Bubble year . . . [and] shows how investors lost their bearings . . . in much the same way as during the dot.com boom'.[24]

Given how widespread the rhetoric of learning from the past is, it is tempt-ing to say that individuals, groups and governments have proved to be exceptionally poor pupils. Perhaps more attention should be paid to why the past is used so little and highly selectively, why it is deployed so badly in making decisions and in forming opinions. It is arguable that if there were anything to the idea of lessons from history, it might be reasonable to expect wars to have ceased long ago. A counter-argument might be that leaders and states have, using historical evidence, identified the gains to be made and hence have indeed learned their lessons well. Such claims, with stark contemporary resonance, demonstrate the point that lessons from history are profoundly contentious. It might be productive to distinguish between lessons – fires burn and knives cut – and understanding. While it is not easy to transfer precepts from one historical case to another, a sophisticated grasp of the patterns of the past, of the background to the context of contemporary events, could be used to inform intelligent and humane decision-making. In this respect, the role of belief systems and their links with political, social and economic phenomena might be considered an urgent priority. Yet there is actually very little evidence of the most powerful decision-makers genuinely, openly turning to history and allowing themselves to be changed by what they find there. Nor is there tangible evidence, so far as I know, that the study of the past prevents man's inhumanity to man. Thus while historians should rightly be alive to shifts in the world as in their own practices, they need to be equally attentive to continuities.

CONTINUITIES

Some aspects of the practice of history have not changed very much. Routine research tasks, like familiar forms of publishing, remain the centrepiece. Information technology has made conventional historical tasks, such as cataloguing source materials and comparing versions of key texts, easier rather than obviating them. The content and style of much history writing remains relatively unchanged. Despite the refreshed interest in seas,[25] most historians work on traditionally delineated chunks of land – villages, towns, cities, regions and nations. In practical terms it is, after all, easier, and in many cases the zones of the archive and the zone of the study more or less match. But this is hardly the explanation for the continuing appeal of familiar boundaries, which has as much to do with immediacy, identity, language use, pedagogic patterns and the organisation of professional life as with practicality. Each geographical area still gives priority to its own history. There is an obvious immediacy here: the vivacity and prominence of directly perceived issues continue to shape historical practice. The point applies to national as well as to local history writing.

In noting that closeness is a common impetus to the writing of histories, it is necessary to think once again about the impact this has on the knowledge produced. While it may count as an advantage, familiarity with an area also means that aspects of its history are simply taken for granted, not easily held up for critical inspection, for re-evaluation. If an understanding of the past has to be produced painstakingly from the ground up, then working on unfamiliar territory may make that process more rigorous. Yet intimate engagement is a precondition of serious history. Hence there is a growing awareness of the historian's equivalent of going on a dig and doing anthropological fieldwork.[26] Sometimes this occurs through the process of learning another language, spending time in the area and undertaking interviews. Citizens undertaking the history of their own nation would rarely think that such conscious familiarisation was required. Yet just as anthropologists have engaged in deliberate *de*familiarisation when working on their own cultures, historians might do the same.

A particularly significant continuity of historical practice concerns the nation state, which, like empires, remains a favoured unit of analysis. Rulers and governments tend to insist, using all the means at their disposal, on the significant contours of national history and on the moral values to be associated with it – the significant moments of triumph and disaster, the victors and the demons. There is a commonsensical appeal in telling the story of a nation, precisely as nations themselves are proliferating and taken as the paradigmatic unit of government. The concept 'nation' is certainly not taken for granted by historians. There was already considerable interest in nations, nationalism and nationhood over the 1980s and 1990s. In the early twenty-first century these issues retain their urgency. The contemporary political order takes nations as the most significant political entities; the United Nations, however ineffectual or marginal it sometimes appears, remains central in world news, and its name, as well as the ways in which events are reported, keeps the concept of the nation to the fore. Developments in Eastern Europe and the Middle East, as in Africa and elsewhere, serve as constant reminders of the fragility of nations and the arbitrariness of borders, yet the ideal of a clearly delineated country, with its own history, remains strong. Partly this is about the use of names, and possibly the spread of tourism, an industry which, like businesses that operate in a number of geographical areas, reinforces an awareness of the wealth of nations.

FINAL WORDS

Simply the advent of the year 2000, marking simultaneously the end of a millennium and a century, has shaped historical practice.[27] All such dates are arbitrary, but their imaginative grip is not lessened by that token. It now seems attractive to look back, not just at the twentieth century, but on a thousand years of history, to take a millennium as a time period.[28] There is an appealing grandeur in taking such a panoramic view. In principle this was always possible, it just did not seem so apt before the year 2000. Such transitions also elicit anxieties about the future, which endow big-picture histories with an added significance. If this millennialism is an imaginative and symbolic phenomenon, it is also a commercial one. The marketing of history is helping to underwrite ambitious thinking, bold attempts at pattern recognition, history writing on a grand scale. The results need to be subjected to critical scrutiny, and it is arguable that some of these enterprises primarily repackage familiar ideas rather than generating new ones. The persistence of a type of superstar history, which privileges political leaders – monarchs, dictators, charismatic leaders or just exceptionally powerful people – is

193

striking. Nonetheless, there does seem to be more enthusiasm for *longue durée* history of all kinds. Partly this builds on books that are written, published and marketed for broad audiences that take big topics, whether in terms of subject matter, place, period or personality. But there is a wider trend at all levels of history publishing.

This trend was already evident in the 1990s when Paul Kennedy published *Preparing for the Twenty-First Century*, a self-conscious attempt at both 'large history' and at generating an account not dominated by world politics and great powers, but by demography, technology, education and the environment. Understood as a world history, a genre discussed already, the title of this work is significant. It subtly suggests the idea of lessons from history – preparing for the future entails comprehending the past – while giving historical analysis the glamour of being associated with the unknown frontier, what is yet to come. In the last chapter Kennedy speaks directly about the future and in quite prescriptive ways, contrasting those nations that seem relatively 'well-positioned' for the twenty-first century, including Japan, Korea, Germany and Switzerland, with those that are not, which include the USA and the UK.[29]

Other forms of *longue durée* history are in the public eye. Again, these draw on trends that were already evident before 2000, but have become more prominent subsequently. Stories built around monarchies remain popular in many countries. The less conventional example of commodity history is useful here. A single item, such as sugar, tobacco or nutmeg, provides a neat way into patterns of producing, trading, consuming, representing and experiencing commodities – topics that exercise particular fascination at the moment.[30] The historical method can be used of any object that is at all popular, valued or noteworthy, but probably works best when it is either alluring or topical. Mark Kurlansky won a best food book award for the beautifully designed *Cod: A Biography of the Fish that Changed the World*. Kurlansky provides recipes as well as narrative, hence *Cod* taps into and elegantly blends a number of current preoccupations. It weaves together oral, written and visual sources; it speaks to environmental history and, more specifically, it examines an important aspect of the Atlantic's past. Since it charts interconnected declines – of the fish itself as of the communities dependent upon it – caused by human action, there is indeed a lesson from history here. 'It is harder to kill off fish than mammals. But after 1000 years of hunting the Atlantic cod, we know that it can be done' are Kurlansky's sombre closing words.[31]

Longue durée approaches are evident in other types of historical writing. Take David Moon's student textbook on *The Abolition of Serfdom in Russia*, for example, which covers the period 1762 to 1907 – the law in question was enacted in 1861. For many students, pieces of legislation constitute excellent examples of clear-cut events, with antecedent causes and subsequent consequences, certainly, but in both cases quite immediate. The recasting of events in terms of multiple overlapping but distinct historical processes that occur over long swathes of time is valuable. There are many areas of history where such an approach has long been practised, such as the history of population and of the environment.[32]

The trends I have sketched in suggest that, as a field, history is not only flourishing, but diversifying into new areas and market niches. Accordingly, public history is becoming more and more important, not just as a phenomenon in its own right, but as an aspect of historical practice to which all professional historians need to pay critical attention. Ways still need to be found of bringing historians who practise in quite different settings closer together. Part of this burgeoning of history is the striking rise in publications about history as a discipline. How is this to be explained? It is just as plausible to suppose that it marks a new prominence of and interest in a confident field as it is to wonder whether it indicates continuing anxieties about the status of historical knowledge and the claims that historians make. No doubt it confirms the marketability of history, which should act as a spur to historians of all kinds to continue to think, feel and write about the past in a self-aware and intellectually robust manner. It would be a shame, however, if reading about the discipline displaced the doing of history. Naturally the two are, ideally, complementary. So much already hangs on accounts of the past, and I have argued that intellectually sophisticated histories should play a far greater role in public life. Entertaining though they may be, blockbuster films and books that retell familiar stories are not what I have in mind. The alternatives, which include finding new slants, delineating fresh topics and bringing unusual sources to the fore, may be of many different kinds. The discipline will indeed thrive from openness and diversity, and also from a combination of honest toil, analytical self-awareness and excellent writing. Marrying established scholarly values with passionate engagement and reflexivity must continue to be history's destiny.

NOTES

Introduction

1 F. Bédarida (ed.), *The Social Responsibility of the Historian*, Providence, RI, 1994; and chapter 8.

2 The popularity of exhibitions and museum displays, like fiction and films on ancient Egypt and its archaeology, are well known. Cf. B. Waterson, *Ancient Egypt*, Stroud, 1998, part of the series Sutton Pocket Histories.

3 *The Medieval Historian*, which claimed to be the first magazine dedicated to the medieval era, was published monthly until February 2005. The contours of this particular trend, then, remain unclear.

4 A good example is Bryce Lyon's 1997 historiographical essay, 'Henri Pirenne's *Réflexions d'un Solitaire* and his re-evaluation of history', *Journal of Medieval History* 23: 285–99, which examines Pirenne's changing attitudes towards German historiography in the light of his experiences during the First World War. Such insights into how history is written are a fundamental part of the discipline. Cf. M. Berg, *A Woman in History: Eileen Power 1889–1940*, Cambridge, 1996.

5 For this reason I accord special significance to successful global histories; see chapter 8, pp. 185–6.

6 See the multi-volume *Science and Civilisation in China*, Cambridge, 1954 onwards, which Joseph Needham initiated.

7 M. Bentley, *Companion to Historiography*, London, 1997, chs 24–27 and 29 on historiographical traditions outside Europe and North America.

8 See chapter 8, p. 194.

Chapter 1

1 *Subaltern Studies* was the name of a series of books produced from 1982 in India. They promoted, from a radical and theoretical perspective, a form of people's history that addressed power relations from the point of view of the colonised. The determination to use the past for fresh purposes has been widespread: see, for example, the introduction to the magazine *Amistad* (1970), which attacks the '"intellectual" racism' of, among other things, the teaching of American history. It published material suitable for use on black studies courses. D. Chakrabarty, *Habitations of Modernity: Essays in the Wake of Subaltern Studies*, Chicago and London, 2002. Cf. F. Krantz (ed.), *History from Below*, Oxford, 1988.

2 Dates after journals indicate the year in which the first part appeared.

3 See, for example, J.W. Chambers and D. Culbert (eds), *World War II, Film and History*, New York, 1996.

4 I. Clendinnen, *Reading the Holocaust*, Cambridge, 1999, is a moving example of a historian who is not Jewish discussing responses to this 'unthinkable' phenomenon.

5 'One of the longest-running and most intractable issues in British politics [which] revolved around land, religion and the political conflicts from these': J. Gardiner and N. Wenborn (eds), *The History Today Companion to British History*, London, 1995, p. 423. The phrase, 'the Irish question' was commonly used in the nineteenth century: see, for example, Karl Marx and Friedrich Engels, *Ireland and the Irish Question*, London, 1971, a collection of their writings over several decades; and Joseph Chamberlain, *Home Rule and the Irish Question: A Collection of Speeches Delivered between 1881 and 1887*, London, 1887.

6 M. Ruthven, *Islam: A Very Short Introduction*, Oxford, 1997, pp. 107–11, explains 'sartorial politics'.

7 It is important to remember that the names used for these areas can be misleading, not just by virtue of their inaccuracy – evident, for example, in the way 'Russia' and 'America' are commonly used – but also because of the way in which they lump diverse societies together, as is the case with 'Africa' and African studies.

8 S. Smith, *Like Cattle and Horses: Nationalism and Labor in Shanghai, 1895–1927*, Durham, NC and London, 2002; see the introduction for a lucid discussion of many important historiographical issues.

9 I have taken these examples from the Department of History, King's College London.

10 Cambridge University Press has a number of series in its history lists which nicely illustrate the points I have been making.

11 J. Thompson, *Books in the Digital Age: The Transformation of Academic and Higher Education Publishing in Britain and the United States*, Cambridge, 2005.

12 H. Matthew and B. Harrison (eds), *Oxford Dictionary of National Biography: in association with the British Academy; from the earliest times to the year 2000*, 60 vols, Oxford, 2004.

13 J. Mokyr (ed.), *The Oxford Encyclopedia of Economic History*, New York and Oxford, 5 vols, 2003; the 'Topical outline of articles', which provides an overview of the way in which economic history has been conceptualised for this enterprise, is particularly valuable, vol. 1, xxix–xxxix.

14 Particularly relevant here is the *Companion to Historiography*, a collection of 39 essays edited by Michael Bentley and published in 1997. Routledge has published many companions, including those on the history of science and the history of medicine. See also C. Kleinhenz (ed.), *Medieval Italy: An Encyclopedia*, New York and London, 2004.

15 V. Berghahn and H. Schissler (eds), *Perceptions of History: International Textbook Research on Britain, Germany and the United States*, Oxford, 1987.

16 For example, Paul Johnson's *The Birth of the Modern: World Society 1815–1830*, London, 1991, is definitely a survey, despite its narrow time-span, and it is also polemical. It can easily be used in teaching, but is certainly not a textbook.

17 The *Journal of Interdisciplinary History* was founded in the United States in 1970.

18 For example, *Social History* 23 (1998), 325–30 for a heated exchange prompted by a conference report. The *American Historical Review* encourages debate through thematic fora, e.g. special issue entitled 'Forum: Histories and Historical Fictions', 103, no. 5 (1998).

19 H. Klein, *A Concise History of Bolivia*, Cambridge, 2003.

20 The notion of a 'heritage industry' is associated with Robert Hewison's highly polemical 1987 book of that name. Like many commentators, he perceives close connections between museums, the practice of history and contemporary culture. Cf. R. Samuel, *Theatres of Memory*, 2 vols, London, 1994 and 1998.

Chapter 2

1 We can illustrate the point by trying to imagine what a short dictionary would be like that was called simply *A Dictionary of History*, in the manner of a dictionary of chemistry or of sociology: for example, J. Daintith (ed.), *The Oxford Dictionary of Chemistry*, 5th edn, Oxford, 2004; N. Abercrombie et al., *The Penguin Dictionary of Sociology*, 4th edn, London, 2000.

2 Cf. M. Fulbrook, *Historical Theory*, London and New York, 2002, which 'is about the ways in which all historical writing is inevitably theoretical', p. ix.

3 C. Bayly, *Origins of Nationality in South Asia: Patriotism and Ethical Government in the Making of Modern India*, New Delhi, 1998, in both the preface and the epilogue, is exceptionally insightful on historians and the explanation of change.

4 Anne Frank, who was from a Dutch Jewish family, kept a diary between 12 June 1942 and 1 August 1944, when she and her family were discovered by the Nazis. Only her father survived the war. See D. Barnouw and G. van der Stroom (eds), *The Diary of Anne Frank. The Critical Edition*, New York, 1989. The foreword mentions the controversies surrounding the diary, esp. pp. ix–x; H. Enzer and S. Solotaroff-Enzer (eds), *Anne Frank: Reflections on her Life and Legacy*, Urbana, IL, 2000.

5 J.C. Holt, *Magna Carta*, 2nd edn, Cambridge, 1992, is both a primary source, in that it contains medieval texts, and a secondary source, in that it contains historical arguments and editorial comments related to them.

6 Some chronicles, such as that by Jocelin of Brakelond (1173–1202), are more personal. This case illustrates some of the complexities of sources; the only complete manuscript dates from the mid- to late thirteenth century. Recent editions, i.e. those used by most students, are translations, divided into chapters 'in order to facilitate its use by modern readers'. These are highly mediated texts: Jocelin of Brakelond, *Chronicle of the Abbey of Bury St Edmunds*, translated with an introduction and notes by D. Greenway and J. Sayers, Oxford, 1989, p. xxiv.

7 Cf. C. Jones, *E.H. Carr and International Relations. A Duty to Lie*, Cambridge, 1998.

8 R. Porter, *Edward Gibbon: Making History*, London, 1988.

9 There has been a decline in (primary) source-based undergraduate teaching, which is where these issues are best broached. However, these skills are emphasised in areas of history, such as ancient and medieval history, where the sources, being scarcer, are treated with notable care and sophistication. This approach could be routinely applied to secondary sources too.

10 I have had a go at this issue in *Nature Displayed*, London, 1999, ch. 1, using a rather different vocabulary.

11 For example, P. Finney (ed.), *Palgrave Advances in International History*, Houndmills, Basingstoke and New York, 2005.

12 New York, 1975. Cf. his *Wartime: Understanding and Behaviour in the Second World War*, New York, 1989.

13 P. Barker, *Regeneration, The Eye in the Door* and *The Ghost Road*, London, 1991, 1993 and 1995; examples of what could be called the 'new military history' may be found in *War in History* (1994). On the distinctiveness of medieval warfare, see P. Contamine, *War in the Middle Ages*, Oxford, 1984. On another whole type of war, see R. Asprey, *War in the Shadows: The Classic History of Guerrilla Warfare from Ancient Persia to the Present*, revised edn, London, 1994. On the stakes in how war is written about, see J. Keegan, *The Battle for History. Refighting World War Two*, London, 1995.

14 Concepts, such as community and tradition, that we might consider in this context, carry their own histories and baggage. Historians use them in diverse ways and for a variety of purposes; sometimes, given the emotional connotations of both community and tradition, these are quite manipulative. Cf. E. Hobsbawm and T. Ranger (eds), *The Invention of Tradition*, Cambridge, 1983. Always indispensable in these matters is R. Williams, *Keywords*, London, 1983. Cf. T. Bennett et al. (eds), *New Keywords. A Revised Vocabulary of Culture and Society*, Malden, MA, Oxford and Carlton, Victoria, Australia, 2005, which includes 'community' but not 'tradition'.

15 Williams, *Keywords*, pp. 291–5. His discussion applies to the English term 'society';

it goes without saying that the connotations of such significant words are language-specific. Cf. Bennet et al. (eds), *New Keywords*, pp. 326–9, on 'society'.

16 Among the main journals in the field are: *International Review of Social History* (1956), *Journal of Social History* (1967), *Histoire Sociale–Social History* (1968) and *Social History* (1976).

17 *History Workshop Journal* was originally subtitled 'a journal of socialist historians'. On British traditions of social history, see A. Wilson (ed.), *Rethinking Social History: English Society 1570–1920 and its Interpretation*, Manchester, 1993.

18 The famous journal *Annales: Economies, Sociétés, Civilisations*, changed its name at the end of 1993 to *Annales: Histoire, Sciences Sociales*. P. Burke, *The French Historical Revolution: The Annales School*, Cambridge, 1990.

19 F. Braudel, *The Mediterranean and the Mediterranean World in the Age of Philip II*, 2 vols, London, 1972 and 1973, first published 1949. Cf. P. Horden and N. Purcell, *The Corrupting Sea. A Study of Mediterranean History*, Oxford, 2000; *Mediterranean Historical Review* (1986); *Mediterranean Archaeology* (1988); and *Mediterranean Studies* (1992). An excellent discussion of the question of focus is B. Gregory, '*Is Small Beautiful? Microhistory and the History of Everyday Life*', *History and Theory* 38 (1999), 100–10.

20 These traits are also evident in Braudel's three-volume *Civilization and Capitalism 15th–18th Century*, London, 1981, 1982 and 1984.

21 It may be helpful to think about micro-history in this context, which takes limited geographical areas in order to study as many aspects of them as possible. P. Burke (ed.), *New Perspectives on Historical Writing*, Cambridge, 1991, ch. 5; E. Muir and G. Ruggiero (eds), *Microhistory and the Lost Peoples of Europe*, Baltimore, 1991.

22 L. Stone, 'The Revival of Narrative: Reflections on a New Old History', *Past and Present* 85 (1979), 1–24.

23 S. Schama, *The Embarrassment of Riches: An Interpretation of Dutch Culture in the Golden Age*, London, 1987; *Citizens: A Chronicle of the French Revolution*, London, 1989; *Landscape and Memory*, London, 1995; *A History of Britain*, 3 vols, London, 2000–2. For different kinds of (*longue durée*) narrative, see R. Fletcher, *The Conversion of Europe: From Paganism to Christianity AD 371–1386*, London, 1997; R. Porter, *The Greatest Benefit to Mankind: A Medical History of Humanity from Antiquity to the Present*, London, 1997.

24 S. Baron and C. Pletsch (eds), *Introspection in Biography: The Biographer's Quest for Self-Awareness*, Hillsdale, NJ, 1985.

25 It is no coincidence that the history of science – a field in which the relationships between life and work are highly contested – should have produced some outstanding, and controversial, biographies: R. Westfall, *Never at Rest. A Biography of Isaac Newton*, Cambridge, 1980; G. Cantor, *Michael Faraday: Sandemanian and Scientist. A Study of Science and Religion in the Nineteenth Century*, Basingstoke, 1991; A. Desmond and J. Moore, *Darwin*, London, 1991; E.J. Browne, *Charles Darwin: A Biography*, vol. 1, *Voyaging*, New York, 1995, vol. 2, *The Power of Place*, London, 2002. See also M. Shortland and R. Yeo (eds), *Telling Lives in Science: Essays on Scientific Biography*, Cambridge, 1996.

26 A. Funder, *Stasiland. Stories From Behind the Berlin Wall*, London, 2003, p. 147.

27 R. Chartier, *Cultural History*, Cambridge, 1988; L. Hunt (ed.), *The New Cultural History*, Berkeley, CA, 1989, 'Review Essays: Beyond the Cultural Turn', *American Historical Review* 109 (2002), 1475–520.

28 J. Rendall, *The Origins of Modern Feminism: Women in Britain, France and the United States 1780–1860*, London, 1985.

29 Relevant interdisciplinary journals include *Signs. Journal of Women in Culture and Society* (1975) and *Women. A Cultural Review* (1990). Those with broader remits, such as *Gender and History* (1989), publish a great deal on women. See also the *Journal of Women's History* (1989) and *Women's History Review* (1992).

30 See, for example, P. Ariès, *Centuries of Childhood*, Harmondsworth, 1973; G. Scarre (ed.), *Children, Parents and Politics*, Cambridge, 1989; C. Steedman, *Strange Dislocations. Childhood and the Idea of Human Interiority 1780–1930*, London, 1995.

31 The museum is part of the Centre d'Histoire de la Résistance et de la Déportation; a catalogue of their permanent exhibition, edited by S. Zeitoun and D. Foucher, was published in 1997. For an English summary of the Centre, see http://www.lyon.fr/vdl/sections/en/culture/musees/centre_histoire_resistance_1/ (accessed 31 August 2005).

32 C. Phythian-Adams, *Re-thinking English Local History*, Leicester, 1987, puts local history in a broad intellectual context and considers local/national relationships. Cf. A. Wood, *The Politics of Social Conflict: The Peak Country, 1520–1770*, Cambridge, 1999.

33 An interesting example is the role of Francis Bacon as Chancellor during the reign of James I. Recent accounts stress the aggressive state-building they engaged in: J. Martin, *Francis Bacon, the State, and the Reform of Natural Philosophy*, Cambridge, 1992.

34 This issue is elegantly addressed by John Iliffe in *Africans: The History of a Continent*, Cambridge, 1995. 'Europe' is equally problematic, as the editorial makes clear in the first issue of the *Journal of Modern European History* (2003), p. 6.

35 This is precisely what the recent wave of work in environmental history has been doing; see, for example, A. Crosby, *Ecological Imperialism. The Biological Expansion of Europe, 900–1900*, Cambridge, 1986; W. Beinart and P. Coates, *Environment and History. The Taming of Nature in the USA and South Africa*, London, 1995; D. Worster, *Rivers of Empire: Water, Aridity, and the Growth of the American West*, 2nd edn, New York, 1992.

36 D. Sabean, *Power in the Blood: Popular Culture and Village Discourse in Early Modern Germany*, Cambridge, 1984, is based on 15 years of 'piecing together all of the material I could find on the village of Neckarhausen', p. ix, before broadening out to regional and state archives; cf. L. Roper, *The Holy Household: Women and Morals in Reformation Augsburg*, Oxford, 1989; A. Rowlands, *Witchcraft Narratives in Germany: Rothenburg, 1561–1652*, Manchester, 2003.

37 R. Floud, *An Introduction to Quantitative Methods for Historians*, 2nd edn London, 1979, introduction, sets out a strong case; C. Tilly, *As Sociology Meets History*, New York, 1981, ch. 2.

38 Distinguished work on demography includes L. Henry, *On the Measurement of Human Fertility*, Amsterdam, 1972, and *Population: Analysis and Models*, London, 1976; P. Laslett, *The World We Have Lost*, London, 1965; E. Wrigley and R. Schofield, *The Population History of England 1541–1871: A Reconstruction*, Cambridge, new ed., 1989. Cf. E. Wrigley et al., *English Population History from Family Reconstitution, 1580–1837*, Cambridge, 1997.

39 One of the most contentious uses of quantitative techniques has been in relation to American slavery. A recent assessment is M. Smith, *Debating Slavery: Economy and Society in the Antebellum American South*, Cambridge, 1998. Cf. J. Walvin, *Questioning Slavery*, London, 1996.

40 R. Schofield, 'Did the Mothers Really Die? Three Centuries of Maternal Mortality

in "The World We Have Lost"', in L. Bonfield et al. (eds), *The World We Have Gained: Histories of Population and Social Structure*, Oxford, 1986, pp. 231–60.

41 W. Ashley, 'The Place of Economic History in University Studies', *Economic History Review* 1 (1927), 1–11, at 1. For a poignant assessment of the state of economic history, which, although it concerns Great Britain, raises broad historiographical issues, see D. Coleman, *History and the Economic Past. An Account of the Rise and Decline of Economic History in Britain*, Oxford, 1987.

42 For example, Sheilagh Ogilvie; see her 'Guilds, efficiency, and social capital: evidence from German proto-industry', *Economic History Review* 57 (2004), 286–333.

43 P. Thompson, *The Voice of the Past: Oral History*, Oxford, 2000, first published 1978. See also *Oral History* (1972); R. Perks and A. Thomson (eds), *The Oral History Reader*, London, 1997; L. Passerini (ed.), *Memory and Totalitarianism*, Oxford, 1992, contains work by scholars from many countries (it was the first *International Yearbook of Oral History and Life Stories*); L. Passerini, *Fascism in Popular Memory. The Cultural Experience of the Turin Working Class*, Cambridge, 1987.

44 See, for instance, the *Journal of the History of Ideas* (1940) and *History of European Ideas* (1985).

45 Cf. A. Lovejoy, *Essays in the History of Ideas*, New York, 1960 (which contains a complete list of Lovejoy's publications), and *The Great Chain of Being: A Study in the History of an Idea*, Cambridge, MA, 1936.

46 D. Lowenthal, *The Past Is a Foreign Country*, Cambridge, 1985, and *The Heritage Crusade and the Spoils of History*, London, 1997; P. Mandler, *History and National Life*, London, 2002.

47 See, for example, H. Ritvo, *The Animal Estate: The English and Other Creatures in the Victorian Age*, Cambridge, MA, 1987, and *The Platypus and the Mermaid and Other Fragments of the Classifying Imagination*, Cambridge, MA, 1998.

48 M. Jenner, 'The Great Dog Massacre', in W.G. Naphy and P. Roberts (eds), *Fear in Early Modern Society*, Manchester, 1997, pp. 44–61.

49 Of course, there are exceptions, Arnold Toynbee being one, but in most countries his work is all but ignored.

50 See *Comparative Studies in Society and History* (1958). A particularly thoughtful and lucid discussion of comparative history may be found in G.M. Frederickson, *The Comparative Imagination: On the History of Racism, Nationalism, and Social Movements*, Berkeley, CA, 1997. See also Forum: Comparative Historiography: Problems and Perspectives, in *History and Theory* 38 (1999), no. 1.

51 Cf. G. Stedman Jones, introduction to K. Marx and F. Engels, *The Communist Manifesto*, London, 2002, pp. 1–184.

52 It is vital to distinguish between the diverse and pragmatic uses of psychoanalytic theories, which are somewhat more acceptable to the majority of historians, and psychohistory, a formalised field, practitioners of which are committed to psychoanalysis as their principal explanatory device. Even within psychohistory there are huge variations in approach. See, for example, E. Erikson, *Young Man Luther. A Study in Psychoanalysis and History*, London, 1959, and *Gandhi's Truth. On the Origins of Militant Nonviolence*, London 1970; P. Lowenberg, *Fantasy and Reality in History*, New York, 1995, and *Decoding the Past: The Psychohistorical Approach*, New York, 1983.

53 D. Stannard, *Shrinking History: On Freud and the Failure of Psychohistory*, New York, 1980; *The Psychohistory Review. Studies of Motivation in History and Culture* (1972); *The Journal of Psychohistory. A Publication of the Institute for Psychohistory* (1976), which was founded in 1973 as the *History of Childhood Quarterly*; for an exceptionally creative

use of psychoanalytic ideas in history, see L. Roper, *Oedipus and the Devil: Witchcraft, Sexuality and Religion in Early Modern Europe*, London, 1994; W. Runyan (ed.), *Psychology and Historical Interpretation*, New York, 1988.

54 F. Manuel's biographical study of Sir Isaac Newton prompted particular fury: *A Portrait of Isaac Newton*, Cambridge, MA, 1968; the preface and introduction discuss methodological issues.

55 *History Workshop Journal* has been notably receptive to psychoanalysis: for example, the special issues 26 in 1988 and 45 in 1998.

56 The best discussion of these points remains P. Gay, *Freud for Historians*, New York, 1985. Psychohistorical accounts that engage with leadership include C.B. Strozier and D. Offer (eds), *The Leader. Psychohistorical Essays*, New York, 1985; B. Mazlish, *The Leader, the Led and the Psyche. Essays in Psychohistory*, Hanover, 1990; and the books by Peter Lowenberg cited in footnote 52.

Chapter 3

1 Pliny the Elder lived between *c.* AD 23 and 79; he studied grammar, philosophy and rhetoric as well as nature.

2 On the writing of history, see M. Bentley (ed.), *Companion to Historiography*, London, 1997. Cf. M. Finley, *Ancient History. Evidence and Models*, London, 1985.

3 With the exception of David Ramsay, the historian of the American Revolution, all these figures are mentioned in J. Black and R. Porter (eds), *The Penguin Dictionary of Eighteenth-Century History*, London, 1994. On Ramsay, see A. Shaffer, *To Be an American. David Ramsay and the Making of the American Consciousness*, Columbia, SC, 1991. See also M. Phillips, *Society and Sentiment: Genres of Historical Writing in Britain, 1740–1820*, Princeton, NJ, 2000.

4 C. Tomalin, *Samuel Pepys: The Unequalled Self*, London, 2002; A. Fraser, *King Arthur and the Knights of the Round Table*, London, 1970; M. Holroyd, *Augustus John*, London, 1996; B. Tuchman, *A Distant Mirror: The Calamitous 14th Century*, London, 1979.

5 Cf. *History and Theory: Studies in the Philosophy of History* (1961). Also relevant is B. Fay et al. (eds), *History and Theory: Contemporary Readings*, Malden, MA, 1998.

6 C.E. Black, *The Dynamics of Modernization. A Study in Comparative History*, New York, 1966; B. Dmystryshyn (ed.), *Modernization of Russia under Peter I and Catherine II*, New York, 1974; C. Calhoun (ed.), *Habermas and the Public Sphere*, Cambridge, MA and London, 1992.

7 Cf. P. Kennedy, *Preparing for the Twenty-First Century*, London, 1993.

8 On comparative approaches to revolution, see T. Skocpol, *States and Social Revolutions: A Comparative Analysis of France, Russia and China*, Cambridge, 1979; and on the Mexican case, A. Knight, *The Mexican Revolution*, 2 vols, Cambridge, 1986.

9 A particularly interesting example is S. Allen, *Finding the Walls of Troy: Frank Calvert and Heinrich Schliemann at Hisarlik*, Berkeley, CA, Los Angeles, CA and London, 1999; the author's doctorate was on Late Bronze Age pottery at the site.

10 See the splendid chapter by Guy Halsall in Bentley (ed.), *Companion to Historiography*, pp. 805–27. Note that this section of the book is called 'Hinterlands', a term dense with assumptions about the relationships between history and other disciplines. Also D.P. Dymond, *Archaeology and History: A Plea for Reconciliation*, London, 1974; S. Tarlow and S. West (eds), *The Familiar Past? Archaeologies of Later Historical Britain*, London, 1999; P. Courbin, *What is Archaeology? An Essay on the Nature of Archaeological Research*, Chicago, 1988, esp. ch.

11; and, for a standard textbook, C. Renfrew and P. Bahn, *Archaeology, Theory, Methods and Practice*, 3rd edn, London, 2000.

11 R. Butlin, *Historical Geography. Through the Gates of Space and Time*, London, 1993; L. Guelke, *Historical Understanding in Geography. An Idealist Approach*, Cambridge, 1982; M. Bell et al. (eds), *Geography and Imperialism 1820–1920*, Manchester, 1995.

12 See Peter Burke's volume, which, when first published was called *Sociology and History*, London, 1980, becoming *History and Social Theory*, Ithaca, NY, 1993. In the preface to the latter he explains his thinking about 'sociology', 'social sciences' and 'social theory', pp. vii–ix. Also, C. Tilly, *As Sociology Meets History*, New York, 1981.

13 The history of sociology may be helpful here: see, for example, G. Hawthorn, *Enlightenment and Despair: A History of Sociology*, Cambridge, 1976. Cf. S. Bruce, *Sociology: A Very Short Introduction*, Oxford, 1999. See also *American Journal of Sociology* (1894), *British Journal of Sociology* (1950) and, for a journal that examines these issues from a critical perspective, *History of the Human Sciences* (1988). See also *Social Science History: The Official Journal of the Social Science History Association* (1976).

14 See A. Smith, *The Concept of Social Change: A Critique of the Functionalist Theory of Social Change*, London, 1973.

15 It is significant that an outstanding intellectual biography of Spencer was written by a practising sociologist: J. Peel, *Herbert Spencer: The Evolution of a Sociologist*, London, 1971.

16 P. Corfield (ed.), *Language, History and Class*, Oxford, 1991; R. Williams, *Keywords*, pp. 60–9; P. Joyce (ed.), *Class*, Oxford, 1995; Bennett et al. (eds), *New Keywords*, pp. 39–42.

17 E. Genovese, *The Political Economy of Slavery*, New York, 1965; Genovese has written many other important works on slavery: for a brief assessment, see Smith, *Debating Slavery*, esp. pp. 16–23. See also M. Finley, *Ancient Slavery and Modern Ideology*, expanded edn, Princeton, NJ, 1998.

18 See Rigby's essay on 'Marxist Historiography', in Bentley (ed.), *Companion to Historiography*, pp. 889–928.

19 On history and anthropology, see ch. 31 by J. Goodman, in Bentley (ed.), *Companion to Historiography*. Cf. D. Gaunt, *Memoir on History and Anthropology*, Stockholm, 1982, which surveys the relationships between history and anthropology in many countries. It should be stressed that anthropology has a number of branches, not all of which are concerned with culture. Historians have been most responsive to social and cultural anthropology.

20 For example, the classic article by E.P. Thompson, 'Eighteenth-Century English Society: Class Struggle without Class?', *Social History* 3 (1978), 133–65.

21 For example, E.P. Thompson, *Customs in Common*, London, 1993, pp. 10–11. Cf. R. Williams, *Marxism and Literature*, Oxford, 1977.

22 A. Giddens, *The Third Way. The Renewal of Social Democracy*, Cambridge, 1998; A. Giddens and C. Pierson, *Conversations with Anthony Giddens. Making Sense of Modernity*, Stanford, CA, 1998; M. Mann, *Incoherent Empire*, London and New York, 2003, where Mann calls himself in the preface 'a historical sociologist (who works) on the nature of power in human societies'; D. Held, *Democracy and the Global Social Order*, Stanford, CA, 1995.

23 E.P. Thompson, *The Making of the English Working Class*, Harmondsworth, 1968, p. 11. Cf. Joyce (ed.), *Class*.

24 R. Smith, *Fontana History of the Human Sciences*, London, 1997; C. Fox et al. (eds), *Inventing Human Science: Eighteenth-Century Domains*, Berkeley, CA, 1995. See also G. Stocking, *The Ethnographer's Magic and Other Essays in the History of Anthropology*, Madison, WI, 1992; K. Sloan (ed.), *Enlightenment: Discovering the World in the Eighteenth Century*, London, 2003; M. Caygill et al. (eds), *Enlightening the British: Knowledge, Discovery and the Museum in the Eighteenth Century*, London, 2004.

25 For example, P. Garnsey, *Food and Society in Classical Antiquity*, Cambridge, 1999.

26 One of the best-known historical pieces in which the influence of anthropology is visible is N. Davis, 'Women on top', in her *Society and Culture in Early Modern France*, Stanford, CA, 1975, pp. 124–51. Cf. L. Hunt (ed.), *The New Cultural History*, Berkeley, CA, 1989, ch. 2.

27 Keith Thomas's *Religion and the Decline of Magic: Studies in Popular Beliefs in Sixteenth- and Seventeenth-Century England*, Harmondsworth, 1973, is often taken as exemplary of this trend – it was first published in 1971. For a recent approach to magic, see L. Kassell, *Medicine and Magic in Elizabethan London. Simon Forman: Astrologer, Alchemist, & Physician*, Oxford, 2005.

28 Marcel Mauss's *The Gift*, London 1990, is an anthropological classic. First published in 1925, it continues to offer inspiration to historians. N. Davis, *The Gift in Sixteenth-Century France*, Oxford, 2000.

29 A splendid example of these points is Clifford Geertz's famous article on Balinese cockfights, which appeared in his *The Interpretation of Cultures*, New York, 1973, and which has wielded extraordinary influence over historians. Geertz is particularly associated with the notion of 'thick description' – detailed accounts of behaviour that serve as a starting point for deeper understanding. What we could call historians' infatuation with Geertz illustrates the influence of anthropological method and of its general mindset. See also Hunt (ed.), *The New Cultural History*, ch. 3.

30 See, for example, R. Williams, *Culture*, London, 1981; J. Bremmer and H. Roodenburg (eds), *A Cultural History of Gesture*, Cambridge, 1991; C. Ginzburg, *The Cheese and the Worms: the Cosmos of a Sixteenth-Century Miller*, Baltimore, 1980.

31 For a different approach, see K. Scott, *The Rococo Interior: Decoration and Social Spaces in Early Eighteenth-Century Paris*, New Haven, CT, 1995.

32 This can be seen in terms of the growing interest in a history of everyday life, which was already more valued in countries with a tradition of studying the history of folklore. Two examples that suggest the impact of anthropology on history are clothing and popular healing: D. Roche, *The Culture of Clothing: Dress and Fashion in the 'Ancien Régime'*, Cambridge, 1994; D. Gentilcore, *Healers and Healing in Early Modern Italy*, Manchester, 1998.

33 The work of Marilyn Strathern, who both draws upon and influences historians, is worth noting; see, for example, *Commons and Borderlands: Working Papers on Interdisciplinarity, Accountability and the Flow of Knowledge*, Wantage, 2004.

34 The term orientalism is primarily associated with the literary critic Edward Said, whose book of that name appeared in 1978. Although hugely fêted, the work is not without its critics: J. MacKenzie, *Orientalism: History, Theory and the Arts*, Manchester, 1995; B. Turner, *Orientalism, Postmodernism and Globalism*, London, 1994; E. Sivan, *Interpretations of Islam: Past and Present*, Princeton, NJ, 1985, ch. 5.

35 S. Shapin, *The Scientific Revolution*, Chicago, 1996; M. Lessnoff (ed.), *Social Contract Theory*, Oxford, 1990.

36 The journals *History and Theory* and *Rethinking History* (1997) bear testimony to this.

37 On Hegel, see M.A. Gillespie, *Hegel, Heidegger and the Ground of History*, Chicago, 1984.

38 Foucault will be discussed below. On Barthes, see S. Sontag (ed.), *Barthes: Selected Writings*, London, 1982; and on Bourdieu, R. Jenkins, *Pierre Bourdieu*, London, 1992. See also Q. Skinner (ed.), *The Return of Grand Theory in the Human Sciences*, Cambridge, 1985.

39 A good introduction to Foucault's writings is P. Rabinow (ed.), *The Foucault Reader*, New York, 1984, although it contains nothing from *The Birth of the Clinic*, London, 1973, which has been particularly influential in the history of medicine. For commentary on Foucault, see J. Goldstein (ed.), *Foucault and the Writing of History*, Cambridge, MA, 1994; G. Gutting (ed.), *The Cambridge Companion to Foucault*, Cambridge, 1994; and D.C. Hoy (ed.), *Foucault: A Critical Reader*, Oxford, 1986. The best short introduction remains J. Weeks, 'Foucault for Historians', *History Workshop Journal* 14 (1982), 106–18.

40 P. Burke (ed.), *Critical Essays on Michel Foucault*, Aldershot, 1992, is a convenient collection of reviews and commentaries.

41 See, especially, *The Archaeology of Knowledge*, London, 1972 (first published in French in 1969), and *The Order of Things*, London, 1970.

42 Volume 2 was entitled *The Use of Pleasure: English edition*, New York, 1985; volume 3, *The Care of the Self*, New York, 1986. A compelling critique is J. Davidson, *Courtesans and Fishcakes. The Consuming Passions of Classical Athens*, London 1997.

43 I stand by this claim, despite Foucault's famous discussion of Velasquez's *Las Meninas* in *The Order of Things*, pp. 3–16.

44 As critiques of a supposedly scientific taxonomy of sexuality were formulated, new oppositional vocabularies arose, such as 'gay' and 'queer', which then entered historical usage.

45 On 'ideology', see Williams, *Keywords*, pp. 153–7; J. Larrain, *The Concept of Ideology*, London, 1979; and F. Lentricchia and T. McLaughlin (eds), *Critical Terms for Literary Study*, 2nd edn, Chicago, 1995, ch. 22; M. Freeden, *Ideology: A Very Short Introduction*, Oxford, 2003; Bennett et al. (eds), *New Keywords*, pp. 175–8.

46 R. Nash (ed.), *American Environmentalism. Readings in Conservation History*, 3rd edn, New York, 1990 (1st edn, 1968); W. Cronon, *Changes in the Land. Indians, Colonists, and the Ecology of New England*, New York, 1983; R. Grove, *Green Imperialism. Colonial Expansion, Tropical Island Edens and the Origins of Environmentalism 1600–1800*, Cambridge, 1995.

47 Cf. Lentricchia and McLaughlin (eds), *Critical Terms for Literary Study*; M.H. Abrams, *A Glossary of Literary Terms*, 6th edn, Fort Worth, TX, 1993; D. Lodge (ed.), *20th Century Literary Criticism: A Reader*, London, 1972.

48 M. Nicolson, *Mountain Gloom and Mountain Glory*, Ithaca, NY, 1959. I. Boal, 'Marjorie Nicolson and the Aesthetics of Nature', *Antipode* 28 (1996), 304–15 is a discussion of her legacy.

49 For example, M. Holroyd, *Bernard Shaw*, 4 vols, London, 1988–92; N. Boyle, *Goethe: The Poet and the Age: Poetry of Desire, 1749–90*, vol. 1, Oxford, 1991, and *Revolution and Renunciation, 1790–1803*, vol. 2, Oxford, 2000; H. Brogan, *The Life of Arthur Ransome*, London, 1984.

50 *New Literary History* (1969) and *Literature and History* (1975).

51 For example, M. Poovey, *Making a Social Body: British Cultural Formation, 1830–1864*, Chicago, 1995.

52 For example, N. Armstrong, *Desire and Domestic Fiction: A Political History of the Novel*, New York, 1987.

53 J. Culler, *Saussure*, London, 1976.

54 This does not mean that the documents are useless as evidence; rather the con-
    trary, as distinguished recent work on witchcraft shows: for example, R. Briggs,
    Witches and Neighbours: the Social and Cultural Context of European Witchcraft,
    London, 1996, L. Roper, *Oedipus and the Devil: Witchcraft, Sexuality and Religion in
    Early Modern Europe*, London, 1994, and *Witch Craze: Terror and Fantasy in Baroque
    Germany*, New Haven, CT and London, 2004.

55 J. Moran, *Interdisciplinarity*, London and New York, 2002, written from the per-
    spective of literary studies, is useful.

56 See, for example, M. Baxandall, *Painting and Experience in Fifteenth-Century Italy*,
    revised edn, Oxford, 1988, and *The Limewood Sculptors of Renaissance Germany*, New
    Haven, CT, 1980. The special issue of *Art History* 21 (1998), no. 4, dedicated to
    Michael Baxandall, is illuminating. S. Alpers, *The Art of Describing*, Chicago, 1983,
    and *Rembrandt's Enterprise: The Studio and the Market*, Chicago, 1988. It should be
    emphasised that Baxandall and Alpers work on 'high' art, placing it in a rich his-
    torical context. For different approaches, see D. Donald, *The Age of Caricature:
    Satirical Prints in the Reign of George III*, New Haven, CT, 1996; M. Pointon, *Strategies
    for Showing: Women, Possession and Representation in English Visual Culture
    1665–1800*, Oxford, 1997.

57 Cf. *Journal of Material Culture* (1996); S. Lubar and W. Kingery (eds), *History from
    Things: Essays on Material Culture*, Washington, 1993; S. Pierce (ed.), *Experiencing
    Material Culture in the Western World*, London, 1997.

58 For example, Debra Silverman: see her *Art Nouveau in Fin-de-Siècle France: Politics,
    Psychology and Style*, Berkeley, CA, 1989.

59 Cf. H. Bloom, *The Western Canon: The Books and School of the Ages*, London, 1994,
    on the western literary canon.

60 P. Bahn, *Bluff Your Way in Archaeology*, Horsham, 1989, p. 5; see also his
    Archaeology: A Very Short Introduction, Oxford, 1996.

61 C. Chippindale, '"A Day at Old Stones": Four Hundred Years of the Stonehenge
    Excursion', *The Hatcher Review*, vol. 2 (1983), 268–77, 268; M. Myrone and L. Peltz
    (eds), *Producing the Past: Aspects of Antiquarian Culture and Practice, 1700–1850*,
    Aldershot, 1999 (ch. 4 is on Stonehenge and Avebury).

62 For example, A. Verhulst, *The Carolingian Economy*, Cambridge, 2002; L. Syson
    and D. Thornton, *Objects of Virtue, Art in Renaissance Italy*, London, 2001, esp. pp.
    78–134 on the importance of medals.

63 'Geography', *Encyclopedia Britannica*, 11th edn, New York, 1910–11, vol. XI,
    619–38, 619.

64 See, for example, the work of Richard Smith, who was trained as a geographer,
    has been affiliated to both history and geography departments and currently
    edits the *Economic History Review*. 'Geographers, Annaliste Historians and the
    Roots and Divergent Pathways of English and French Historical Geography', in
    A. Encisco (ed.), *Histories and Historiographies: Post-War European Pathways*,
    Rochester, NY, 2004, pp. 210–29, and (ed.), *Land, Kinship and Life-Cycle*,
    Cambridge, 1984, which contains two essays by him.

65 See the journal *Environment and Planning* (1969), section D *Society and Space*
    (1983), which publishes a wide range of material that could be termed 'histori-
    cal geography'. It is markedly international in scope and overtly engaged with
    contemporary issues. The *Journal of Historical Geography* is yet more 'historical'.

66 For example, P. Hulme, *Remnants of Conquest: The Island Caribs and their Visitors,
    1877–1998*, Oxford, 2000.

67 For example, R. Scribner, *For the Sake of Simple Folk: Popular Propaganda for the German Reformation*, Oxford, 1981. Cf. D. Freedberg, *The Power of Images: Studies in the History and Theory of Response*, Chicago and London, 1989.

Chapter 4

1 I have in mind especially scares about rising crime and child abuse, which are rarely based on the meticulous evaluation of historical evidence. This would involve, for instance, assessing changes in record-keeping and analysing the intricate relationships between occurrence, prosecutions and convictions.

2 For two very different approaches to truth, see S. Shapin, *A Social History of Truth: Civility and Science in Seventeenth-Century England*, Chicago, 1994, and F. Fernandez-Armesto, *Truth: A History*, London, 1997. O. Handlin, *Truth in History*, Cambridge, MA, 1979, is less about the concept 'truth' than about historical practice in the USA over the previous 50 years.

3 There have long been some historians who were sceptical of the suitability of the natural sciences to provide epistemological paradigms for their field, e.g. R. Collingwood, *The Idea of History*, Oxford, 1946.

4 Fernandez-Armesto distinguishes between four ways in which truth has been understood: 'the truth you feel', 'the truth you are told', 'the truth of reason' and 'the truth you perceive through your senses'.

5 See Williams, *Keywords*, pp. 308–12, for the tortuous history of 'subjective' in English.

6 But see R. Evans, *Telling Lies about Hitler: The Holocaust, History and the David Irving Trial*, London and New York, 2002.

7 Onora O'Neill's influential Reith Lectures on the theme of trust, published as *A Question of Trust*, Cambridge, 2002, are indicative of the current interest in these matters.

8 See, for example, W. Stott, *Documentary Expression and Thirties America*, New York, 1973.

9 P. Curtin (ed.), *Africa Remembered: Narratives by West Africans from the Era of the Slave Trade*, Madison, WI, 1967, is an interesting collection. The interest in the subjectivities of slavery has been greatly encouraged by literary works such as Toni Morrison, *Beloved*, London, 1987.

10 A compelling account of the trickiness of memories and records of the Holocaust is Bernard Schlink's novel *The Reader*, London, 1997, first published in Zurich in 1995 as *Der Vorleser*. See also C. Browning, 'German Memory, Judicial Interrogation, and Historical Reconstruction: Writing Perpetrator History from Postwar Testimony', in S. Friedländer (ed.), *Probing the Limits of Representation: Nazism and the 'Final Solution'*, Cambridge, MA, 1992, pp. 22–36.

11 On the Farm Security Administration, see S. Baldwin, *Poverty and Politics: The Rise and Decline of the Farm Security Administration*, Chapel Hill, NC, 1968.

12 On Walker Evans, see J. Thompson, *Walker Evans at Work*, New York, 1982; on the Depression, A. Badger, *The New Deal: the Depression Years, 1933–40*, Basingstoke, 1989, and R. McElvaine, *The Great Depression: America, 1929–1941*, New York, 1984. See also J. Tagg, *The Burden of Representation*, Basingstoke, 1988; G. Clarke, *The Photograph*, Oxford, 1997, ch. 8. *Robert Capa: Photographs*, New York, 1996, is useful for thinking about documentary photography and received understandings of historical events.

13 Cf. A. Grafton, *The Footnote: A Curious History*, Cambridge, MA, 1997.

14 This is not to say such works are uncontroversial. See, for example, C. Webster,

The Great Instauration: Science, Medicine and Reform 1626–1660, London, 1975; J. Gage, *Colour and Culture: Practice and Meaning from Antiquity to Abstraction*, London, 1993; I. Kershaw, *Hitler 1889–1936: Hubris*, London, 1998, and *Hitler 1936–1945: Nemesis*, London, 2000.

15 B. Tuchman, *The March of Folly*, London, 1997, p. 2.

16 Cf. L. Gossman, 'Anecdote and History', *History and Theory* 42 (2003), 143–68.

17 M. Baxandall, *Painting and Experience in Fifteenth-Century Italy*, p. 152, is particularly eloquent on historians' sloppy use of pictures. Television is becoming an increasingly important source of such historical 'knowledge', with serialisations of novels and costume dramas easily blurred in viewers' minds with documentaries, themselves works of art.

18 O. Hufton, *The Poor of Eighteenth-Century France 1750–1789*, Oxford, 1974, and *The Prospect Before Her. A History of Women in Western Europe, vol. 1: 1500–1800*, London, 1995.

19 For example, her moving piece, 'Women in Revolution 1789–1796', *Past and Present* 53 (1971), 90–108.

20 N. Zemon Davis, *The Return of Martin Guerre*, Cambridge, MA, 1983, and 'Remaking Imposters: from Martin Guerre to *Sommersby*', Hayes Robinson Lecture Series no. 1, London, 1997; see also her *Fiction in the Archives: Pardon Tales and their Tellers in Sixteenth-Century France*, Cambridge, 1988, and the French film, *The Return of Martin Guerre*, 1982.

21 M. Stanford, *An Introduction to the Philosophy of History*, Oxford, 1998, chs 3 and 4; C. Lloyd, *Explanation in Social History*, Oxford, 1986 (his definition of key terms at the beginning is useful). See also R. Atkinson, *Knowledge and Explanation in History. An Introduction to the Philosophy of History*, London, 1978, esp. ch. 4. Such works can be rather 'technical' in that they presuppose an acquaintance with philosophical matters, and their applicability to historical practice can be unclear.

22 For example, Atkinson, *Knowledge and Explanation in History*, ch. 5; Stanford, *An Introduction*, ch. 3; P. McClelland, *Causal Explanation and Model Building in History, Economics, and the New Economic History*, Ithaca, NY, 1975. Note the large number of books with 'the causes of' in their titles.

23 These historiographical shifts are evident in writings that blend culture and economics, such as P. Curtin, *Cross-Cultural Trade in World History*, Cambridge, 1984; J. Goodman, *Tobacco in History: The Cultures of Dependence*, London, 1993; M. Finn, *The Character of Credit: Personal Debt in English Culture, 1740–1914*, Cambridge, 2003.

24 See, for example, the special feature on 'Psychoanalysis and History', in *History Workshop Journal* 26 (1988).

25 See, for example, M. Bakhtin, *Rabelais and his World*, Bloomington, IN, 1984; P. Stallabrass and A. White, *The Politics and Poetics of Transgression*, London, 1986.

26 On the Hitler diaries, see R. Harris, *The Media Trilogy*, London, 1994, which includes *Selling Hitler: The Story of the Hitler Diaries*, first published in 1986. We should note the persistent claims that Anne Frank's diary was a fake, and that special tests were undertaken to disprove the allegations: see the foreword to Barnouw and van der Stroom (eds), *The Diary of Anne Frank. The Critical Edition*.

27 Friedländer (ed.), *Probing the Limits of Representation: Nazism and the 'Final Solution'*; *History of the Human Sciences*, special issue, vol. 9, no. 4 (1996); I. Gutman (ed.), *Encylopedia of the Holocaust*, 4 vols, New York, 1990 (see vol. 4, pp. 1797–802, on 'Estimated Jewish Losses in the Holocaust').

28 N. Ferguson (ed.), *Virtual History: Alternatives and Counterfactuals*, London, 1997; Stanford, *An Introduction*, pp. 89–93.

29 S. Wilson, 'The Myth of Motherhood a Myth: The Historical View of European Child-rearing', *Social History* 9 (1984), 181–98; I. Kershaw, *The 'Hitler Myth': Image and Reality in the Third Reich*, Oxford, 1987; and N. Henshall, *The Myth of Absolutism: Change and Continuity in Early Modern European Monarchy*, London, 1992.

Chapter 5

1 J.K. Galbraith, *The Age of Uncertainty*, London, 1977; P. Guiral, *La vie quotidienne en France à l'âge d'or du capitalisme 1852–1857*, Paris, 1976; A. Calder-Marshall, *The Grand Century of the Lady: Regency and Georgian Elegance in the Age of Romance and Revolution*, London, 1976.

2 B. Lewis, *What Went Wrong? Western Impact and Middle Eastern Response*, New York, 2002, unpaginated preface; cf. C. Hughes, 'Reflections on Globalisation, Security and 9/11', *Cambridge Review of International Affairs* 15 (2002), 421–33; T. Kean et al., *The 9/11 Commission Report: Final Report of the National Commission on the Terrorist Attacks upon the United States, Authorised Edition*, New York, 2004.

3 Cf. G. Kubler, *The Shape of Time: Remarks on the History of Things*, New Haven, CT, 1962.

4 D. Ewing Duncan, *The Calendar: The 5000-Year Struggle to Align the Clock and Heavens – And What Happened to the Missing Ten Days*, London, 1998; S. Burnaby, *Elements of the Jewish and Muhammadan Calendars*, London, 1901; R. Sewell and S. Dikshit, *The Indian Calendar*, London, 1896.

5 The Scottish company Craig and Rose divide their colours into seven periods, from the 'ancient world period' to 'arts and craft movement', including 'Ming', and provide a brief historical description for each colour and for each period.

6 See, for example, S. Faroqhi, *Approaching Ottoman History: An Introduction to the Sources*, Cambridge, 1999.

7 This has become possible largely through the power of film, which has conveyed, in both documentary and fictional form, an exceptionally vivid sense of what we mean by 'Hitler': less an individual than an ensemble of historical phenomena and emotional reactions.

8 P. Burke, *The Fabrication of Louis XIV*, New Haven, CT, 1992.

9 J. Mordaunt Crook, *The Dilemma of Style: Architectural Ideas from the Picturesque to the Post-Modern*, London, 1987, 1989; B. Allsop, *Style in the Visual Arts*, Newcastle, 1968; M. Finch, *Style in Art History: An Introduction to Theories of Style and Sequence*, Metuchen, NJ, 1974. Rococo is primarily associated with French art of the first half of the eighteenth century: 'in France it fell out of fashion in the 1740s to be decisively superseded by the earnest ideals and Republican Roman virtue of Neoclassicism': P. and L. Murray, *Dictionary of Art and Artists*, Harmondsworth, 1960, p. 277. Scholars debate the definition and usefulness of such terms, but for our purposes the point is that they become loaded with other associations, which shape the sense of a period. For example, rococo suggests femininity, ancien régime decadence, neoclassicism austere masculinity. Cf. S. Slesin et al., *Japanese Style*, New York, 1994 (first published 1987).

10 R. Samuel, 'Mrs Thatcher and Victorian Values', in *Island Stories: Unravelling Britain* (vol. 2 of *Theatres of Memory*), London, 1998, pp. 330–48 (article first published 1992).

11 C. Totman, *A History of Japan*, Malden, MA and Oxford, 2000, p. 141.

12 D. Weiner, *The Citizen Patient in Revolutionary and Imperial Paris*, Baltimore, 1993; L. Brockliss and C. Jones, *The Medical World of Early Modern France*, Oxford, 1997, esp. the conclusion.

13 On Lavoisier, see S. French, *Torch and Crucible: The Life and Death of Antoine Lavoisier*, Princeton, NJ, 1941; D. McKie, *Antoine Lavoisier, Scientist, Economist, Social Reformer*, London, 1952; A. Donovan, *Antoine Lavoisier: Science, Administration and Revolution*, Oxford, 1993.

14 On the revolutionary calendar, see C. Jones, *The Longman Companion to the French Revolution*, Harlow, 1988, pp. 425–30; F. Furet and M. Ozouf (eds), *A Critical Dictionary of the French Revolution*, Cambridge, MA, 1989, pp. 538–47.

15 L. Woolf, *After the Deluge: A Study of Communal Psychology*, London, 1931, started with a discussion of the war as 'a catastrophe and a landmark in history'. Cf. A. Marwick, *The Deluge: British Society and the First World War*, 2nd edn, Basingstoke, 1991.

16 R. Leys, *Trauma: A Genealogy*, Chicago, 2000.

17 A. Mayer, *The Persistence of the Old Regime: Europe to the Great War*, New York, 1981. On poetry, see J. Silkin, *Out of Battle: The Poetry of the Great War*, 2nd edn, Basingstoke, 1998; D. Hibberd (ed.), *Poetry of the First World War: A Casebook*, London, 1981; J. Silkin (ed.), *The Penguin Book of First World War Poetry*, Harmondsworth, 1979.

18 Williams, *Keywords*, pp. 208–9; Bennett et al. (eds), *New Keywords*, pp. 219–24.

19 R. Jones, *Ancients and Moderns: A Study of the Rise of the Scientific Movement in Seventeenth-Century Europe*, 2nd edn, Berkeley, CA, 1961.

20 It is vital to distinguish between 'modern', 'modernism', 'modernity' and 'modernisation'. 'Modern', the adjective, is discussed in the text above. 'Modernism' generally refers to cultural movements, especially in art, architecture and literature, and when applied to other phenomena implies a cultish or celebratory approach to what is 'modern'. 'Modernity' concerns a general state or condition, and is what sociologists have focused upon. 'Modernisation' refers to broad processes of transformation, especially social and economic change. See M. Berman, *All That Is Solid Melts into Air: The Experience of Modernity*, London, 1983; M. Abrams, *A Glossary of Literary Terms*, 6th edn, Fort Worth, TX, 1993, pp. 118–21; H. Ritter, *Dictionary of Concepts in History*, New York, 1986, pp. 273–7; D. Peters Corbett, *The Modernity of English Art 1914–30*, Manchester, 1997, esp. the introduction. Note that the *Journal of Modern History* (1929) accepts articles across a wide chronological span, including 'early modern'.

21 A. Koyré, *From the Closed World to the Infinite Universe*, Baltimore, MD, 1957.

22 The Australian case is particularly interesting in relation to the broad implications of all forms of periodisation. It had been seen and visited by Europeans for some time before Cook's voyage of 1769–71. One history starts with the declaration, 'Australia was conceived officially . . . on 22 January 1787', which gives priority to its status as a British penal colony: F. Crowley (ed.), *A New History of Australia*, Melbourne, 1974, p. 1. The whole approach to periodisation in the volume is striking. Cf. Manning Clark's *History of Australia*, Melbourne, 1993 (an abridgement by M. Cathcart), p. 3: 'Civilization did not begin in Australia until the last quarter of the eighteenth century.' He also privileges 1787.

23 M. Freeman, 'Human Rights and the Corruption of Governments, 1789–1989', in P. Hulme and L. Jordanova (eds), *The Enlightenment and its Shadows*, London, 1990, pp. 163–83; cf. M. Mazower, 'The Strange Triumph of Human Rights, 1933–1950', *The Historical Journal* (2004), 379–98.

24 D. Bien, *The Calas Affair: Persecution, Toleration, and Heresy in Eighteenth-Century Toulouse*, Princeton, NJ, 1960; F. Venturi, *Utopia and Reform in the Enlightenment*, Cambridge, 1971; E. Peters, *Torture*, expanded edn, Philadelphia, 1996.

25 P. Hudson, *The Industrial Revolution*, London, 1992; P. Kriedke, H. Medick and J. Schlumbohm, *Industrialization before Industrialization: Rural Industry in the Genesis of Capitalism*, Cambridge, 1981.

26 For example, Klein, *A Concise History of Bolivia*, who entitled the first chapter, which forms less than 10 per cent of the book, 'Geography and Pre-Columbian Civilization'. Subsequent chapters use a range of political and economic concepts to demarcate subsequent periods. His 'Political Chronology', pp. 266–9, covering 2500 BC to 2002, reveals the range of criteria historians consider in order to shape past times.

27 Cf. H.S. Hughes, 'Is Contemporary History Real History?', in his *History as Art and as Science: Twin Vistas on the Past*, New York, 1964, pp. 89–107; A. Seldon (ed.), *Contemporary History: Practice and Method*, Oxford, 1988; *Journal of Contemporary History* (1966).

28 W. Speck, 'The Eighteenth Century in Britain: Long or Short?', *The Historian*, autumn 1996, 16–18, is a brief useful discussion of this idea. Cf. F. O'Gorman, *The Long Eighteenth Century. British Political and Social History 1688–1832*, London, 1997; W. Prest, *Albion Ascendant. English History 1660–1815*, Oxford, 1998; D. Blackbourn, *The Fontana History of Germany, 1815–1918: The Long Nineteenth Century*, London, 1997.

29 The ongoing and extremely intricate relationships between Britain and the United States two centuries after independence would be a case in point: W. Louis and H. Bull (eds), *The 'Special Relationship': Anglo-American Relations Since 1945*, Oxford, 1986; J. Baylis, *Anglo–American Defence Relations 1939–1984: The Special Relationship*, 2nd edn, London, 1984.

30 A variety of perspectives on the Enlightenment can be gleaned from: N. Hampson, *The Enlightenment*, Harmondsworth, 1968; R. Darnton, *Mesmerism and the End of the Enlightenment in France*, Cambridge, 1968; P. Gay, *The Enlightenment*, 2 vols, New York, 1966 and 1969; R. Porter and M. Teich (eds), *The Enlightenment in National Context*, Cambridge, 1981; R. Porter, *The Enlightenment*, Basingstoke, 1990; D. Outram, *The Enlightenment*, Cambridge, 1995; A. Herman, *The Scottish Enlightenment. The Scots' Invention of the Modern World*, London, 2001, which takes a *longue durée* approach.

31 For example, A. Marwick, *The Sixties. Cultural Revolution in Britain, France, Italy and the United States, c.1958–c.1974*, Oxford, 1998.

32 M. Teich and R. Porter (eds), *Fin de Siècle and its Legacy*, Cambridge, 1990; B. Dijkstra, *Idols of Perversity: Fantasies of Feminine Evil in Fin-de-siècle Culture*, New York, 1986; C. Schorske, *Fin-de-siècle Vienna: Politics and Culture*, New York, 1979; A. Danchev (ed.), *Fin de Siècle: The Meaning of the Twentieth Century*, London, 1995; R. Pahl, *After Success: Fin-de-Siècle Anxiety and Identity*, Cambridge, 1995.

33 E. Williams, *The Ancien Régime in Europe: Government and Society in the Major States 1648–1789*, London, 1970; C.B.A. Behrens, *The Ancien Régime*, London, 1967; A. de Tocqueville, *L'Ancien Régime et la Révolution*, Paris, 1856.

34 A particularly explicit discussion of periodisation is J. Webster, 'The Eighteenth Century as a Music-Historical Period?', *Eighteenth-Century Music*, vol. 1, no. 1 (2004), 47–60.

35 C. Friedrich, *The Age of the Baroque, 1610–60*, New York, 1952; W. Park, *The Idea of Rococo*, Newark, NJ, 1992; D. Irwin, *Neo-classicism*, Oxford, 1997. 'Biedermeier',

which is both a style term and a period term, illustrates a number of my points: see M. Fulbrook, *A Concise History of Germany*, 2nd edn, Cambridge, 1992, p. 122.

36 On taste, see, for example, S. Bayley, *Taste, the Secret Meaning of Things*, London, 1991; J. Curl, *Egyptomania: The Egyptian Revival, a Recurring Theme in the History of Taste*, Manchester, 1994.

37 For a range of approaches to the Reformation, see R. Scribner, *The German Reformation*, Basingstoke, 1986; P. Chaunu (ed.), *The Reformation*, London, 1989; J. Bossy, *Christianity in the West 1400–1700*, Oxford, 1985; E. Cameron, *The European Reformation*, Oxford, 1991; E. Duffy, *The Stripping of the Altars. Traditional Religion in England*, New Haven, CT and London, 1992; D. MacCulloch, *Reformation Europe's House Divided 1490–1700*, London, 2003.

38 J. Harrison, *The Second Coming: Popular Millenarianism, 1780–1850*, London, 1979; E. Gaustad, *The Great Awakening in New England*, Gloucester, MA, 1965.

39 S. Dunant and R. Porter (eds), *The Age of Anxiety*, London, 1996; W. Burn, *The Age of Equipoise: A Study of the Mid-Victorian Generation*, London, 1964; J. Cannon, *Aristocratic Century: The Peerage of Eighteenth-Century England*, Cambridge, 1984. The phrase 'golden age' appears in the title of hundreds of books, relating to many countries, such as Spain, Italy, the Netherlands, Brazil and Scotland, and to many periods; e.g. H. Kamen, *Golden Age Spain*, Basingstoke, 1988.

40 J. Galbraith, *The Age of Uncertainty*, London, 1977. His aim was to 'contrast the great certainties in economic thought in the last century with the great uncertainty with which problems are faced in our time', p. 7.

41 N. Branson and M. Heinemann, *Britain in the Nineteen Thirties*, London, 1971; A. Badger, *The New Deal: The Depression Years, 1933–40*, Basingstoke, 1989; J. Garraty, *The Great Depression: An Inquiry into the Causes, Course and Consequences of the Worldwide Depression of the Nineteen-Thirties*, San Diego, 1986.

42 *The Great Depression: A Historical Bibliography*, Santa Barbara, CA, 1984. Cf. S.B. Saul, *The Myth of the Great Depression, 1873–1896*, 2nd edn, London, 1985.

43 The Italian Risorgimento would be another example: see L. Riall, *The Italian Risorgimento: State, Society and National Unification*, London, 1994.

44 F. Braudel, *Civilization and Capitalism, 15th–18th Century*, 3 vols, London, 1981, 1982 and 1984; cf. his *On History*, London, 1980, esp. the essay on 'La longue durée'. See also the works cited below in note 45.

45 E. Wrigley and R. Schofield, *The Population History of England 1541–1871*, London, 1981, and new edition, 1989; K. Patterson, *Pandemic Influenza 1700–1900: A Study in Historical Epidemiology*, Totowa, NJ, 1986; D. Hackett Fisher, *The Great Wave. Price Revolutions and the Rhythm of History*, New York, 1996 (covers the medieval period to the present day).

46 A classic example would be the work of Philippe Ariès: for example, *Centuries of Childhood*, Harmondsworth, 1973 (first published in French in 1960), and *The Hour of Our Death*, Harmondsworth, 1983 (first published in French in 1977).

47 See, for example, J. Gillis (ed.), *Commemoration: The Politics of National Identity*, Princeton, NJ, 1993; J. Winter, *Sites of Memory, Sites of Mourning: The Great War in European Cultural History*, Cambridge, 1995; B. Taithe, 'Monuments aux Morts? Reading Nora's *Realms of Memory* and Samuel's *Theatres of Memory*', *History of the Human Sciences* 12 (1999), 123–39.

48 K. Figlio, 'Oral History and the Unconscious', *History Workshop Journal* 26 (1988), 120–32.

Chapter 6

1 For example, B. Howe and E. Kemp (eds), *Public History: An Introduction*, Malabar, FL, 1986; J. Liddington, 'What is Public History? Publics and their Pasts, Meanings and Practices', *Oral History* 33 (2002), 83–93.

2 A useful introduction to the issues is S. Benson, S. Brier and R. Rosenzweig (eds), *Presenting the Past: Essays on History and the Public*, Philadelphia, PA, 1986, based on articles in the *Radical History Review*. In the introduction they distinguish between three types of public history: a slick form, found in the media and serving dominant interests; professional public history; and a radical people's history. In my view there is increasing overlap and interplay between these types. See also the special issue of *Gender and History*, vol. 6, no. 3 (1994), esp. the useful introduction by Barbara Melosh.

3 For example, R. Samuel, *Theatres of Memory*, vol. 1: *Past and Present in Contemporary Culture*, London, 1994, esp. part 3, 'Heritage', and particularly the brilliant essay, 'Semantics', pp. 205–26. Cf. D. Lowenthal, 'Fabricating Heritage', *History and Memory* 10 (1998), 5–24.

4 The connections are closest in archaeology, where the work of museums and that of academics are inseparable. Renfrew and Bahn, *Archaeology: Theories, Methods and Practice*, ch. 14, on 'Whose Past? Archaeology and the Public', is an excellent introduction to the issues of this chapter from the point of view of archaeology. For most historians there are few or no links with the museums/heritage world. For the general public it is difficult if not impossible to discern the academic history in what they see displayed. In this general area, see *International Journal of Heritage Studies* (1994); J. Arnold et al. (eds), *History and Heritage: Consuming the Past in Contemporary Culture*, Shaftesbury, 1998; T. Bennett, *The Birth of the Museum: History, Theory, Politics*, London, 1995; P. Vergo (ed.), *The New Museology*, London, 1989; J. Elsner and R. Cardinal (eds), *The Cultures of Collecting*, London, 1994; D. Horne, *The Great Museum: The Re-presentation of History*, London, 1984; P. Mandler, *History and National Life*, London, 2002.

5 See, for example, *Museums Journal* (1901), *Journal of the History of Collections* (1989) and items cited in footnote 4, above. The collecting of works by native peoples raises particularly challenging issues: see J. Berlo and R. Phillips, *Native North American Art*, Oxford, 1998.

6 Williamsburg is an attempt to reconstruct life in colonial America in considerable detail. Longleat in Wiltshire, England, is a stately home that has long promoted other attractions, such as wildlife, in the search for commercial success.

7 In the USA, the *Radical History Review* has played an important part in bringing these issues to historians. The huge amounts of money available, for example, from the Disney Corporation for theme parks with historical dimensions, fuels public discussion. In Britain, a country intensely anxious about its historic past, this has focused on 'heritage' issues and on organisations, such as the National Trust and English Heritage, with interests in the area.

8 Their author, Mrs Montagu Barstow, published under the name Baroness Orczy: see J. Neild, *A Guide to the Best Historical Novels and Tales*, London, 1911. The most famous film was made in 1934 and remade in 1950, and there have been several television versions.

9 Statements about the Trust's aims may be found in their annual handbook. Its holdings include 'over 200 historic houses and gardens and 49 industrial monuments and mills'. The 2004 edition features properties associated with The Beatles on p. 6 as one of the Trust's 'highlights'.

10 The full title of the novel is *Brideshead Revisited: The Sacred and Profane Memories of Captain Charles Rider*. F. Scott Fitzgerald's *The Great Gatsby* (1925) and the film version of 1974 have had a comparable effect.

11 Gillis (ed.), *Commemoration: The Politics of National Identity*; Winter, *Sites of Memory, Sites of Mourning*, ch. 4.

12 M. Agulhon, *Marianne into Battle: Republican Imagery and Symbolism in France: 1789–1880*, Cambridge, 1981, brings out just these points. The study of public sculpture is an important area for historians, although such research is generally undertaken by specialists in art history. On war memorials, see A. Borg, *War Memorials: From Antiquity to the Present*, London, 1991; A. King, *Memorials of The Great War in Britain: the Symbolism and Politics of Remembrance*, Oxford, 1998.

13 See J. Hodge, *The Private World of Georgette Heyer*, London, 1984.

14 Not all genres are 'written'; there are a number of distinct genres, for example, within the medium of film. See R. Rosenstone (ed.), *Revisioning History. Film and the Construction of a New Past*, Princeton, NJ, 1995; N. Davis, *Slaves on Screen. Film and Historical Vision*, Cambridge, MA, 2000, explores these issues through a study of five films about slavery made between 1960 and 1998. Another non-written genre that is relevant here is maps: see, for example, L. Smart, *Maps that Made History*, London, 2004.

15 Although not primarily about (public) history, the following works are useful: G. Levine (ed.), *Realism and Representation: Essays on the Problem of Realism in Relation to Science, Literature, and Culture*, Madison, WI, 1993; L. Cooke and P. Wollen (eds), *Visual Display: Culture Beyond Appearances*, Seattle, WA, 1995; D. Haraway, *Primate Visions. Gender, Race and Nature in the World of Modern Science*, New York, 1989, ch. 3 (about the New York Museum of Natural History).

16 J. Habermas, *The Structural Transformation of the Public Sphere: An Inquiry into a Category of Bourgeois Society*, Cambridge, MA, 1989. Cf. D. Castiglione and L. Sharpe (eds), *Shifting the Boundaries. Transformation of the Languages of Public and Private in the Eighteenth Century*, Exeter, 1995.

17 On the gendering of public and private, see J. Elshtain, *Public Man, Private Woman: Women in Social and Political Thought*, Oxford, 1981; A. Vickery, 'Golden Age to Separate Spheres? A Review of the Categories and Chronology of English Women's History', *Historical Journal* 36 (1993); L. Davidoff, *Worlds Between: Historical Perspectives on Gender and Class*, Cambridge, 1995, ch. 8; J. Landes, *Women and the Public Sphere in the Age of the French Revolution*, Ithaca, NY, 1988.

18 E. Miller, *That Noble Cabinet: A History of the British Museum*, London, 1973.

19 Cf. Castiglione and Sharpe, *Shifting the Boundaries*.

20 W. Sellar and R. Yeatman, *1066 and All That. A Memorable History of England*, London, 1930; Goscinny and Uderzo, *Asterix the Gaul*, Leicester, 1969. Samuel, 'One in the Eye: *1066 And All That*', in *Island Stories: Unravelling Britain*, pp. 208–13.

21 Particularly useful is the special section in *Technology and Culture* 39 (1998), 457–82, which discusses not only the *Enola Gay* fiasco, but also broad issues around public history. The Allied bombing of Dresden in 1945 has raised similar issues.

22 The chain of shops that retails 'historical' items, Past Times, demonstrates the point. The idea that the eighteenth century was 'elegant' is commonplace, for example, in relation to clothes and music. Other public, marketable images coexist, which are equally politically freighted, such as the 'romp', bodice-ripping view of the eighteenth century, which ignores class tensions and is based on a selective reading of fiction from the period. Other retailers selling 'historical'

items produce catalogues that are instructive about public history: see, for example, Museum Selection: Gifts and Cards from the Great Museums of the World, www.museumselection.com (accessed 31 August 2005) and Nauticalia: Where the Past Meets the Present, www.nauticalia.com (accessed 31 August 2005).

23 C. Webster, *The Health Services Since the War*, 2 vols, London, 1988 and 1996, was commissioned by the government. Cf. his *The National Health Service: A Political History*, Oxford, 1998. Business history is a growing field: see, for example, the journals *Business History* (1959) and *Business History Review* (1926).

24 Figures such as the steel magnate and philanthropist Andrew Carnegie exemplify the point: H. Livesay, *Andrew Carnegie and the Rise of Big Business*, Boston, MA, 1975; J. Wall, *Andrew Carnegie*, New York, 1970; L. Hacker, *The World of Andrew Carnegie 1865–1901*, Philadelphia, PA, 1968. Cf. *Autobiography of Andrew Carnegie*, Boston, MA, 1920; J. Wall, 'A Second Look at Andrew Carnegie', in S. Baron and C. Pletsch (eds), *Introspection in Biography: The Biographer's Quest for Self-Awareness*, Hillsdale, NJ, 1985, pp. 209–22.

25 Jesse Foot's defamatory life of the celebrated surgeon John Hunter, who died in 1793, is a good example: *The Life of John Hunter*, London, 1794. When historians write biographies of those, such as Joseph Stalin, who are deemed 'evil', they face a challenge that is closely related to the question of how and why writers identify, or not, with their subjects; cf. Robert Service, *Stalin*, London, 2004.

26 I. McBryde (ed.), *Who Owns the Past?*, Melbourne, 1985.

27 I am emphatically not making a global statement here. Notions of ownership are historically specific. I refer to the political and intellectual traditions that I, and most of my readers, have been shaped by, whether we like it or not.

28 Cf. B. Anderson and J. Zinsser, *A History of Their Own: Women in Europe from Prehistory to the Present*, 2 vols, London, 1989. More generally, we should note periodical publications such as *Our History* (1956) and *Our History Journal* (1977).

29 The phrase 'identity politics' is widely used in the United States, and it has helped to shape the type of history I am discussing here.

30 Charles Maier addresses just this question in *The Unmasterable Past*, Cambridge, MA, 1988. See also A. Rosenbaum, *Is the Holocaust Unique? Perspectives on Comparative Genocide*, Boulder, CO, 1996.

31 For example, the Museum of the Resistance, Lyon, and the Memorial to the Deported, Paris. See also J. Young, *The Texture of Memory: Holocaust Memorials and Meaning*, New Haven, CT, 1993; J. Young (ed.), *The Art of Memory: Holocaust Memorials in History*, Munich, 1994.

32 The ferocity of responses to D. Goldhagen's *Hitler's Willing Executioners: Ordinary Germans and the Holocaust*, London, 1996, makes the point. See also C. Browning, *The Path to Genocide: Essays on Launching the Final Solution*, Cambridge, 1992; J. Stern, *Hitler, the Führer and the People*, Glasgow, 1975. I return to these questions in chapter 8.

33 D. Irving, *The Destruction of Dresden*, London, 1963; *Hitler's War*, London, 1977; *Nuremberg: the Last Battle*, London, 1996. For a critical view of this work, see Harris, *The Media Trilogy*, esp. pp. 374–9. A defence of Irving is N. Jackson, *The Case for David Irving: The Selective Censorship of History and Free Speech*, Cranbrook, Western Australia, 1994. Holocaust denial is a criminal offence in Germany. See also Evans, *Telling Lies about Hitler. The Holocaust, History and the David Irving Trial*. I return to these issues in chapter 8.

34 See, for example, P. Finney, 'Ethics, Historical Relativism and Holocaust Denial', *Rethinking History* 2 (1998), 359–69.

35 W. Cronon, *Changes in the Land. Indians, Colonists, and the Ecology of New England*, New York, 1983; R. White, *Land Use, Environment and Social Change: The Shaping of Island County*, Seattle, WA, 1980.

36 Work on the aristocracy has included L. Stone, *The Crisis of the Aristocracy, 1558–1641*, Oxford, 1965, and *The Family, Sex and Marriage in England*, London, 1977; D. Lieven, *The Aristocracy in Europe, 1815–1914*, Basingstoke, 1992; S. Tillyard, *Aristocrats: Caroline, Emily, Louisa and Sarah Lennox, 1750–1832*, London, 1994, and a TV series; D. Cannadine, *Aspects of Aristocracy: Grandeur and Decline in Modern Britain*, New Haven, CT and London, 1994; P. Mandler, *The Fall and Rise of the Stately Home*, New Haven, CT, 1997.

37 On servants, see C. Fairchilds, *Domestic Enemies: Servants and their Masters in Old Regime France*, Baltimore, MD, 1984; A. Kussmaul, *Servants in Husbandry in Early Modern England*, Cambridge, 1981; J. Hecht, *The Domestic Servant Class in Eighteenth-Century England*, London, 1956. Similar issues are raised by any kind of historical research on unequal power relationships where one side is widely castigated.

38 Irving, *Hitler's War*; cf. Kershaw, *Hitler: 1889–1936: Hubris* and *Hitler 1936–1945: Nemesis*.

39 An outstanding example of a work that is of the highest scholarly standard, avows its values and makes a case of the greatest possible public interest is I. Katznelson, *When Affirmative Action was White. An Untold History of Racial Inequality in Twentieth-Century America*, New York, 2005. Thus scholarly history and public history can sometimes be one and the same.

Chapter 7

1 See, for example, the journal *Comparative Studies in Society and History* (1958); also E. Acton, *Nazism and Stalinism: A Suitable Case for Comparison?*, London, 1998; R. Smith, 'Social institutions and demographic regimes in non-industrial societies: a comparative approach', in H. Macbeth and P. Collinson (eds), *Human Population Dynamics: Cross-Disciplinary Perspectives*, Cambridge, 2002, pp. 103–23.

2 J. Pound, *Tudor and Stuart Norwich*, Chichester, 1988; B. Ayers, *English Heritage Book of Norwich*, London, 1994; F. Meeres, *A History of Norwich*, Chichester, 1998; R. Wilson and C. Rawcliffe (eds), *Norwich since 1550*, London, 2004.

3 See, for example, R. Schulte, *The Village in Court: Arson, Infanticide and Poaching in the Court Reports of Upper Bavaria, 1848–1910*, Oxford, 1994; M. Jackson, *New-Born Child Murder: Women, Illegitimacy and the Courts in Eighteenth-Century England*, Manchester, 1996; L. Rose, *The Massacre of the Innocents: Infanticide in Britain 1800–1939*, London, 1986.

4 C. Brinton, *French Revolutionary Legislation on Illegitimacy, 1789–1804*, Cambridge, MA, 1936.

5 R. Phillips, *Family Breakdown in Late Eighteenth-Century France; Divorces in Rouen 1792–1803*, Oxford, 1980.

6 P. Laslett et al. (eds), *Bastardy and its Comparative History*, London, 1980.

7 On illegitimacy, see the works by Jackson, Brinton and Laslett, cited above.

8 *Journal of Family History* (1976); *Journal of Marriage and the Family* (1939); *Continuity and Change: A Journal of Social Structure, Law and Demography in Past Societies* (1986). A useful introduction is J. Casey, *The History of the Family*, Oxford, 1989.

9 On demographic methods, see J. Willigan and K. Lynch (eds), *Sources and Methods in Historical Demography*, New York, 1982; D. Reher and R. Schofield (eds), *Old and New Methods in Historical Demography*, Oxford, 1993.

10 Floud, *An Introduction to Quantitative Methods for Historians*, p. 3; C. Feinstein and

M. Thomas, *Making History Count. A Primer in Quantitative History*, Cambridge, 2002. On quantitative history, see also J. Le Goff and P. Nora (eds), *Constructing the Past: Essays in Historical Methodology*, Cambridge, 1985, chs 1, 2 and 5; O. Handlin, *Truth in History*, Cambridge, MA, 1979, ch. 8; C. Harvey and J. Press, *Databases in Historical Research. Theory, Methods and Applications*, Basingstoke, 1996; P. Hudson, *History by Numbers: An Introduction to Quantitative Approaches*, London, 2000.

11 M. Cullen, *The Statistical Movement in Early Victorian Britain: The Foundations of Empirical Social Research*, Hassocks, 1975; T. Porter, *The Rise of Statistical Thinking: 1820–1900*, Princeton, NJ, 1986, and *Trust in Numbers: The Pursuit of Objectivity in Science and Public Life*, Princeton, NJ, 1995; A. Desrosières, *The Politics of Large Numbers: A History of Statistical Reasoning*, Cambridge, MA, 1998.

12 *Medieval Prosopography* (1980); K. Keats-Rohan, *Family Trees and the Roots of Politics: The Prosopography of Britain and France from the Tenth to the Twelfth Century*, Woodbridge, 1996. Arnold Thackray has been a promoter of prosopographic approaches in the history of science. His joint book with J. Morrell, *Gentlemen of Science: Early Years of the British Association for the Advancement of Science*, Oxford, 1981, explores the nature of scientific communities.

13 M. Camille, *Images on the Edge: The Margins of Medieval Art*, London, 1992, and *Mirror in Parchment: The Luttrell Psalter and the Making of Medieval England*, London, 1998; R. Gameson (ed.), *The Early Medieval Bible: Its Production, Decoration and Use*, Cambridge, 1994; M. Clanchy, *From Memory to Written Record: England 1066–1307*, London, 1979; B. Bischoff, *Latin Palaeography: Antiquity and the Middle Ages*, Cambridge, 1990.

14 For example, G. Vernadsky, *A Source Book for Russian History from Early Times to 1917*, New Haven, CT, 1972; B. Szczesniak (ed.), *The Russian Revolution and Religion: A Collection of Documents Concerning the Suppression of Religion by the Communists, 1917–1925*, Notre Dame, IN, 1959; S. Page (compiler), *Russia in Revolution. Selected Readings in Russian Domestic History since 1855*, Princeton, NJ, 1965.

15 Cf. M. Lindemann, 'Confessions of an Archive Junkie', in P. Karsten and J. Modell (eds), *Theory, Method, and Practice in Social and Cultural History*, New York, 1992, pp. 152–80.

16 For example, C. King, *Renaissance Women Patrons: Wives and Widows in Italy c.1300–1550*, Manchester, 1998; S. Cavallo and L. Warner (eds), *Widowhood in Medieval and Early Modern Europe*, New York, 1999.

17 A stimulating account of the concept of interpretation is S. Sontag, *Against Interpretation*, New York, 1966. See also R. Nelson and R. Shiff (eds), *Critical Terms for Art History*, Chicago, 1996, pp. 87–100; Lentricchia and McLaughlin (eds), *Critical Terms for Literary Study*, part 2, esp. pp. 121–34.

18 See the two special issues of *History of the Human Sciences* on 'The Archive', vol. 11, no. 4 (1998) and vol. 12, no. 2 (1999); C. Steedman, *Dust*, Manchester, 2001.

19 For example, *Print Quarterly* (1984); R. Porter, 'Seeing the Past', *Past and Present* 118 (1988), 186–205; D. Jarrett, *England in the Age of Hogarth*, St Albans, 1976; L. Colley, *Britons: Forging the Nation, 1707–1837*, New Haven, CT, 1992; D. Donald, *The Age of Caricature: Satirical Prints in the Reign of George III*, New Haven, CT, 1996.

20 P. Burke, *Eyewitnessing: The Uses of Images as Historical Evidence*, London, 2001, explores historians' use of visual evidence.

21 M. Baxandall, *Painting and Experience in Fifteenth Century Italy*, Oxford, 1988, p. 152.

22 For some very different examples of the use of music, see E. Said, *Musical Elaborations*, London, 1991; R. Leppert, *Music and Image: Domesticity, Ideology and Socio-Cultural Formation in Eighteenth-Century England*, Cambridge, 1988; J. Brewer,

The Pleasures of the Imagination, London, 1997, ch. 14; T. Tolley, *Painting the Cannon's Roar*, Aldershot, 2001.

23 Thus the heterogeneity of those included in M. Hughes-Warrington, *Fifty Key Thinkers on History*, London, 2000, is striking.

Chapter 8

1 Written responses to these events have been legion, but see, for example, A. Sinclair, *An Anatomy of Terror*, Basingstoke and London, 2004, which covers the ancient world to the present day. The need for continuing critical analysis of the concept 'terror' is urgent.

2 The highly accessible works in the Oxford University Press series 'A Very Short Introduction' make a positive contribution: see, for example, K. Knott, *Hinduism*, 1998; S. Hamilton, *Indian Philosophy*, 2001; M. Ruthven, *Islam*, 1997; D. Keown, *Buddhism*, 1996.

3 H. Macdonald, *Falcon*, London, 2006, cover blurb, and p. 7. This is part of a series published by Reaktion Books, London, called simply 'Animal'.

4 The *Journal of Military History* has a complex history: it was first published in 1937 as *The Journal of the American Military History Foundation*, subsequently going through a number of changes of name and format, assuming the current one in 1989; since 1992 it has been published for the Society of Military History. The issue of gender and war is a historical topic in its own right: see, for example, S. Dudink, K. Hagemann and J. Tosh (eds), *Masculinities in Politics and War. Gendering Modern History*, Manchester, 2004. See also the important journal *War in History* (1994).

5 *Civil Wars* (1998), editorial in the first issue by C. Kennedy-Pipe and C. Jones, pp. 1–15, esp. pp. 1–3.

6 A. Bennett, *The History Boys*, London, 2004, pp. 70–4, is characteristically perceptive on this point. Cf. M. Howard, *The Lessons of History*, Oxford, 1991. I owe the phrase 'battlefield hikes' to English Heritage, who organise 'walks around some fascinating historical battlefields and the lovely scenery surrounding them', according to recent publicity.

7 The answer seems to be no. Gettysburg, the site of an exceptionally important battle of the American Civil War in 1863 and made into a National Military Park in the 1890s, has an elaborate series of explanatory tablets: G. Large, *Battle of Gettysburg, The Official History by the Gettysburg National Military Park Commission*, Shippenburg, PA, 1999, explains the complexities. Bannockburn, the site of a much earlier but no less legendary encounter in Scotland, has prompted a visually virtuosic book aimed at general readers: P. Armstrong, *Bannockburn 1314 Robert Bruce's Great Victory*, Oxford, 2002, illustrated by Graham Turner, which also indicates just how much 'reconstruction' – both verbal and visual – is required for a battle and the site to be at all accessible after the event.

8 It would be a mistake to suppose that the fascination with war is confined to the recent past. See, for example, J. Phillips, *The Fourth Crusade and the Sack of Constantinople*, London, 2004; A. Chaniotis, *War in the Hellenistic World: A Social and Cultural History*, Oxford, 2004; A. Spalinger, *War in Ancient Egypt: The New Kingdom*, Oxford, 2004.

9 For example, E. Barkan, *The Guilt of Nations. Restitution and Negotiating Historical Injustices*, New York and London, 2000; M. Cunningham, 'Prisoners of the Japanese and the Politics of Apology: A Battle over History and Memory', *Journal of Contemporary History* 39 (2004), 561–74.

10 D. Goldhagen, *A Moral Reckoning: the Role of the Catholic Church in the Holocaust and*

Its Unfulfilled Duty of Repair, New York, 2002. The commentaries by V. Lapomarda and R. Herzstein in *The Journal of the Historical Society* 3 (2003), 493–502 and 470–92 are revealing.

11 Hence, for example, the importance of continuing historical scholarship about slavery: see, for example, I. Berlin, *Generations of Captivity. A History of African American Slaves*, Cambridge, MA and London, 2003; S. Miers, *Slavery in the Twentieth Century. The Evolution of a Global Problem*, Walnut Creek, CA, 2003.

12 Evans, *Telling Lies about Hitler. The Holocaust, History and the David Irving Trial*, p. 5. The secondary literature on the Holocaust is staggeringly vast, hence D. Stone (ed.), *The Historiography of the Holocaust*, Basingstoke, 2004, is useful.

13 The secondary literature on globalisation is huge: see, for example, A. Giddens, *Runaway World. How Globalization is Reshaping our Lives*, London, 1999; P. O'Meara, H. Mehlinger and M. Krain (eds), *Globalization and the Challenges of a New Century: A Reader*, Bloomington and Indianapolis, IN, 2000; M. Steger, *Globalization: A Very Short Introduction*, Oxford, 2003; A. Hopkins (ed.), *Globalization in World History*, London, 2002.

14 See, for example, S. Broughton et al. (eds), *World Music: the Rough Guide*, 2 vols, new edn, London, 1999–2000.

15 D. Reynolds, *One World Divisible: A Global History since 1945*, London, 2000, pp. 3–4.

16 Steger, *Globalization*, ch. 2.

17 J. Roberts, *The New Penguin History of the World*, London, 2004; J. Palmowski, *A Dictionary of Contemporary World History from 1900 to the Present Day*, 2nd edn, Oxford, 2003, and *Oxford Dictionary of World History*, Oxford, 2000. Also relevant is R. Moore, 'World History', in Bentley (ed.), *Companion to Historiography*, pp. 941–59. Moore edits The Blackwell History of the World series.

18 J. Brotton, *The Renaissance Bazaar From the Silk Road to Michelangelo*, Oxford, 2002.

19 C. Bayly, *The Birth of the Modern World 1780–1914*, Malden, MA, Oxford and Carlton, Victoria, Australia, 2004, pp. 12–19 on 'bodily practice', p. 14 on defining uniformity, p. 160 on 1848 revolutions. This is part of the series of 18 volumes on the history of the world published by Blackwell's.

20 *Rethinking History* 8 (2004), 253–332, contains a 'Forum on History and the Web'. In addition, see C. Gere, *Digital Culture*, London, 2002; S. Schreibman et al., *A Companion to Digital Humanities*, Oxford, 2004. For the purposes of this book, websites come in two main kinds: those that enable historians to find information and those that contain significant amounts of sources in an electronic form. While these may be combined, the latter are the product of research and may be used for further research, even if funders are keen for them to appeal to the general public. See, for example, www.oldbaileyonline.org (accessed 31 August 2005) (the Proceedings of London's 'Old Bailey' court 1674–1834) and www.the-clergydatabase.org.uk (accessed 31 August 2005) (information on English clergymen 1540–1835). Electronic library and museum catalogues are examples of the former type. Since many books are now purchased on the internet, there is an opportunity for historians to reflect upon what in their field sells. The best-selling history books on the Amazon site for January 2005 confirm the points made in this chapter, with the following themes predominating: war and violence, especially the Second World War; modern politics; biography; and family history (*The Economist*, 5 February 2005, p. 83).

21 R. Hillenbrand (ed.), *Shahnama The Visual Language of the Persian Book of Kings*, Aldershot, 2004, describes the project. An existing database on the Shahnama is www.princeton.edu/~shahnama/ (accessed 31 August 2005).

22 For example, the hugely successful *Small Island*, London, 2004, by Andrea Levy, who is the daughter of Jamaican immigrants, on their experiences in Britain.

23 For example, I. Malkin, 'Networks and the Emergence of Greek Identity', *Mediterranean Historical Review* 18 (2003), 56–74, who comments on the current resonance of the concept of networks.

24 R. Dale, *The First Crash, Lessons from the South Sea Bubble*, Princeton, NJ and London, 2004. Cf. J. Mickelthwaite and A. Wooldridge, *The Company, A Short History of a Revolutionary Idea*, London, 2003; B. Mclean and P. Elkind, *The Smartest Guys in the Room. The Amazing Rise and Scandalous Fall of Enron*, New York, 2003, which concerns the largest bankruptcy in history.

25 In addition to current interest in the Mediterranean mentioned elsewhere, the rise of Atlantic studies is striking. While the interest in this idea was present after the end of the Second World War, the recent foundation of journals in the area suggests a new wave of enthusiasm: *Journal of Transatlantic Studies* (2003) is an interdisciplinary journal which emphasises post-1945 and also publishes pieces that reflect on the field. *Atlantic Studies* (2004) is also interdisciplinary, but places no period restrictions on articles – in the first issue William O'Reilly's article on 'Genealogies of Atlantic History' is particularly helpful. The opening editorial presents Atlantic studies as a new form of area studies that examines a space rather than nation states.

26 For example, in his foreword to David Reynolds's book, Paul Kennedy emphasises the genuinely global reach of the book: 'Reynolds's conscious decision to visit and study in Japan and Southeast Asia as part of the preparation for writing this book has paid off amply', p. xviii. See also C. Bayly, *Origins of Nationality in South Asia. Patriotism and Ethical Government in the Making of Modern India*, Delhi, 1998, pp. 307–22, who makes the comparisons between history and anthropology explicit and describes his encounters with India from 1965 on.

27 See R. Lacey and D. Danziger, *The Year 1000: What Life was Like at the Turn of the First Millennium: An Englishman's World*, London, 1999, for a book that trades on the topicality of the millennium.

28 For example, P. Brown, *The Rise of Western Christendom. Triumph and Diversity 200–1000 AD*, 2nd edn, Oxford, 2002.

29 Kennedy, *Preparing for the Twenty-First Century*. Kennedy attributes the idea of 'large history' to David Landes: see, for example, *The Unbound Prometheus: Technological Change and Industrial Development in Western Europe from 1750 to the Present*, 2nd edn, Cambridge, 2003. Claims about the future are made in the publisher's blurb for C. Totman, *A History of Japan*, 2nd edn, Oxford, 2004: 'an epilogue has been added looking at Japan today and tomorrow'.

30 For example, G. Milton, *Nathaniel's Nutmeg: How One Man's Courage Changed the Course of History*, London, 1999.

31 M. Kurlansky, *Cod: A Biography of the Fish that Changed the World*, London, 1998, p. 233.

32 D. Moon, *The Abolition of Serfdom in Russia*. Cf. P. Browning, *The Changing Nature of Warfare. The Development of Land Warfare from 1792 to 1945*, Cambridge, 2002.

FURTHER READING

Health warning: the English-language works cited below illustrate a variety of perspectives. No attempt has been made to produce a comprehensive or exhaustive list. This section is designed to provide suggestions for going further into matters mentioned in the text, and includes items that are often referred to in debates about the nature of history. Many are available in cheap paperbacks; some have been published in a number of editions; others are out of print.

General works

Appleby, J., Hunt, L. and Jacob, M., *Telling the Truth about History*, New York, 1994.

Arnold, J., *A Very Short Introduction to History*, Oxford, 2000.

Bennett, T., Grossberg, L. and Morris, M., *New Keywords. A Revised Vocabulary of Culture and Society*, Malden, MA, Oxford and Carlton, Victoria, Australia, 2005.

Berkhofer, R., *Beyond the Great Story: History as Text and Discourse*, Cambridge, MA, 1995.

Bloch, M., *The Historian's Craft*, New York, 1953.

Braudel, F., *On History*, London, 1980.

Burke, P. (ed.), *New Perspectives on Historical Writing*, Cambridge, 1991.

Butterfield, H., *The Whig Interpretation of History*, Harmondsworth, 1973.

Carr, E.H., *What is History?*, London, 1961.

Collingwood, R.G., *The Idea of History*, Oxford, 1946.

Elton, G., *The Practice of History*, London, 1967 (2nd edn, Oxford, 2002).

Evans, R., *In Defence of History*, new edn, London, 2001 (first published 1997).

Galbraith, V.H., *An Introduction to the Study of History*, London, 1964.

Gardiner, J. (ed.), *What Is History Today?*, Basingstoke, 1988.

Gay, P., *Freud for Historians*, New York, 1985.

Jenkins, K., *On What Is History? From Carr and Elton to Rorty and White*, London, 1995.

Jenkins, K., *Re-thinking History*, London, 2003 (first published 1995).

Marwick, A., *The Nature of History*, London, 1970.

Marwick, A., *The New Nature of History: Knowledge, Evidence, Language*, Basingstoke, 2001.

Ritter, H., *Dictionary of Concepts in History*, New York, 1986.

Smith, B., *The Gender of History: Men, Women and Historical Practice*, Cambridge, MA, 1998.

Southgate, B., *History: What and Why?*, 2nd edn, London, 2001 (first published 1996).

Stanford, M., *A Companion to the Study of History*, Oxford, 1994.

Stern, F. (ed.), *The Varieties of History from Voltaire to the Present*, London, 1970 (first published 1956).

Tosh, J., *The Pursuit of History*, revised 3rd edn, London, 2002 (first published 1984).

Tuchman, B., *Practicing History*, New York, 1981.

Vincent, J., *An Intelligent Person's Guide to History*, London, 1995.

White, H., *Metahistory: The Historical Imagination in Nineteenth-Century Europe*, Baltimore, MD, 1973.

Williams, R., *Keywords*, 2nd edn, London, 1983.

Introduction

Since the introduction sets out my position, I list below two types of publication: first, a small number of my own writings that relate to the themes of this book, and second, a selection of works that are important to me.

Jordanova, L., 'Cultural Effort: An Introductory Essay', ch. 1 of *Nature Displayed: Gender, Science and Medicine 1760–1820*, London, 1999, pp. 1–18.
Jordanova, L., 'Gender', in P. Burke (ed.), *History and Historians in the Twentieth Century*, Oxford, 2002, pp. 120–40.
Jordanova, L., 'Angels Writing on the Shoulders of Time?', in *Historia Magistra Vitae?*, a special issue of *Österreichische Zeitschrift für Geschichtswissenschaft*, autumn 2005.

Appleby, J., 'Locke, Liberalism and the Natural Law of Money', *Past and Present* 71 (1976), 43–69.
Baxandall, M., *Patterns of Intention: On the Historical Explanation of Pictures*, London, 1985.
Bayly, C.A., *The Birth of the Modern World 1780–1914*, Malden, MA, Oxford and Carlton, Victoria, Australia, 2004.
Crow, T., *Emulation: Making Artists for Revolutionary France*, New Haven, CT, 1995.
Davidoff, L., *Worlds Between: Historical Perspectives on Gender and Class*, Cambridge, 1995.
Douglas, M., *Purity and Danger: An Analysis of Concepts of Pollution and Taboo*, London, 1966.
McManners, J., *Death and the Enlightenment: Changing Attitudes to Death among Christians and Unbelievers in Eighteenth-Century France*, Oxford, 1981.
Pointon, M., *Strategies for Showing: Women, Possession and Representation in English Visual Culture 1665–1800*, Oxford, 1997.
Porter, R., *Health for Sale: Quackery in England, 1660–1850*, Manchester, 1989.
Schaffer, S., 'States of Mind: Enlightenment and Natural Philosophy', in G. Rousseau (ed.), *Languages of Psyche: Mind and Body in Enlightenment Thought*, Berkeley, CA, 1990, pp. 233–90.
Strathern, M., *After Nature: English Kinship in the Late Twentieth Century*, Cambridge, 1992.

Chapter 1 History in general

Bartlett, R. (ed.), *History and Historians. Selected Papers of R.W. Southern*, Malden, MA, Oxford and Carlton, Victoria, Australia, 2004.
Bentley, M. (ed.), *Companion to Historiography*, London, 1997.
Bentley, M., *Modern Historiography. An Introduction*, London and New York, 1999.
Booth, A., 'Rethinking the Scholarly: Developing the Scholarship of Teaching in History', *Arts and Humanities in Higher Education* 3 (2004), 247–66.
Burke, P., *The French Historical Revolution: The Annales School 1929–89*, Cambridge, 1990.
Fuchs, E. and Stuchtey, B. (eds), *Across Cultural Borders: Historiography in Global Perspective*, Lanham, MD, 2002.
Hewison, R., *The Heritage Industry*, London, 1987.
Lambert, P. and Schofield, P., *Making History. An Introduction to the History and Practices of a Discipline*, London and New York, 2004, part I.
Lamont, W. (ed.), *Historical Controversies and Historians*, London, 1998.
Levine, P., *The Amateur and the Professional: Antiquarians, Historians and Archaeologists in Victorian England*, Cambridge, 1986.
Munslow, A., *The Routledge Companion to Historical Studies*, London, 2000.
Samuel, R., *Theatres of Memory*, 2 vols, London, 1994 and 1998.
Tosh, J. (ed.), *Historians on History*, Harlow, 2000.

Chapter 2 Mapping the discipline of history

Boyd, K. (ed.), *Encyclopedia of Historians and Historical Writing*, 2 vols, London and Chicago, IL, 1999.

Burke, P. (ed.), *New Perspectives on Historical Writing*, Cambridge, 1991.

Burke, P., *What Is Cultural History?*, Cambridge, 2004.

Chartier, R., *Cultural History: Between Practices and Representations*, London, 1988.

Coleman, D., *History and the Economic Past. An Account of the Rise and Decline of Economic History in Britain*, Oxford, 1987.

Gay, P., *Freud for Historians*, New York, 1985.

Gottschalk, L., *Understanding History: A Primer of Historical Method*, New York, 1963 (first published 1950).

Hunt, L. (ed.), *The New Cultural History*, Berkeley, CA, 1989.

Lambert, P. and Schofield, P., *Making History. An Introduction to the History and Practices of a Discipline*, London and New York, 2004, part II.

Porter, R., *Gibbon*, London, 1988.

Renier, G., *History: Its Purpose and Method*, New York, 1965 (first published 1950).

Ritter, H., *Dictionary of Concepts in History*, New York, 1986.

Wilson, A. (ed.), *Rethinking Social History: English Society 1570–1920 and its Interpretation*, Manchester, 1993.

Chapter 3 History and other disciplines

Abrams, M., *A Glossary of Literary Terms*, 7th edn, Fort Worth, TX and London, 1999 (first published 1941).

Bentley, M. (ed.), *Companion to Historiography*, London, 1997, esp. part 5.

Bruce, S., *Sociology: A Very Short Introduction*, Oxford, 1999.

Burke, P., *History and Social Theory*, Ithaca, NY, 1993.

Douglas, M., *Natural Symbols: Explorations in Cosmology*, London, 1970.

Geertz, C., *The Interpretation of Cultures*, New York, 1973.

Haskell, F., 'Visual Sources and the Embarrassment of Riches', *Past and Present* 120 (1988), 216–26.

Haskell, F., *History and its Images: Art and the Interpretation of the Past*, New Haven, CT, 1993.

Hastrup, K., *Other Histories*, London, 1992.

Lambert, P. and Schofield, P. (eds), *Making History. An Introduction to the History and Practices of a Discipline*, Abingdon and New York, 2004, part III.

Leff, G., *History and Social Theory*, London, 1969.

Lentricchia, F. and McLaughlin, T. (eds), *Critical Terms for Literary Study*, 2nd edn, Chicago, IL, 1995.

Lodge, D. (ed.), *20th Century Literary Criticism: A Reader*, London, 1972.

Monaghan, J. and Just, P., *Social and Cultural Anthropology. A Very Short Introduction*, Oxford, 2000.

Nelson, R. and Shiff, R. (eds), *Critical Terms for Art History*, Chicago, IL, 1996.

Pointon, M., *History of Art: A Student's Handbook*, 4th edn, London, 1997 (first published 1980).

Rabinow, P. (ed.), *The Foucault Reader*, New York, 1984.

Rotberg, R. and Rabb, T. (eds), *Art and History: Images and their Meaning*, Cambridge, 1988.

Smith, D., *The Rise of Historical Sociology*, Cambridge, 1991.

Thomson, E.P., *Customs in Common*, London, 1993.

Tilly, C., *As Sociology Meets History*, New York, 1981.

Chapter 4 The status of historical knowledge

Breisach, E., *On the Future of History. The Postmodernist Challenge and its Aftermath*, Chicago, IL and London, 2003.

Fay, B. et al. (eds), *History and Theory: Contemporary Readings*, Oxford, 1998.

Fulbrook, M., *Historical Theory*, London, 2002.

Gardiner, P. (ed.), *Theories of History*, New York, 1959.

Kramer, L. and Maza, S. (eds), *A Companion to Western Historical Thought*, Malden, MA, Oxford and Carlton, Victoria, Australia, 2002.

Lemon, M., *The Discipline of History and the History of Thought*, London, 1995.

Lloyd, C., *Explanation in Social History*, Oxford, 1986.

Mandelbaum, M., *The Status of Historical Knowledge: An Answer to Relativism*, New York, 1967.

Munslow, A., *The New History*, Harlow, 2003.

Phillips, M., 'Distance and Historical Representation', *History Workshop Journal* 57 (2004), 123–41.

Schlink, B., *The Reader*, London, 1997.

Stanford, M., *An Introduction to the Philosophy of History*, Oxford, 1998.

Tosh, J., *The Pursuit of History*, 3rd revised edn, London, 2002, chs 6 and 7.

Chapter 5 Periodisation

Best, G. (ed.), *The Permanent Revolution: The French Revolution and its Legacy*, London, 1988.

Briggs, A. and Snowman, D. (eds), *Fins de Siècle: How Centuries End 1400–2000*, New Haven, CT, 1996.

Freeman-Grenville, G., *Chronology of World History. A Calendar of Principal Events from 3000 BC to AD 1973*, London, 1975.

Hunt, L., 'The Challenge of Gender', in H. Medick and A.-C. Trepp, *Geschlechtergeschichte und Allgemeine Geschichte*, Göttingen, 1998, pp. 59–97.

Kubler, G., *The Shape of Time: Remarks on the History of Things*, New Haven, CT, 1962.

Reynolds, D., 'The Origin of the Two "World Wars": Historical Discourse and International Politics', *Journal of Contemporary History* 38 (2003), 29–44.

Roberts, J., *The New Penguin History of the World*, London, 2003.

Scott, J., *England's Troubles*, Cambridge, 2000, ch. 1.

Stearns, P. (ed.), *The Encyclopedia of World History, Ancient, Medieval, and Modern. Chronologically Arranged*, 6th edn, Cambridge, 2001.

White, H., *Metahistory: The Historical Imagination in Nineteenth-Century Europe*, Baltimore, MD, 1973.

Williams, N., *Chronology of the Modern World 1763–1965*, revised edn, Harmondsworth, 1975.

Chapter 6 Public history

Benson, S. et al. (eds), *Presenting the Past: Essays on History and the Public*, Philadelphia, PA, 1986.

Friedländer, S. (ed.), *Probing the Limits of Representation: Nazism and the 'Final Solution'*, Cambridge, MA, 1992.

Gillis, J. (ed.), *Commemoration: The Politics of National Identity*, Princeton, NJ, 1993.

Lambert, P. and Schofield, P. (eds), *Making History. An Introduction to the History and Practices of a Discipline*, London and New York, 2004, part V.

History Workshop Journal 59 (2005), Feature: Rethinking Memory.

Horne, D., *The Great Museum: The Re-presentation of the Past*, London, 1984.

Lowenthal, D., *The Past Is a Foreign Country*, Cambridge, 1985.

Maier, C., *The Unmasterable Past*, Cambridge, MA, 1988.

Moeller, R., *War Stories: The Search for a Usable Past in the Federal Republic of Germany*, Berkeley and Los Angeles, CA, 2001.

Nora, P. (ed.), *Realms of Memory*, 3 vols, New York, 1996, 1997 and 1998.

Samuel, R., *Theatres of Memory*, 2 vols, London, 1994 and 1998.

Stille, A., *The Future of the Past. How the Information Age Threatens to Destroy Our Cultural Heritage*, New York, 2002.

Vergo, P. (ed.), *The New Museology*, London, 1989.

Waterfield, G. and French, A., *Below Stairs. 400 Years of Servants' Portraits*, London, 2003.

Chapter 7 Historians' skills

Abbott, M. (ed.), *History Skills: A Student's Handbook*, London, 1996.

Bédarida, F. (ed.), *The Social Responsibility of the Historian*, Providence, RI, 1994.

Black, J. and MacRaild, D., *Studying History*, 2nd edn, Basingstoke, 2000 (first published 1997).

Clanchy, M., *From Memory to Written Record: England 1066–1307*, London, 1979.

D'Aniello, C., *Teaching Bibliographic Skills in History*, London, 1993.

Edmonds, G., *The Good Web Site Guide 2005*, London, 2004.

Floud, R., *An Introduction to Quantitative Methods for Historians*, 2nd edn, London, 1979.

Hockett, H., *The Critical Method in Historical Research and Writing*, New York, 1955.

Hudson, P., *History by Numbers: An Introduction to Quantitative Approaches*, London, 2000.

Karsten, P. and Modell, J. (eds), *Theory, Method, and Practice in Social and Cultural History*, New York, 1992.

Lambert, P. and Schofield, P. (eds), *Making History. An Introduction to the History and Practices of a Discipline*, Abingdon and New York, 2004.

Le Goff, J. and Nora, P. (eds), *Constructing the Past: Essays in Historical Methodology*, Cambridge, 1985.

Lloyd, C., *The Structures of History*, Oxford, 1993.

Seldon, A. (ed.), *Contemporary History: Practice and Method*, Oxford, 1988.

Tuchman, B., *Practicing History*, New York, 1981, esp. part 3, 'Learning from History'.

Vansina, J., *Oral Tradition: A Study in Historical Methodology*, London, 1985.

Chapter 8 Trends

Bayly, C.A., *The Birth of the Modern World 1780–1914*, Malden, MA, Oxford and Carlton, Victoria, Australia, 2004.

Breisach, E., *On the Future of History. The Postmodernist Challenge and its Aftermath*, Chicago, IL and London, 2003.

Buruma, I. and Margalit, A., *Occidentalism: A Short History of Anti-Westernism*, London, 2004.

Daddow, O., *Britain and Europe since 1945. Historiographical Perspectives on Integration*, Manchester, 2004.

David, P. and Thomas, M. (eds), *The Economic Future in Historical Perspective*, Oxford, 2003.

Diamond, J., *Guns, Germs and Steel. A Short History of Everybody for the Last 13,000 Years*, London, 1998.

Edmonds, G., *The Good Web Site Guide 2005*, London, 2004.

Gere, C., *Digital Culture*, London, 2002.

Grove, R., *Ecology, Climate and Empire. Colonialism and Global Environmental History 1400–1940*, Cambridge, 1997.

Harris, W. (ed.), *Rethinking the Mediterranean*, Oxford, 2005.

History of the Human Sciences 17, no. 2/3 (2004), Special Issue: 'Theorizing from the Holocaust: What is to be Learned?'

Hogan, M. and Paterson, T. (eds), *Explaining the History of American Foreign Relations*, 2nd edn, Cambridge, 2004.

Howard, M., *The Lessons of History*, Oxford, 1991.

Howe, S., *Empire. A Very Short Introduction*, Oxford, 2002.

Mann, M., *Incoherent Empire*, London and New York, 2003.

May, E.R., *'Lessons' of the Past. The Use and Misuse of History in American Foreign Policy*, New York, 1973.

Pols, R., *Family Photographs 1860–1945*, Richmond, 2002.

Reynolds, D., *One World Divisible. A Global History since 1945*, London, 2000.

Roberts, J.M., *The New Penguin History of the World*, London, 2003.

Staley, D., *Computers, Visualization, and History: How New Technology Will Transform our Understanding of the Past*, Armonk, NY, 2002.

Thompson, J., *Taking Responsibility for the Past: Reparation and Historical Injustice*, Cambridge, 2002.

GLOSSARY

(All words are nouns unless otherwise stated.)

anachronism: something that is out of its own time; specifically, historians using ideas that are alien to the period under discussion.

bricolage: a French term for something that is assembled from disparate pieces.

canon: an authoritative body of writings or art works that are deemed of special value and worthy of academic study.

citation index: a list of where a particular publication is made reference to, i.e. cited, by other scholars.

cliometrics: the application of mathematical and statistical methods to historical data.

counterfactuals: speculative claims that are contrary to known facts and deployed to examine alternative, hypothetical sequences of events. This is generally undertaken to help clarify issues of causation.

critical theory: a set of approaches to knowledge loosely indebted to Marxism, which is sympathetic to **social constructionism** and develops politically informed critiques of the uses to which knowledge is put.

diplomatic: the systematic study of handwritten documents, especially medieval ones, which has as its object both deciphering the writing and ascertaining the authenticity of the documents themselves.

discourse: a more or less coherent body of statements that can be analysed using approaches deriving from linguistics, and underlying which is a particular view of the world.

documentary (noun and adjective): a cultural artefact, such as a photograph, film or television programme, which purports to report actual events, persons and circumstances.

episteme(s): the dominant mode of knowledge of a specific era, common to many, even all, forms of knowledge produced at the time.

epistemology: a branch of philosophy concerned with theories of knowledge, that is, the nature and quality of knowledge and how we know what we know.

exoticism: infatuation with or admiration for what is exotic, foreign, unfamiliar.

genre: a type of text or cultural product with its own conventions; a way of classifying works of art and literature.

globalisation: a set of processes whereby disparate parts of the world are linked together, economically, culturally and possibly ideologically; sometimes used pejoratively to mean 'Americanisation'.

hagiography: literally, lives of saints and martyrs written to glorify their subjects; more loosely, uncritical, reverential accounts of a life.

hegemony: all-embracing dominance, especially of a political and/or ideological kind, wielded by states, classes or, by extension, other groupings.

heritage industry: the marketing of the past for leisure purposes; the development of forms of tourism that promote 'historic' places, such as old towns, villages, museums, rural activities, and so on. Associated with this is the selling of objects, for example, in museum shops, that evoke past times.

heuristic device: an assumption that assists in taking research further, a useful tool to think with.

histoire totale: a French term meaning history written so that a number of levels or aspects of the past are brought together.

historiography: the writing of history and the study of historical writings. More broadly, an awareness of different ways of doing history.

history from below: history for and about the majority of the population; the serious and committed study of non-elite groups; historical writing that is highly accessible and relevant to the people as a whole; a type of history that rejects elite perspectives.

holistic (adjective): the tendency or ability to perceive wholes, that is, to see how the parts of a historical situation are related to one another, and to embrace apparently disparate phenomena.

human sciences: a name for all the fields of knowledge that focus on human beings, principally psychology, anthropology and sociology. It is possible to see history and philosophy as human sciences.

hypothesis: an untested proposition, used as a basis for argument and research, which will be (or ought to be) empirically tested.

ideology: a set of ideas, held with deep commitment by individuals or groups, which shapes their view of the world, and which serves their material interests, if only indirectly.

imaginary: originally a psychoanalytic term, used loosely to suggest a way of imagining the world that is widely held at a given time and place.

keywords: those words in any language that carry special weight because they are contested, highly value-laden, ideologically fraught or unusually emotive. As a result they are exceptionally revealing historically.

linguistics: the systematic study of the elements of language and of the principles governing their organisation; the science of language.

longue durée (adjective): a French term to describe a piece of historical writing or research that covers a long period of time.

mediation: in everyday use the term 'mediators' refers to go-betweens, who bring together two groups, but remain separate from them. Mediation is the name given to the whole process. 'Mediation', the noun, and 'mediate', the verb, can also be used metaphorically in relation to ideas and the transformations they undergo, which is how I use them in this book. Mediation can be a useful way of drawing attention to the centrality of interpretation in any commentary. Behind these terms is a strong conviction that ideas perform major social work. Scholars who deploy them have generally been influenced by Marxian traditions.

medicalisation: the process of making phenomena medical, that is, under the control of doctors, which were not so previously. The term implies criticism of this process.

mentalités: a French word for which there is no precise English equivalent, but 'attitudes' and 'outlook' come fairly close. It is used of a kind of history that is concerned with people's mental lives and attitudes, and especially those aspects of them that remain tacit, but which nonetheless shape daily lives, child-rearing, for example.

meta- (prefix): when attached to nouns it indicates a higher, more abstract or general level of the noun in question.

micro-history: a level of social analysis that is concerned with everyday life; historical research, often of a single community, on a small scale.

modernism: a western artistic movement usually associated with the late nineteenth and early twentieth centuries and with a repudiation of settled, traditional approaches; especially evident in literature, music, architecture and art. More broadly, the cult of what is modern, self-consciously innovative and dismissive of established ways.

modernisation: the processes whereby supposedly traditional societies become modern ones; and the ways in which these processes are conceptualised. Modernity is the state of being modern, where modern can be defined in a variety of ways.

monograph: a piece of writing, generally a book, on a specific historical phenomenon, person, place or event and the result of specialised research.

myth: stories, often involving supernatural or exceptional persons, actions or events, that are endowed by a society with special significance, and that speak to its most cherished concerns, such as its origins, leadership or destiny; a fictional account; a view that is deeply ingrained and resistant to contradictory evidence.

narrative: an account, or narration of events, in the form of a story or tale, and often conforming to a recognisable type, such as a life history.

orientalism: the cult of the orient; the development of an aesthetic based on (imagined) ideas of the east; the term now implies a criticism of such attitudes on the grounds that they distort and homogenise 'the east' inappropriately. Its flipside, occidentalism, sometimes associated with anti-westernism, is best seen in this context.

other/otherness: that which is not the self, and which possesses the quality of being different and sometimes alien; the tendency of dominant groups to see and exploit the differences they find between themselves and distinct groups, who thereby become subordinate.

palaeography: the study of documents, generally ancient or old ones, with special attention to the handwriting and to their authenticity, including accurate dating.

paradigm: a model or pattern, sometimes a coherent world view or set of theories.

pedagogy: the art or science of teaching; the principles according to which instruction is given.

people's history: see **history from below**.

postmodernism: a reaction to modernism that is both dependent upon and highly critical of it; a scepticism of totalising explanations, assumptions about progress and so-called grand narratives, an insistence on the impossibility of objective knowledge, and an acceptance of what is partial and fragmentary, both in human experience and in accounts of it; sometimes an amorphous term for recent cultural trends.

prosopography: the study of collective biography; a historical method involving the examination of significant numbers of lives, for example, in a given occupation, institution or place.

quadrivium: the division of the curriculum into four parts, current in medieval and early modern times; the trivium comprised the three liberal arts – grammar, rhetoric and logic.

relativism: the view that there can be no objective standards, for example, of historical truth, hence theories, values, and so on, must be understood as relative to the people and circumstances that produced them.

research assessment exercise: the periodic review and assessment of the quality of research produced in universities, the results of which are sometimes used to determine the amount of government money each department receives for its research activities.

rhetoric: a field of study since classical times that systematically analyses how language produces its effects; loosely, the art of using language effectively, for instance, to persuade or influence others. Sometimes used pejoratively to suggest merely superficial verbal effects without underlying substance.

second-wave feminism: the forms of feminism that developed over the 1960s and that have been continuously developing both intellectually and politically since then.

semiotics: the systematic study of signs; analysis of the wider meanings and social functions of sign systems, both verbal and non-verbal.

sign: a basic element of communication, not objects or referents themselves, but the device, whether verbal or non-verbal, that refers to them.

social construction(ism): theories that emphasise the socially created nature of collective life; the idea that human existence is made up not of natural givens, but of social products or constructs.

structuralism: an approach in the social sciences that studies the structures that underlie and generate observable phenomena; these structures are often thought to be rooted in the basic characteristics of the mind. Accordingly the study of language is of fundamental importance. **Post-structuralism** is a set of influential cultural theories that departs from structuralism but that refuses the possibility of a scientific study of structures. Instead they stress the indeterminacy of meaning.

subaltern (adjective): subordinate or inferior; in the phrase 'subaltern studies', it involves looking at colonial situations from the vantage point of the colonised.

teleology: explanation in terms of goals or purposes; the assumption that ends or outcomes are present in and/or explain earlier stages of a process.

topos (plural, **topoi**): a motif or theme in a literary or artistic composition, a convention or formula.

trivium: see **quadrivium**.

Whiggish (adjective): history that is written either from the point of view of the winners or from an unthinking commitment to progress. The term implies criticism of such an approach.

BIBLIOGRAPHY

Abercrombie, N., Hill, S. and Turner, B., *The Penguin Dictionary of Sociology*, 3rd edn, London, 1994.

Abrams, M., *A Glossary of Literary Terms*, 6th edn, Fort Worth, TX, 1993.

Baldick, C., *The Concise Oxford Dictionary of Literary Terms*, Oxford, 1990.

Bennett, T., Grossberg, L. and Morris, M. (eds), *New Keywords. A Revised Vocabulary of Culture and Society*, Malden, MA, Oxford and Carlton, Victoria, Australia, 2005.

Bullock, A. and Trombley, S. (eds), *The New Fontana Dictionary of Modern Thought*, London, 1999.

Cook, C., *A Dictionary of Historical Terms*, 3rd edn, Basingstoke, 1998.

Marshall, G. (ed.), *A Dictionary of Sociology*, 2nd edn, Oxford, 1998.

Munslow, A., *The Routledge Companion to Historical Studies*, London, 2000.

Ritter, H., *Dictionary of Concepts in History*, New York, 1986.

Weigall, D., 'Historical Terms', in M. Abbott (ed.), *History Skills: A Student's Handbook*, London, 1996, pp. 107–16.

Williams, R., *Keywords: A Vocabulary of Culture and Society*, revised edn, London, 1983.

INDEX

Bien, D., 211

Biography/ies, 16, 27, 45–6, 47, 59, 95, 142, 143, 155, 179, 194, 197, 202, 203, 215, 219, 229

Bischoff, B., 217

Black history, 14, 48, 144

Black, C.E., 202

Black, J., 202, 225

Blackbourn, D., 211

Bloch, M., 221

Bloom, H., 206

Boal, I., 205

Bolivia, 32

Bonfield, L., 201

Booth, A., 222

Borg, A., 214

Bossy, J., 212

Bourdieu, P., 74, 205

Boyd, K., 223

Boyle, N., 205

Branson, N., 212

Braudel, F., 16, 44, 45, 123, 199, 212, 221

Bremmer, J., 204

Breisach, E., 224, 225

Brewer, J., 218

Bricolage, 56, 227

Brier, S., 213

Briggs, A., 224

Briggs, R., 206

Brinton, C., 216

Brockliss, L., 210

Brogan, H., 205

Brotton, J., 185, 219

Broughton, S., 219

Brown, P., 220

Browne, E.J., 199

Browning, C., 207, 215

Browning, P., 220

Bruce, R., 218

Bruce, S., 203, 223

Bull, H., 211

Bullock, A., 231

Burke, P., 199, 203, 205, 209, 217, 221, 222, 223

Burn, W., 212

Burnaby, S., 209

Buruma, I., 225

Butlin, R., 203

Butterfield, H., 221

Calas, Jean, 115, 211

Calder-Marshall, A., 209

Calhoun, C., 202

Calvert, F., 202

Cameron, E., 212

Camille, M., 217

Cannadine, D., 216

Cannon, J., 212

Canon, 81, 206, 227

Cantor, G., 199

Capa, R., 207

Capitalism, 29, 105, 114, 115, 123, 199, 209, 211, 212

Cardinal, R., 213

Carnegie, A., 215

Carr, E.H., 39, 198, 221

Case studies, 61–2, 67, 84, 152, 167

Casey, J., 216

Castiglione, D., 214

Cathcart, M., 210

Causality, 41, 74, 101, 102, 124, 185, 208, 227

Cavallo, S., 217

Caygill, M., 204

Chamberlain, J., 196

Chambers, J.W., 196

Chaniotis, A., 218

Charles I, 107

Charles II, 107

Chartier, R., 199, 223

Chakrabarty, D., 196

Chaunu, P., 212

Childhood, 41, 57, 127, 212

Chippindale, C., 206

Chinese Revolution, 100

Christ, Jesus, 109

Christianity, 59, 109, 120–1, 180–1, 212, 220

Churchill, W., 108

Citation index, 227

Clanchy, M., 217, 225

Clark, C. Manning, 210

Clarke, G., 207

Class/es, 16, 17, 23, 44, 56, 66, 67, 68, 69, 71, 76, 87, 91, 144, 145, 201, 203, 214

Classification, 37, 41, 69, 83, 108, 120, 162, 201, 205

Clendinnen, I., 196

Cliometrics, 87, 151, 227